# TÓCHAR

# TÓCHAR

## Walking Ireland's Ancient Pilgrim Paths

Darach MacDonald

NEW ISLAND

TÓCHAR
First published 2013
by New Island
2 Brookside
Dundrum Road
Dublin 14

www.newisland.ie



PRINT ISBN: 978-1-84840-247-8
EPUB ISBN: 978-1-84840-248-5
MOBI ISBN: 978-1-84840-249-2



British Library Cataloguing Data. A CIP catalogue record for this book is available from the British Library

Typeset by JVR Creative India
Cover design by Andrew Brown
Printed by Bell & Bain Ltd, Glasgow

The author acknowledges with thanks an SIAP grant from the Arts Council of Northern Ireland.

New Island received financial assistance from
The Arts Council (An Comhairle Ealaíon), Dublin, Ireland

10 9 8 7 6 5 4 3 2 1

# Contents

# Foreword

## By Fr Brian D'arcy

It's my belief that too often we are so preoccupied with our destinations that we miss the joy of the journey. That is why this book is such a fascinating read. For Darach MacDonald, the journey is almost always more interesting than the destination. The genuine pilgrim must journey in a reflective, prayerful way. What makes a pilgrimage fruitful are the stops along the way where we look back with gratitude on where we've come from, enjoy where we are now and discern the most fulfilling way ahead. The pilgrim is not a tourist.

What I find most appealing in Darach's approach is his selection of familiar destinations. He rightly acknowledges that 'people of faith still travel to sacred places' for prayer and renewal. Christians, Muslims and Hindus all have their own special places of prayer and penance. The author admits he is a struggling Catholic – the best kind – about to 'set out on a personal odyssey along the paths of our fathers'. He is right to tell us that his reflections will be his own; there is no guarantee that others will have the same experience. That's as it should be.

Not surprisingly, he begins with St Patrick's Purgatory in Lough Derg, a short drive from where he lives. Of equal interest is his less-organised ramble in the footsteps of Patrick, around Downpatrick on the saint's feast day, the 17th of March. He fills us in on the history of the places he visits from the time of the saint's burial to the present day. He observes with interest and accuracy the foibles and the attitudes of the pilgrims he meets.

To me, his journeys in Mayo are perhaps most interesting. Clew Bay, Ballintubber Abbey, Croagh Patrick – and, of course, Knock – all come alive through the author's vivid descriptions. Some observations I recognise; others don't tally with my own experience. Once again, that's as it should be, because everyone's journey is different.

For me, going to Knock as a boy was boring. We sat on a bus for hours and prayed three full Rosaries on the journey. There were three more Rosaries during our time in Knock and three tedious, sleepy Rosaries on our way home. Yet it was to Knock that my mother took me when I first indicated that I wanted to enter the seminary and become a priest. Both of my parents tried to discourage me. Eventually, my mother suggested that if we both went to Knock and I still wanted to enter the Graan when we came home, they'd let me do it. In the summer of 1962 we made our pilgrimage to the west of Ireland; in September I was in the Graan, and that's still where I live and work.

Nowadays I visit Knock at least once a year to pray for direction and a renewed commitment. I have no idea whether or not Mary appeared to the people of that village in the nineteenth century, but I believe that the sincere prayers of generations of pilgrims have made Knock a holy place of peace and healing.

*Tóchar* is an excellent, thought-provoking, enjoyable jaunt down memory lane and at the same time a challenging reflection on the ever-changing face of modern Ireland.

Darach shares his inner thoughts and often reveals his spiritual hunger too. His journeys are not in vain.

He concludes:

> *The path of the pilgrim is as long as life itself. It has many starting points, yet it has only one destination. As I have endeavoured to follow it, I have learned that it is a path worth taking, for it leads the true pilgrim through wondrous places to the most wondrous place of all … thanks be to God.*

Deo gratias indeed.

Fr Brian D'Arcy, CP

# Introduction

## Walk the Walk

We live in a sceptical world, a place where the rituals and practices of our past are forgotten, the places where we performed them neglected. Even for those who profess Christianity, fundamental faith crumbles in the face of scandal, duplicity and betrayal by those once trusted as ministers of Christ. As we despair of institutional religion, most have only sketchy memories and scant knowledge of the faith that sustained previous generations in the darkest times. Our beliefs and practices were corralled into empty rituals at prescribed places, carefully controlled by the hierarchical, repressive and sex-obsessed Catholic Church. For many of my generation and younger, a deep sense of loss compounds our helplessness in the face of material and spiritual collapse.

Perhaps we have experienced this most in Ireland, a land where our most sacred places of pilgrimage have a spiritual significance that echoes back to pre-Christian beliefs. For centuries and millennia, we persisted in visiting these places in time-honoured rituals, even against the strictures of an authoritarian church. Yet in modern times the joy and liberation of rebirth, inherent in time-honoured pilgrimage, have been traded for dour repression at approved Marian shrines – places that rob us of spontaneity and the fundamental spiritual resonance of ancient traditions.

In just a few generations of travelling abroad, we have traded penitence for exotic experience using jet airliners and air-conditioned coaches. Even the great walking pilgrimage of the Camino de Santiago de Compostela across northern Spain has been repackaged into manageable bites, with luggage transferred to the next boutique hotel while modern *peregrinos* have their passports stamped for salvation. Yet pilgrimage remains a central facet of most world religions. People of faith still travel to sacred places and assert belief in acts of repentance, renunciation and renewal. Today's great gatherings of Muslims at Mecca and of Hindus at Kumbh Mela are only the most spectacular pilgrimages for believers seeking spiritual renewal.

For the two millennia since his death on the cross, followers of Jesus Christ have gone to sacred shrines. They have endured tribulations, recited prayers, performed rituals and sought indulgences to allow them to conquer mortal weakness and attain salvation. Yet this Christian practice of pilgrimage is much more than a religious tradition for true believers. It is at the very core of western culture. From the Nativity trek of the Magi to Arthurian quests for the Holy Grail, the Crusades to the Holy Land, Chaucer's *Canterbury Tales*, Dante's *Divine Comedy*, the discovery of the New World and John Bunyan's *Pilgrim's Progress*, an understanding of pilgrimage – and the search for truth that is at its core – is vital to a full appreciation of literature, art and the revealed truths of the natural world, never mind religious belief. We are enthralled by quests. So, even as our faith in Christ wavers, our desire for rebirth persists in acts of faith that harbour a hope of relief from our fragile human condition. Each quest is a journey based on instinct and follows the example of honourable ancestors who have gone before us. Pilgrimage fulfils a fundamental desire to transcend the woes of the world and focus on our essential spirit. Never before have so many needed it.

This pilgrim could best be described as a healthy sceptic on matters of belief. I have had a strong aversion to religious rite without reason, and I steer well clear of blind obedience – twin components of the Roman Catholic faith as I experienced it growing up. If I remain a card-carrying member, I could best be described as an à-*la-carte* Catholic, a disparaging term spat out by 'traditionalists'. The Second Vatican Council liberated me, and my lapses of faith have coincided with subsequent attempts to roll back its influence. Yet in times of personal trouble, crisis or trauma, I have turned instinctively to the faith of my fathers. During and after the break-up of my marriage I found comfort and succour in familiar expressions of religion, even if my divorced status would render me ineligible for the sacraments in the eyes of some of my fellow Catholics. Over time, I have come to appreciate the fundamental spiritual appetite that lurks within me. While it has remained unfed for long periods, I believe it to be as important as my physical well-being (which I also neglected for much of my life). While I choose the intellectual over the obedient, I am also in awe of spiritual practices that stretch back to the rituals adapted by Celtic Christianity from previously existing belief. I believe that the ancient sites of Christianity, where these rituals were enacted, form a mother-lode of spirituality that we can tap – but that we must replenish also.

So I have set out on a personal odyssey along the paths of our fathers. In doing so, I have experienced rare opportunities for spiritual reflection and honest reassessment of my life. This is my pilgrimage. I offer it only as a personal testimony, with no promise or expectation that others will experience what I have experienced. In my spiritual quests I have always had a precise destination, but the act of getting there is the pilgrimage. I have endeavoured to follow the code prescribed and to avoid advance preparation beyond the most basic, so that my experiences can be put down to good or bad fortune, karma or destiny. Wherever possible, my journeys have been timed to coincide with traditional observance; and some have been made in the company of other pilgrims. When I have travelled alone, I have sought guidance on the rituals of observance. Most importantly, perhaps, I have walked the pilgrim path whenever possible. In this I have followed the practice of pilgrims from time immemorial, including one of the modern world's most admired literary chroniclers on the practice. In his pivotal work, *The Pilgrimage*, Paulo Coelho explains:

> *When you travel, you experience, in a very practical way, the act of rebirth. You confront completely new situations, the day passes more slowly, and on most journeys you … are like a child just out of the womb. You begin to attach much more importance to the things around you because your survival depends on them. You begin to be more accessible to others because they may be able to help you in difficult situations. And you accept any small favour from the gods with great delight, as if it were an episode you would remember for the rest of your life. At the same time, since all things are new, you see only the beauty in them, and you feel happy to be alive. That's why a religious pilgrimage has always been one of the most objective ways of achieving insight.*[1]

In my quest for insight, I have sought the company of many writers besides Coelho. Between trails and along each path, their words and observations have shown me that poets are the priests of a secular age, shamans who touch our spiritual essence even when religion has become anathema. They are guardians of belief who remind us that truth often resides in the rejected past. Louis MacNeice wrote:

*His father gave him a box of truisms*
*Shaped like a coffin, then his father died;*
*The truisms remained on the mantelpiece*
*As wooden as the playbox they had been packed in*
*Or that other his father skulked inside.*
*Then he left home, left the truisms behind him*
*Still on the mantelpiece, met love, met war,*
*Sordor, disappointment, defeat, betrayal,*
*Til through disbeliefs he arrived at a house*
*He could not remember seeing before,*
*And he walked straight in;*
*It was where he had come from*
*And something told him the way to behave.*
*He raised his hand and blessed his home;*
*The truisms flew and perched on his shoulders*
*And a tall tree sprouted from his father's grave.*[2]

This is my quest for truth and solace. I hope it provides guidance and encouragement for others to walk these pilgrim paths to sacred places. For nothing can match the sheer exhilaration of those final, faltering steps when muscles ache and satisfaction soars. In the act of emptying the body, the soul opens for joy.

# Chapter 1

# Pulled to Purgatory

## St Patricks Purgatory, Lough Derg, Donegal

For months I am drawn to St Patrick's Purgatory. I drive there from my home in Castlederg, a 20-minute journey over moorland and forests to a small stone bridge on Tulnashane Road. As I cross the border from Tyrone into Donegal, there is no shortage of bad news on the radio – faltering banks, rising unemployment, corporate greed, public fiddling, plummeting tax revenues, soaring deficits and dashed hopes. I park at Tievetooey, where the river tumbles out in a torrent and gushes north towards Derry, and set off on foot along the north-eastern shore of Donegal's most expansive body of fresh water. It is a relief to feel the bracing air in my face as I march towards Croaghbrack Mountain and on my back as I return to Tievetooey. In the lee of Tullyglass and Crockmore, I ponder the travails of Ireland and my eyes are drawn to Station Island and the dome of St Patrick's Basilica. In a district almost bereft of human habitation, it looms across the misty waters, a holy refuge in a sea of turmoil.

Home for Easter from Rome, my son Sam joins me on the walk and is captivated also by the haunting spectre. We drive down to the lakeshore complex, below the big arch proclaiming '*Purgatorio Sancti Patricii*', to the car parks, the modern reception building and chapel and the big concrete jetty poking out towards Station Island. Around us are the stirrings of a new season. Staff trim lawns and ply back and forth in motor launches. We wander and gaze at a thriving manifestation of religious belief rooted in the pious pilgrimages of barefoot people rather than the splendour of the Eternal City. This quiet and remote place of reflection and self-denial has stood the test of time; that seems particularly pertinent in the current collapse of a world built on greed.

A statue of Patrick the Pilgrim by sculptor Ken Thompson presides over the jetty, and almost hidden behind it is an information board with a map of the path to Saints Island, inviting us to follow in the footsteps of medieval pilgrims. It says:

> *By the late twelfth century, the cave known as St Patrick's Purgatory on Station Island in Lough Derg had become famous across Europe as a place of pilgrimage. Pilgrims made their way there via the Priory of the Canons Regular of St Augustine on the larger Saints Island. The old pilgrimage road or Tóchar was marked on Ordnance Survey maps of the nineteenth century.*

The notice points out that the route is a circuit of 12 kilometres and it offers the good advice that pilgrims should wear proper clothing and footwear. We have already completed our walk for that day, but I resolve to return and walk the pilgrim path.

*Tuesday, 21 April 2009*
2.00 p.m.
President Mary McAleese sets off on a pilgrimage along the Camino de Santiago de Compostela in Spain. I join her on the pilgrim path, but in Donegal. And if previous walks have been comforting, this is an invigorating hike along the shore, up, down and around small inlets, sometimes disappearing into thick woodland, but emerging to yet another view of the purgatorial penitentiary on Station Island. The island forms a reference point on the right as my perspective changes and the route unfolds, with the help of waymarker signs put there by the Heritage Council of Ireland. The waymarkers have a distinctive yellow logo – a medieval pilgrim with staff. Other features are indicated by fingerpost signs. The first of these is for the picnic spot, pointing out a beaten path through shoreline thicket to a promontory where a rough wooden table offers unimpeded views of fasting pilgrims. From here, the pilgrim path continues along a high ledge, which is actually a rugged forest road, around a deep inlet, rising higher again and on to the second fingerpost for St Brigid's Chair, about 1.5 kilometres from the starting-point. This points down steps with a handrail to what was possibly a resting-place among the rocks. Today, the steps lead down to brambles and a rocky recess harbouring no more than a crushed beer can. A short distance further along the path, however, is the third fingerpost, pointing towards St Davog's Chair, up a steep mountain path about 200 metres away. The first prior of St Patrick's Purgatory; Davog was a devotee of Patrick. The 'chair' is his burial cairn, overlooking the lake.

2.30 p.m.
The path drops almost to lake level for another little cove and a final fingerpost for St Brigid's Well. It is more than

worth walking the 2 kilometres from the jetty, even for those who baulk at the full route. The lake is high, but the well peeks above ripples that swirl around the stone-rimmed circle. A metal cross from a foundry in Glasgow, almost hidden beneath overhanging shoreline trees, adorns this ancient place of pilgrimage. The cross and tree branches are festooned with rags, tiny garments, Rosary beads, holy medals and other votive offerings from those who come to this ancient place in search of Brigid's intercession. The pain of pilgrims is evident in such offerings as baby bootees and a child's prayer-book. My attention is drawn to a school tie from CBS Grammar in Omagh. I sense it was put there about seven years previously, during the desperate search for a classmate of my son, Sam; a boy of 15 from Castlederg who went missing on a night out in Donegal. The dragnet included this area, before it emerged that he had drowned below a sea wall across from Donegal town's garda station after a garda patrol had declined to help him. I stand in silent prayer for Brendan Rushe at St Brigid's Well and reflect that each ragged offering represents a story of heartbreak for loved ones who came on pilgrimage to this receptacle of tears.

3.00 p.m.
Just beyond a gate, the pilgrim path veers off the forestry road and hugs the shoreline as it meanders along for a couple of kilometres. The trail now resonates with the past, when medieval pilgrims from all over Christendom walked this route to purgatory. With frequent glimpses of the lake, and one substantial break for a view of Station Island, the path rises, falls and turns gently under overhanging trees until the tiny, cobbled lane crosses a small burn. It rises again to rejoin the forestry road at a waymarker pointing

right. Here the road dips to a long straight trail and the view opens up with Station Island looming again, further offshore. Then at a T-junction, another waymarker points right and the land balloons out into the lake. About a kilometre on, the forestry has been cut down and another distinctive pilgrim-path waymarker points across the boggy terrain to the lakeshore, where Saints Island almost nudges the shore. There is no path, so I pick my way carefully across the heath for the final hundred metres.[3] It is well worth the effort. Here, as a line of rocks peeping above the water and stretching across the rippling lake, are the remnants of the causeway and bridge that once brought pilgrims to the Augustinian monastery, where monks helped penitents to prepare for St Patrick's Purgatory over on Station Island. The monastic island is deserted now; a thicket on its southern end seems the most likely location of the monastery and monks' graveyard. From the mainland, it seems close enough to touch, but there is no way across the cold waters of Lough Derg. I cast a longing eye towards the island shore and turn for home.

4.20 p.m.

The return route of the pilgrim path continues around the headland, past the Black Lough, where Donegal's Bluestack Mountains take off from Tyrone's Sperrins. After about 1.5 kilometres, the path rejoins the outward route for a straight stretch of almost a kilometre, bypassing the turn for the old woodland trail that hugs the shore. It then turns left at a quarry and continues for a couple of kilometres to St Brigid's Well. While this part of the trail is higher, it has little of interest to the pilgrim hiker because it runs through dense forestry that precludes any view of the lake or mountains. From the well, however, the path finishes in a flurry, with magnificent vantages, especially at St Davog's Chair with its panoramic view. Finally, it's over the stile at Patrick the Pilgrim's statue and into the car park, turning my back at last on what poet Patrick Kavanagh called:

> *Christendom's purge. Heretical*
> *Around the edges: the centre's hard*
> *As the commonplace of a flamboyant bard.*[4]

The second time I take this trail, I opt to return along the lakeshore path and I begin to delve into the story of Lough Derg and its spiritual significance down the ages. Clíodhna, a Celtic goddess, is said to have had a castle here of marble, gold and precious stones. It guarded the portal of Tír na nÓg, where nobody aged. In this story, Clíodhna entices men there before their time. Dazzled by her beauty, they follow her into a cave and thence from the mortal coil. However, she falls in love with a mortal, Ciabhán. As they try to escape together from the fairy world, he is drowned by a huge wave, the Tonn Chlíodhna at Glandore Bay in Cork, and Clíodhna is washed off to Tír na nÓg forever.[5]

A variation of the Clíodhna tale tells of Lough Finn (meaning Fair Lake) in south Donegal, home of a monster that has devoured more than two thousand men, taking the guise of an alluring woman to entice them into her cave. When Finn McCool and his Fianna warriors come to the lake, the monster agrees to leave humans alone in exchange for 50 horses and 50 cattle daily. But the Fianna forget to feed her. In a rage, the monster devours scores of men, including Finn's son. But the quick-witted Finn grabs the monster and flips her onto her back, while his son (having been swallowed whole) cuts his way out and kills her. The monster's blood turns Lough Finn to Loch Derg (*dearg* meaning red).[6] An alternative translation of the name Lough Derg suggests that it derives from the Gaelic word *deirc*, meaning cave.

Fast forward, then, to AD 445, when St Patrick arrives, despondent that his work of persuading the Irish away from belief in pagan deities (like Clíodhna) has faltered. The Irish have no concept of right and wrong, much less of Judgement Day. Patrick decides to fast and pray for guidance in the isolation of the lough. He goes to an island, banishes a serpent (which, having nowhere to go, explodes and dyes the lake red) and takes up residence in its cave. Here he receives a vision of purgatory that reaffirms his Christian mission. Patrick then leaves his companion Davog to take care of this 'termon', or sanctuary, and this area of Pettigo becomes a monastic settlement of anchorite (hermit) monks living in stone cells near the cave.

While Patrick earns the plaudits for the pilgrimage, Davog is the first saint known to have been associated with Lough Derg.[7] From all areas of Christendom, however, others follow to St Patrick's Purgatory. The earliest surviving maps of Ireland record Lough Derg – one place-name in a land almost totally bereft of them. David, rector of Würzburg, describes the pilgrimage in 1120.[8]

In 1135, St Malachy of Armagh, primate of Ireland and a devotee of Rome, gains control of Lough Derg by establishing a monastery of Augustinian canons on Saints Island, where pilgrims prepare through prayer and fasting (bread and water) for their vigil in the cave on Station Island. Among them is the knight Owein, whose 1153 pilgrimage is described by Henry of Saltrey in *Tractatus de Purgatorio Sancti Patricii*, which survives in libraries throughout Europe.[9] Owein descends into purgatory in the cave of Lough Derg and is visited by demons, which try to inveigle him into renouncing his religion. Each time, he resists by saying the name of Jesus Christ. After passing an entire night in purgatory he emerges, purged of his sins.

Around the same time, Giraldus Cambrensis describes Lough Derg in *Topographica Hibernica* (1188). A 1346 fresco at a convent in Todi, Italy, depicts Patrick in the cave and his vision. Lough Derg becomes one of the most venerated places of pilgrimage in Christendom. In 1397, Ramon de Perillos, a former page of King Charles V of France, who went on to become chamberlain of King Juan I of Aragon and special adviser to the pope, describes his pilgrimage to Lough Derg.[10] He begins at Avignon, with papal permission to go to St Patrick's Purgatory, and travels to Paris, across the sea to Canterbury and on to Oxford, to be received by King Richard of England. He crosses the Irish Sea from Chester and is met by Roger Mortimer, the king's cousin and heir presumptive. He then visits the archbishop of Armagh and Niall, the O'Neill, who gives him permission to take the path to Lough Derg. Ramon de Perillos describes his purgatorial vision and his return journey, including how he spends Christmas with the O'Neill and New Year's Day in the Pale before returning to serve the pontiff.

Others of courtly credentials flock to the Irish lake island. In 1411, Laurentius Tar from the court of Sigismund of Luxembourg, king of Hungary, writes his account, which survives in the original Magyar. In 1482, *Legenda Aurea*, written by Jacubus de Voragine two hundred years previously, becomes one of the first books to be printed. It contains a lengthy description of a Lough Derg pilgrimage by a nobleman named Nicholas, who endures 15 days' mortification before the monks allow him to enter the cave, warning him of the temptations and advising him to call out, 'Jesus Christ, Son of the living God, have mercy on me, a sinner!'[11]

The demons appear and, when Nicholas refuses to obey them, they roar like wild beasts until he silences them with the invocation. The demons cast him into a great fire, but he uses the invocation again. He does so again when being burned alive with other men, whose limbs are devoured by serpents. He is taken to the pit of hell, where there is a horrific stench and acrid smoke. He is so terrified of being cast down he can no longer speak and can only invoke God's help in his heart. The torment ends when he crosses a bridge as smooth as ice over a fire of burning sulphur, invoking Christ with each step. He is met in a sweet-smelling meadow by two youths, who show him paradise. He wishes to enter, but the youths say he must return to his people for 30 days. He emerges from the Lough Derg cave and tells of his experiences. Thirty days later, he 'calmly rest[s] in the Lord'.

There are many other notable literary allusions to Lough Derg in early published literature.[12] Stories of the visions of pilgrims in the cave on Station Island are an inspiration for Dante Alighieri's lengthy sequence on purgatory in his *Divine Comedy*, written in the early fourteenth century.[13] The fascination continues with William Caxton's popular encyclopaedia of 1481, the first illustrated book published in England, which includes a lengthy entry on the pilgrimage. While such stories draw devout pilgrims to Lough Derg, the site also draws sceptics. In 1497, a Dutch monk from Eymstede goes to the pope, complaining that he has not had a vision in the cave. Shortly thereafter, Pope Alexander VI closes St Patrick's Purgatory. The cave is sealed and the Augustinians removed. Such a papal decree might cause lasting concern but for the fact that it came from the most infamous of the Borgia 'secular popes'. Alexander VI's pontificate is described as follows by the man who would become Pope Leo X: 'Now we are in the power of a wolf, the most rapacious perhaps that this world has ever seen.'[14] Pope Pius III says Alexander VI is 'damned' at death and the Vatican is hard put to find a cleric to perform his Requiem Mass.

Yet his rapaciousness does not extend to Donegal, where the Franciscan friars step into the breach and the pilgrimage resumes under a new edict of Pope Pius III in 1603. The pontifical blessing is confirmed when Papal Nuncio Chiericati visits Lough Derg in 1617. By then, the Plantation of Ulster is under way. Lough Derg remains in the control of the MacGrath family, whose title is secured under English law. Yet, under government order, the Protestant bishop of Clogher, James Spottiswoode, comes to the island in October 1632 to supervise the destruction of everything there. The interruption of service is temporary, however, and by 1660, when references first record women making the pilgrimage, Michael O'Clery is prior. Fr Art MacCullen takes over as prior from 1672 to 1710, when the Franciscans return. In 1763, a friary and an oratory are built on Station Island. In 1780, St Patrick's Church is built. Five years later, priests of Clogher Diocese take on the priory and in 1790 the cave is filled in and replaced by a chapel. The current facilities and modern pilgrimage then take shape. A substantial hospice opens in 1882, allowing thousands of pilgrims to 'do Lough Derg' during a season that is set from the start of June to 15 August.

But enough pussyfooting around the pilgrim path. It is time to take the penitential plunge into Lough Derg as a barefoot pilgrim for three days of prayer and fasting.

*Monday, 8 June 2009*
9.55 a.m.
On the car journey to St Patrick's Purgatory, the radio news tells of the Irish government taking a battering in the

European and local elections. A senior government member maintains that it's because of tough decisions that have to be taken on the economy. Asked whether their failure is more likely because of anger that tough decisions were not taken before now, he avoids the question.

10.45 a.m.
I pay the ferryman, Chris, with the token from registration and we are greeted by Zoltan, who helps us aboard the *St Columba* for the day's first crossing. Both speak with heavily accented English. As the 11 pilgrims disembark, Zoltan says, 'Have a nice day.' I wonder has he ever 'done Lough Derg'.

11.00 a.m.
We are assigned dorms on the third floor of the cloisters. A woman wrestling with a huge wheeled suitcase asks if there is a lift. There isn't. Her friend says, 'This is the start of the penance.' I am inmate 301D. Two other men are standing in the corridor as I come through. One of them, 301B, asks if I know where his 'room' is. I open the unmarked dorm door in front of him and there are our respective bunkbeds, about a metre apart and the same distance from those opposite. We unpack and take off our shoes and socks. I remark that this must be what it's like on the first day in prison. Neither man smiles, and I reflect that sharing with twin misery-guts cellmates may add to my penance.

11.30 a.m.
I make an exploratory visit to the magnificent basilica, then wander around the island. I see a notice about depositing bags and coats in Davog House and I assume that means the cloisters. So I return and ask the receptionist. She gets

out the brochure and points to Davog House on the map, on the far shore of tiny Station Island.

'You probably know more than me anyway,' she says.

'How could I?' I reply. 'Sure I'm only off the boat.'

I note the general assumption that if you are aged over 30, you have 'done Lough Derg' many times. Armed with the map, I set off for the cloakroom and deposit my small backpack containing 'essentials' – book, notepad, pens, reading glasses, waterproofs (which I pray I won't need) and my Lough Derg mug (which I will need for the vigil). I then find a spot bathed in sunshine, bask in the serenity and decide I am really looking forward to solitude and time to reflect. Then I remember the 'stations', the central component of the Lough Derg pilgrimage. I read the details and discover that this is no flash-in-the-penance exercise. Three stations must be completed by nine o'clock on the first evening. Better get going and enjoy some free time later. So I visit the shop near the ferry jetty. I buy a set of Rosary beads (€5.95) and a bottle of water (€1) and head for the basilica.

1.05 p.m.

Happiness is a smooth stone and absolute luxury is a wee grassy knoll for the knees. I have discovered the basic desires of a penitent and completed the first station of my Lough Derg pilgrimage. Just eight more to go. The station has taken just a little over one hour; I'm back in my sunny spot crunching numbers for the prayers I must recite to complete my pilgrimage. Let's see: for one station, that's 94 Our Fathers, 157 Hail Marys and 29 Apostles' Creeds, besides the triple invocation, 'I renounce the world, the flesh and the devil' at St Brigid's Cross, and a final visit to the basilica to recite Psalm 16 for 'the Pope's intentions'. I could substitute Psalm 16 for another five Our Fathers, five Hail Marys and one Creed, but I decide that a little variety never hurt a pilgrim. Multiplied by nine, it makes a grand total of 846 Our Fathers, 1,413 Hail Marys and 261 Creeds by 8.30 a.m. on day three. Meanwhile, the ferries are still plying from the mainland and I observe that most of the arriving pilgrims launch themselves into the penitential beds for the stations.

As a novice, I had trouble working out the sequence, and most of the others were so absorbed in their own stations they did not notice my dilemma. One nice lady did help, however. So, having visited the Blessed Sacrament in the basilica, I went outside, where I prayed and kissed St Patrick's Cross. Then to St Brigid's Cross, an ancient carving embedded into the basilica walls. There I spread-eagled to renounce the world, the flesh and the devil before four slow circuits outside the basilica, reciting seven decades of the Rosary. And then to bed – the first of the six penitential beds, which are remnants of ancient monastic cells, beginning with St Brigid, then St Brendan, St Catherine, St Columba, St Patrick and finally the shared bed of Saints Davog and Molaise. Then it's over to the lakeshore to pray standing, then kneeling, then bless myself with lake water. Then back to St Patrick's Cross to kneel and pray and finally into the basilica to complete the station with the choice of Psalm 16 or more Paters, Aves and a Creed for the pope's intentions. I opt for the psalm and wonder why the pope doesn't do Lough Derg for himself.

1.45 p.m.

As if I haven't had enough of walking in circles, I try out the labyrinth between the penitential beds and Davog's House. Round and round I go, disturbing a young man taking an illicit nap. It is his second day and he is from Cork. I remark that his county Gaelic-football team, known as the Rebels, threw away a Munster Final win yesterday when they allowed Kerry to draw on the final whistle, took the lead again in extra time, then conceded a free to allow Kerry to equalise.

'Ah, sure, didn't they get the draw at least?' says he. I ask if he's more of a hurling fan. 'Ah, I'd be a bit of a neutral,' he says, shattering the advice I'd been given that Lough Derg is a place of fervent discussion about Gaelic games. I concentrate on the labyrinth, working my way to the centre and out on a path that leads to a small lakeside sentry post. They don't make Rebels like they used to, I decide.

3.10 p.m.
I have just completed my second station and have learned a few things. First, St Brendan is a hard taskmaster and second, St Brigid is an equally taxing mistress. Circling their beds is treacherous, particularly in the corners nearest the Bell Tower mound, said to cover the cave where Patrick vanquished the serpent and had his vision. At this point, you need your hands free to save yourself from a fall on rocks not yet beaten into a smooth path by the bare feet of pilgrims. Also, I learned to watch out for wee blonde women with painted toenails. One such pilgrim took off like a greyhound out of the traps as I was completing my fourth round of the basilica. By St Catherine's Bed (number three) we were neck and neck. Traversing the course with astonishingly sure feet, she was on to St Columba before I got kneeling beside St Catherine for the second time. By the time I got to the double bed of St Davog and St Molaise, she was heading for the water's edge. At this rate, she would have her nine stations done by teatime and have completed her three-day pilgrimage in a day. I wonder do they do a discount for that?

3.25 p.m.
I have just walked past and wee Blondie is back in Brendan's Bed with its speckled rocks. During my second station, the mantra-like praying drifted off into Gerard Manley Hopkins's poem 'Pied Beauty', with its invocation, 'Glory be to God for dappled things.' Since completing the station – with prayers in proper order – I have enjoyed reflecting on the poem, particularly its closing lines: 'He fathers-forth whose beauty is past change: / Praise him.' It really is a beautiful prayer, and appropriate for Lough Derg, so I cannot be faulted for faltering on the Paters. I'm surprised I remember all the lines too. Praying is wonderfully therapeutic.

5.15 p.m.
During the rounds of the basilica for the third station, my new Rosary beads come apart. Luke from Castlederg, who runs the First Aid station, offers to fix them, and does so with forceps. A woman coming in for headache tablets remarks that this is the most versatile First Aid station she has seen. Back on the rounds, the beads go again. Luke fixes them once more.

'Probably made in China,' he remarks, and I agree that they certainly aren't up to the heavy-duty praying of a Lough Derg pilgrim. I finish the station without further mishap and am heading for the dining-room. In the covered walkway of the cloisters I hear, 'Darach, is that you?' It is I, and the voice belongs to Gertie McCabe of Omagh, here as basilica organist until July. I know Gertie through mutual friend Mary Ronayne-Keane, the Cork composer. Gertie is in great form as usual, but then she has proper meals and wears shoes.

6.20 p.m.
My first 'Lough Derg meal' of oatcakes and black coffee. I am at a table with three women and they are excellent company. Nora Pat lives in Roscommon but says she still feels like a Dubliner down the country. Marian and Maria are both nurses and friends from way back. Nora Pat is curious about the male quartet at the next table and wonders if they are a pilgrimage 'fourball' (as in golf), so she comes right out and asks as they are leaving. Paddy O'Sullivan joins us to explain. He is a 79-year-old Corkman on his fifty-second annual pilgrimage. He takes a group to Lough Derg annually and over the years some join and others leave.

'Sure all of them that came with me those first years are dead and gone now and I'm the only one still coming,' he points out.

He describes their itinerary – set off from Cork on Saturday morning and stop for scones and sandwiches in Limerick; then Galway for lunch and from there to Bundoran for a hotel and dinner. Off without breakfast to Lough Derg on Sunday morning and finish on Tuesday morning. Then it's off to visit Belleek Pottery and Drumcliffe Cemetery, to 'cast a cold eye on life and death' at W.B. Yeats's graveside. After that, Knock Basilica for Mass and then a Lough Derg meal and on down the country, with a good break but no breaking of fast in Limerick, arriving into Cork city centre around 10.30 p.m. Having seen the others off, Paddy is home in time to put on the pan for a big fry as his pilgrimage ends at midnight. His wife died six years ago and he lives alone now, but this year he has been invited to break his fast with friends and he knows they'll be having stew. As we munch on our Spartan meal of Lough Derg oatcakes, he relishes the prospect. Paddy enjoys life and even St Patrick's Purgatory is an annual highlight. 'But sure, I don't know if

I'll do it again because I may not be here at all next year,' he remarks. Does he still benefit from pilgrimage? He says he never left the island disappointed. Last year he came with an overwhelming anger after an associate cheated him out of personal savings. During his pilgrimage, he decided he did not need the money: 'It's gone, so let it go.' On the ferry for home he felt a huge serenity and has not felt anger since. 'I don't have a problem with it now, but he does,' says Paddy of his cheating associate.

7.30 p.m.
Lough Derg prior Mgr Richard Mohan shepherds late pilgrims to the front pews for the opening Mass as the congregation practises hymns with a young female cantor and Gertie McCabe's organ. The processional brings in a priest I know, Canon Macartan McQuaid, and two concelebrants, Fr Mick from Cork and Fr David from Tanzania. The homily is about why Mass should not be boring. Then, after Communion, another short homily on how 'Canon Mac' says post-Communion prayers based on the acronym WALTER – Worship, Adore, Love, Thank, Entreat and Repent. I greet Canon Mac outside after Mass and he tells me he is really enjoying life since retiring as parish priest in my native town of Clones. Back in Enniskillen, he combines chaplaincy at the two Catholic grammar schools, St Michael's College and Our Lady of Lourdes Convent. Tomorrow, he heads off on pilgrimage to Knock with a hundred schoolgirls. We talk of Gaelic football, but Derry's recent defeat of our native Monaghan has left too bitter a taste for enthusiasm.

I head up to the dorms then for the pre-vigil rest, but it is too bright and I had too much black coffee earlier. I just lie on my bunk as others snore, some loudly. When the man opposite farts noisily and continues snoring, I rise.

Down the dorm, somebody is talking of how cold it will be tonight, so I add another layer of clothes. When my caffeine rush wears off, I may be in trouble.

*Tuesday, 9 June 2009*
7.45 a.m.
The vigil brings me to the brink several times. It's not hunger but a general build-up of pain in my knees and a feeling that I could just pass out from exhaustion at any moment. The prayers are relentless, repetitive and, depending on who is leading, often hard to follow. The night is bitterly cold, too, with a northerly wind blowing across the lake from Tievetooey, which a fellow pilgrim describes several times as a 'very bleak place'. Yet for hour after hour, we walk slowly around the interior of the basilica, reciting our mantra, kneeling, rising and kneeling again. It is a huge bonus if the kneeling comes when I am at the front. The padded kneelers at the altar rails are sheer luxury. The worst is at the back, where we flop to our knees on the hard floor. Over time, by varying my route up the centre aisle rather than around the sides, I devise little strategies to get to the front. It doesn't work most times, but at least I avoid the back floor. Occasionally, I perch on the pew and lower one knee to the wood. Meanwhile, with shifts of pacing patterns and people diverting, sometimes I find myself following a fellow pilgrim who is praying loudly off the pace. This is unsettling and requires adjustment to a more amenable procession. Energy drains away as the night intensifies and the interlude between prayers seems shorter and shorter.

The night begins at 10 o'clock, after Benediction, when the vigil candle is extinguished for the 80 or so pilgrims who have kept vigil on the Sunday night into Monday. Surprisingly, I find this session very uplifting. The incense and familiar Latin of *'Tantum Ergo'* bring back vivid childhood memories. Then the ex-'vigilantes' go off to bed, smiling with relief, and we are left to our fate. In bare feet across the cold pavement, we file over to the Flood Room (Named after former rector, Monsignor Thomas Flood) shelter used between basilica bouts for a first mug of boiling water from the geyser. Someone advises that a shake of white pepper gives the illusion of more sustenance and I add some, finding the slight kick in the throat a pick-me-up. As the night wears on, I even look forward to my next mug of 'Lough Derg soup'. Yet the constant source of support is the companionship of fellow pilgrims, particularly my recent dining companions. While discussing the Mass, I mention Canon Mac. Marian knows of him and talks of her connection with Clogher Diocese through her uncle, Fr Austin Slowey. I recall him and mention my own late uncle, Fr Vincent. There is a squeal of delight as Marian informs me that her father, Brendan Slowey, was best friends with Vincent during their time as boarders in St Macartan's College, Monaghan. Within minutes, we know seed, breed and generation; their Slowey roots in Clones, my mother Mamo's public profile. Didn't I have a brother in the Northern Bank with their brother Kevin? What of their cousin Sean Slowey, a good friend of mine in Toronto? As the pieces fall into place we are bolstered against the long night ahead by newfound friendship.

At 10.15 p.m. we are back in the pews for our 'Introduction to Vigil' talk by a Mercy sister working here as a counsellor. Several times, she illustrates her talk with New-Age type music. At one point, the singer gets stuck in a rut. The vigilator turns it off, apologising for the technology. I lose it there. While I am sure it is a worthy talk, I can't remember anything afterwards because my caffeine kick has worn off. At the very first juncture of the vigil, I am starting to crash. But back in the Flood Room, 'soup' and good company restores my spirits and I am ready for the Rosary at 11.45 p.m. By this stage, the vigilantes are starting to firm up into more definite characters. Groups coalesce during breaks as we return to where we have left our mugs. The few pilgrim smokers have typically bonded in their addiction. Like pariahs, they have a separate shelter beside the cloakroom, from which they emerge for an even longer traverse to the basilica.

Day two, and the fourth station begins at half past midnight. It is led by an older woman, who sets the pace as we circle inside on our imaginary journey around the outside of the basilica, through the penitential beds to the waterside and back to the basilica, all in just about an hour. The first of the vigil's four stations completed, it's back to the flood room for mutual support before the next and fifth station. This time the prayers of our imaginary tour are led by a pilgrim nun from our group, who seems so overcome with exhaustion she might faint. But she and we survive the pace and earn our next break. That's half the night's complement of stations finished and it's just after three o'clock. By now, groups are more fluid. A friendly woman from Meath joins us. She took a bus to Enniskillen only to discover that the Lough Derg bus from there now only runs on Thursday, Friday and Saturday.

'I ended up sharing a taxi,' she relates.

Marian describes how she came as a young nurse, hitchhiking from Dublin to Pettigo.

'I knew that during the pilgrimage I would probably find somebody who would take me back to Dublin. In the end I plucked up the courage to ask a man that I knew was driving there. Turned out he lived just around the corner from us and he was more than happy to give me a lift home right to our door. Isn't it extraordinary how we can live our lives and not even be aware of people right beside us?'

We shuffle back for the penultimate station of the vigil at 3.30 a.m., in the reassuring knowledge that dawn is on the way. There is general concern for a young couple. He is from Pennsylvania and she is from Argentina, working in Dublin. They are doing Lough Derg together before getting married and moving to the States. They weren't fully aware of what the pilgrimage entails and are finding it overwhelming. He comforts her constantly and holds her through times when she is simply unable to rise from the pew. Others stop occasionally to offer support and encouragement. For the rest of the pilgrimage, they receive a steady stream of solicitude, support and good wishes. In this fifth station, I am impressed by the young man who is leading the prayers. His firm, clear voice leaves no doubt where we are in our imaginary traverse of the penitential beds. Yet at one stage during this station I feel transported. I am staring at the huge penal cross suspended behind the altar. Gradually, as I pray, I see a sequential series of images in the panelled marble behind. It begins in the top left corner with a demonic face. Moving down that panel, the face implodes. The pattern continues over the other panels until all is clear and calm. My eyes are drawn constantly to this image as the station continues and I know it will remain with me through the coming days. Perhaps I have shared a vision with Patrick and all those pilgrims who entered his cave.

But for now, my preferred vision is of the flood room, where we soon return for more meagre comforts. As people scan newspapers there, several remark that final results for the European elections will now be in. We suffering pilgrims know perfectly well the outcome and the reasons for it. Someone raises the huge waste of opportunities in a decade of greed, but soon we drift back to the reassurance that we will come through tough times into a more realistic perspective. Perhaps Ireland's travails are like a purgatorial stint at Lough Derg.

By now we are revealing more personal details of our lives, including our children. Nora Pat's son is doing his Leaving-Certificate exams. Unable to contact him, she wonders how he has got on. The blonde woman who raced around the beds joins us; she turns out to be a wonderful person whose only son is finishing his Ph.D in London. Each time she mentions him, her face lights up with love and she recites precisely the title of his thesis in Education Psychology. For several moments we share pride in our progeny; then it's back to the basilica for the final station at five o'clock.

Now, dawn has fully settled over Lough Derg, a magical mist rising from the lake over at Saints Island, and we have been transported through our darkest hours into a new day. Yet the final station of the vigil proves difficult because the man leading the prayers has an almost impenetrable accent and delivers them in a mumbled monotone. At times I do not know whether he is saying the Our Father, the Hail Mary or the Creed. As a consequence, my pace falters. In frustration, I step out through the basilica door into the dawn to regroup and find calm. I walk briefly down to the lakeside and am heartened immediately as I watch:

> *… the lake waves clapping cold hands together*
> *And … the morning breaking as it breaks*
> *Over a field where a man is watching a calving cow.*[15]

New life, new day.

When I return a few minutes later, the basilica doors are all opened as others snatch a brief spell outside. In the growing warmth of the morning sun, we make it to six o'clock and a final break before we are joined for morning Mass by those pilgrims being roused from sleep in the dorms.

The first Mass of the new day is celebrated by the prior and, despite our exhaustion, we ride through on the accomplishment of lasting the night. The Mass seems inordinately long, however, with a full homily and various wee bits at the end. I note that Mass on Station Island is never curtailed, and it is a full hour and more before we emerge to wash and freshen up in the dorm before the next steps in our pilgrimage – the Sacrament of Reconciliation (Confession) followed by the eighth station around the penitential beds. The prospect of kneeling on the rocks is very daunting, but it is shaping up to be another beautiful day – yet very cold in the shade.

10.30 a.m.

Even during the prior's initial pep-talk, I can feel the dread rising in my chest. My eighth station will be preceded by the Sacrament of Reconciliation – an ordeal that never fails to produce in me a panic-stricken revulsion. It is occasioned by the memory of a tyrannical parish priest who came to our parish in 1960 – long before Vatican II – straight from his two-decade-long posting as prior of Lough Derg.

Mgr Cornelius Ward revelled in his reputation as a tyrant even before my induction as an altar boy under the Latin Mass rite about a year later. During Mass he frequently delivered a vicious elbow dig or even an angry cuff on the side of the head for any perceived laxity. In the sacristy, he bullied us on any pretext and never in my memory did he acknowledge our efforts with even a simple word of kindness. It did not make for a happy relationship, but it was in the supposed secrecy of the confessional that he was at his worst. On Saturdays we were required, on pain of worse retribution than any penance for our relatively frivolous transgressions, to go to Confessions. We had the option of three priests – Mgr Ward and his kindly curates, Fr Dan Ward and Fr Tommie Gormley. The pews outside the monsignor's box were invariably empty, yet he would frequently emerge and chivvy a couple of us into the penitential kiosk. Often the inducement included a firm grip of an earlobe or, even worse, the small hairs of our forelocks. Trapped behind closed doors, I waited for the shutter to draw back, knowing that humiliation would ensue. For, while other priests conducted the sacrament of Confession in a discreet whisper, the hard-of-hearing monsignor demanded loud disclosure of our venial sins before absolution. His strictures on behalf of the Lord were loud enough to be heard by the Hail Marys gathered down at the back of the church, whispering to their beads in breath that seemed to inhale forever and exhale on a burst of 'Amen'. The penitent would emerge as the focus of attention – and perhaps even gossip.

I recall this search-and-embarrass mission of the former prior of purgatory as I watch his successor at the altar rails, clasping the shoulders of penitents who kneel before him as he looks them straight in the eye and challenges them to 'give up their oul' sins'. Having avoided this sacrament, I quake at the prospect of repentance. In the end, I am directed to one of the other priests and, kneeling, find my mind is totally blank. I mumble something non-committal, then repeat it to a priest who seems impatient at my lack of disclosure. In the end, he sighs, 'Well, at least you're on the island.' I'm given a general absolution, a package job of very low specification. As I arise from the kneeler, I am remarkably relieved to be heading for the penitential beds. Meanwhile, I don't feel in the least hungry, but I would love some strong coffee to get rid of the bitter taste of Confession – to which, I fear, I will never be reconciled.

The eighth station, on the rugged rocks, with my sore knees and lower legs, is very difficult. Even on the circuits of the basilica, I find the paving much rougher underfoot than yesterday and the dreaded midges are attacking. Luke is back at the First Aid station, so I interrupt my station briefly to ask if he has anything for the midges. He gets his 'mossy' potion, a foul-smelling unguent guaranteed to keep pests away. Soon after, I am interrupted by Nora Pat, who has been to the shop for mosquito nets, and she hands me one. Doubly protected, I negotiate the beds, kneeling, rising and kneeling again. Moving to the final double bed brings huge relief, and the view from the shore induces ecstasy. I recall Seamus Heaney's lines:

> *… Everything in me*
> *Wanted to bow down, to offer up,*
> *To go barefoot, foetal and penitential,*
> *And pray at the water's edge.*[16]

11.15 a.m.
A few newcomers make their way from the ferry to the cloisters. There seem to be fewer today than our group of 46 yesterday, but there is plenty of time for more to arrive. I walk over to the jetty, calling in to the shop to have my broken beads replaced. They don't have a matching set in deep blue, so I settle for rather striking turquoise beads. With only one station remaining, they won't take much abuse.

2.30 p.m.
Seven and a half hours until bedtime as we emerge from the dining-room where, with liberal libations of caffeine at a table for eight, we have had a great chat. My fellow pilgrims are very different in background and outlook from what I expected. Over the course of an hour and a half we have discussed alternative remedies, cultural contrasts in Europe and beyond, education systems, spiritual influences, our personal difficulties with organised religion and much more besides. After 30 hours with no sleep, practically no food, long sessions of repetitive prayer, constant instruction and admonishment, we have even talked of current economic and political issues on the mainland far away. Nobody here could be described as a Catholic automaton. Our small group has thrown together people of varying ages with real life experiences – people who have many issues, difficulties and challenges in their lives, including major issues with the church to which we belong. What has drawn us here is a common need for answers. Sitting together, sharing a frugal meal of oatcakes and dry toast after prayer, fasting, sleep deprivation and extreme discomfort, a huge sense of shared experience has bonded us as a group. Leaving the dining-room, we know the next hours will be difficult, but there is strong support for those who might waver, or who might simply need it.

4.00 p.m.
Making our Way of the Cross around Harry Clarke's stunning stained-glass basilica windows, I am struck by other exquisite furnishings. The huge penal crucifix behind the altar still embraces us with truncated arms, its simple and stark functionality testimony to a time when art was sacred, simple and heartfelt. Below it, the modern bronze tabernacle

and lectern capture spiritual essence in their swirling Celtic designs in enamel insets. At the rear door, the bog-oak processional cross stands sentinel. Like it, the ceremony is simple yet deeply moving. Afterwards, I accompany Marian and Nora Pat to the 'museum' behind the basilica, where old registers list names and details of pilgrims. Many of the handwritten tomes are in a distressing state, lying in an open cupboard without proper heat and ventilation. Some are waterlogged and have been laid out to dry on an old wagon-wheel. While my companions search for specific entries, I hunt out the earliest volume. I discover that the registers from Mgr Ward's tenure are terse, regimental lists – albeit in beautiful copperplate – while the 1905 register has pilgrim remarks preserved for posterity. Many of these are in Irish, most are enthusiastic about Lough Derg and many are witty. One pilgrim says he has had the happiest days of his life in St Patrick's Purgatory, which might be explained by the fact that he comes from County Cavan. Another poor pilgrim has recorded that his cap has blown away and he now has to 'head off bareheaded to Pettigo'. Another pilgrim has noted that 'the stones are too hard': he can be assured by this pilgrim of a century later that they haven't got any softer. Then there is the observation that 'The fellow feeling among the pilgrims is remarkable! Everyone tries to make everyone else as miserable as himself.' Another has written: 'I came to do penance and I have not been disappointed.' Probably referring to the penitential stations rather than the hostel accommodation, an entry remarks: 'I have never seen so many people in one Bed.' Certainly, however, the 1905 pilgrims are positive:

> *My first visit to Lough Derg[;] was glad to see that the faith of St Patrick is so deeply rooted in the hearts of the Irish*

> *people. I shall come again and hope to bring some friends with me.*

As it is in the twenty-first century, the health of the economy was obviously of concern to at least one 1905 pilgrim, who has written that the 'supply of oatbread is rather limited. Irish manufacture might be prudently and judiciously furthered in the direction of the oatmeal supplied to the hospice.' Always the voice of dissent on the side, someone has scrawled beside that entry: '*Raiméis*' ('Rubbish').

Elsewhere in this trove of the pilgrimage island's past, I come across the following entry on the 'Remuneration of Priests':

> *Beginning with the year 1944, the charge for the boat ticket was fixed at 4/= per pilgrim. Of this sum the ferryman received 1/= and 3/= was assigned to the island and the priests. The distribution being as follows – 2/2 to the general charges of the island, ⅓ of the balance, that is ⅓ of 10d per pilgrim – Prior's rata paid to the general funds of the island. The remainder of the balance – that is ⅔ of 10d per pilgrim was distributed among the Prior and the Attendant Priests in accordance with the numbers of days which each of them served on the island during the season.*

This entry goes on to record that from the year 1955, the charge for the boat ticket was fixed at 4s 6d per pilgrim and the ferryman received one-third of this. Clearly the ferryman was a key figure in the operation of the pilgrimage. The other major cost was bread. One entry records that in June 1955, bread from the Ballyshannon Bakery cost £378 12s 0d, while an entry for 1963 shows that bread for the season cost £899 12s 9d, while other provisions cost £1,319 19s 0d.

Back outside the museum, the weather has turned decidedly colder, yet I am enchanted by the stark beauty of barren moorland that induces the sense of isolation inherent in the Lough Derg experience.

6.10 p.m.
Before Mass – the third since I last slept – I explore Davog House to keep my mind occupied. A plaque in the hallway lists the priors, with several big gaps, starting with St Davog. The recent entries interest me because I am familiar with all who have ruled this purgatory since 1942 – more than a decade before I was born. A noticeboard displays a table from *The Times* of London rating the 'top 10' pilgrimages. It includes Rome, Lourdes, Santiago de Compostela and others; Lough Derg makes the tenth spot. An accompanying article by Scottish theologian Ian Bradley notes that 'as church attendance has plummeted, more people are travelling the old pilgrim routes across Europe or visiting shrines old and new'. The article concludes, 'Many people find it easier to walk than talk their faith and derive encouragement through treading in the footsteps of countless pilgrims before them.'[17] With that, I decide I had better tread in the footsteps of countless pilgrims across to the basilica for evening Mass.

7.30 p.m.
Mass is celebrated by Fr David from Tanzania, whose home parish has nine churches, the furthest 36 kilometres from the centre and the nearest 9 kilometres. He travels to them all by bicycle. He tells of his arrival here, with last-minute changes because he has no transit visa for London Heathrow and the alternative arrangement via Paris to Dublin and on to Lough Derg. He is confused by our water taps because he

is familiar only with taps that turn. He tries this with no effect and then sees the word 'push' on it. Then he sees 'push' everywhere – including on the doors of the basilica. He suggests that PUSH is an acronym for the Lough Derg pilgrimage: 'Pray Until Something Happens'. In our brief exchanges, Fr David comes across as a caring man, but I am struck by the irony that the traffic in missionaries has reversed. I am tempted to ask if children in Tanzania bring a penny to school for the 'white babies'.

On the way out of Mass, I chat to a couple of new pilgrims from Tyrone, who tell me they had to give up on their stations earlier, halfway through their second, because they were 'eaten alive by the midges'. They have to complete them before night prayer and Benediction at 9.20 p.m. and so will miss their pre-vigil rest. But the evening has cleared up, the midges have gone to bed, sated on pilgrim flesh, and the lake is a light shade of grey as ripples lap the shoreline. A swan glides by and I recall being told earlier that its mate has died last year. Alone now on the lake of penance: 'It is with flocks of birds your cries will be heard forever.'[18] At least the Children of Lir, born into a life of wealth and privilege but robbed of their legacy and turned into swans until St Patrick released them, had the comfort of each other's company. I am looking out on the lake when the young American, here with his Argentine fiancée, pauses for a chat. He is really looking forward to bed, but says he has some concern now about where they can get their 'Lough Derg meal' to complete the pilgrimage when they leave the island and head off to Westport. I ask if they plan to climb Croagh Patrick. He says he has only sneakers and has been told he would need boots for the Reek.

'Mind you, after being barefoot here, my sneakers will probably feel like reinforced hiking boots by the morning,' he laughs. Clearly his spirit has not been broken.

8.45 p.m.
Groups of pilgrims find warmth in clusters and chat as we approach the final hour of our vigil. At the basilica, the young man who led the prayers for the sixth station has his feet covered in bandages. The skin has peeled off, he tells me.

'The skin would have been soft because I do a lot of running,' he says, adding happily, 'but we're coming into the final stretch now.' Down at the water's edge near Davog House, two women from Leitrim are also talking about feet. One of them has just put a hot-water bottle in her bed.

'Last year my feet were so cold, I couldn't get to sleep,' she says. 'Imagine not being able to sleep because your feet are too cold and you are absolutely exhausted. Problem is, I'm not used to having to keep myself warm in bed,' she adds with a wink and a smile. I tell her it's just as well she brought the hot-water bottle because her usual feet-warming method would probably be against the pilgrimage rules. Inside Davog House, the conversation of a quartet of Omagh pilgrims jumps from local graveyard politics to tiredness and food. One names a man who used to 'come off Lough Derg and straight away to Bundoran for a big feed. There was no fasting or praying for him once he came off the island.' One of her companions says, 'Eating was never a priority for us. We'd just go on home and go to bed.' Out on the lake, a swift skims the water surface, harvesting the insects. At least one creature is happy about the infestation of midges.

I barely remember the final hour of the vigil. We have night prayers and Benediction with Fr David and then the conclusion as our candle is extinguished. There is a blessing from Pope Benedict, who does not attend personally, and we go off to the dorms. As others are getting into pyjamas, I peel down to t-shirt and boxers and climb into my lower bunk. By the time my head hits the pillow, I am off in the Land of Nod.

6.20 a.m.
I awake around the first glimmer of dawn, take stock of my surroundings, rearrange the blankets, which are tangled, and drift off again until about 10 minutes before the six o'clock alarm. Then I lie in post-sleep slumber and listen to fellow pilgrims snoring. At the first sound of the bell, I am up and quickly washed, dressed and ready for the final hours. I feel well rested and almost ready for home, but my knees are killing me.

8.45 a.m.
Our closing Mass does not seem half as long as yesterday's, although it takes almost exactly the same time. Canon Mohan speaks of how Lough Derg has been changing and how this was initiated by his predecessor, Canon McSorley. The trials of purgatory have been eased for some. Pilgrims say how good it is to have duvets on the beds now, and that the heavy blankets will all be replaced in time. This disclosure that we got the economy-class deal takes something from my good sleep. After Mass, we embark on the ninth station to conclude our pilgrimage. Many opt to do it outside, but my knees simply aren't up to the rocks. I opt to do the station inside the basilica, where prayers are led by one of the Omagh women. Again I notice that those praying off pace are hugely disruptive and have to be avoided, because they can spoil the chances of getting to the cushioned kneelers at the altar rails. After being marooned in a pew at the back, I congratulate Nora Pat on securing the rails for the long concluding sessions.

'You've got to work on it,' she advises.

9.00 a.m.
I've just noticed a fellow pilgrim with his shoes on. He tells me that as soon as he completed his ninth station outside, he went to the dorm, packed and dressed for home, and his shoes and socks feel great.

'I've my bag sitting down at the jetty,' he says, 'and I'm all ready to go.'

*Pilgrims smiled at one another:*
*How good God was,*
*How much a loving Father!*
*How wonderful the punishing stones were!*
*Another hour and the boats will sail*
*Into the port of Time.*
*Are you not glad you came?*[19]

9.30 a.m.
I climb the stairs to 301D, where staff have already stripped the beds. My shoes and socks feel luxurious after almost 48 hours of barefoot praying. On the way up I note the duvets on lower floors and I ask one of the housekeeping staff when the top dorm will get them.

'Any day now,' she tells me.

As I hoist my bag and hobble off, I compute the pilgrimage bonus of old blankets and more stairs to climb. I join my fellow pilgrims over at the jetty with a full half hour to go before the announced departure at 10 o'clock. Someone notes that this is a quarter hour later than the ferry left yesterday. Maybe we are getting another pilgrimage bonus, yet I am content to linger with these new friends, chatting. Marian remarks that our ordeal was nothing compared to the daily lot of children abused in institutions run by religious orders and funded by the state. They had no hope that life would get better, she observes. One of our dining companions from yesterday agrees heartily and then discloses that he is a member of one of the religious orders. Clearly, behind the horror stories, there are caring and good people too. A change of subject to how we will have our final Lough Derg meal and the mood becomes buoyant in our cluster of now-well-heeled pilgrims. Most will head straight for a shop in Pettigo that sells oatcakes. One man tells me his grandchildren look forward to his annual stint on Lough Derg because they enjoy the oatcakes he brings home.

10.20 a.m.
The *St Columba* emerges from the side of the island, surprising most of us, who have been keeping watch on another ferry over on the mainland. As we board, we are handed a Lough Derg candle and literature about retreats, pilgrimages and more. The prior bids an individual farewell to each of us and asks where we are going. I tell him Castlederg, but mention my Clones origins. His face registers recognition and, as I step onto the boat, he calls out my name, which he has just remembered. Then, as soon as we are all seated, Canon Mohan comes to the front to tell us that our Lough Derg pilgrimage will stay with us. He advises us, if we are ever troubled, to light our Lough Derg candle to show the way. He leads us in a rousing rendition of 'Hail Glorious St Patrick', climbs off and waves as we pull away from the jetty. In no time we are putting to on the mainland, where it is considerably warmer, and talking of the superstition that if you look back at Station Island you are bound to return for another pilgrimage. As the boat glides to the jetty, I turn deliberately to gaze at a place that is so redolent of our past and so important for our future. I notice that I am not the only one who stares back.

11.50 p.m.
Approaching midnight of the third day of my Lough Derg pilgrimage, I have prepared ingredients for an omelette of fresh tomatoes and basil, to be ready on the stroke of midnight. I have eaten nothing since the oatcakes from Pettigo around 1.30 p.m. – after a brief nap. Yet I have been on a high all day, energised by my pilgrimage and puzzling over the value of 'doing Lough Derg'. Does it provide answers for our troubled times? It certainly allows time for reflection and, if only for a short time, it totally alters your perspective, not least about what you expect and what you find. Going to Station Island, I expected to encounter people who might otherwise be religious stand-offs, the Hail Marys and Holy Joes who want to do the required penance and a bit extra. Perhaps they were there, but those I met were, without exception, people with real lives, facing all the challenges and problems that brings; people with big hearts who come to support the needs and wants of others; people with their own needs and wants who come to search for solutions within themselves. They are people with failed or troubled relationships, people with addictions or living with addicts. Some have a troubled past and all have an uncertain future. Most are believers, yet many others are searching for something to believe in. Each of these pilgrims can derive as much and more from this penitential exercise as those who come year in year out to purge the flesh and renounce the world and the devil. All come with individual motives for partaking in this ancient three-day pilgrimage and, over the course of three days, they often find answers within themselves. Yes, it is worth every moment and every painful step along the way.

# Chapter 2

# Visions of Paradise

## Gleann Cholm Cille

*22 June 2009*

The ninth *stad* or station on the Turas Cholmcille (St Columba's Pilgrimage) is the Cloch Aonach (Meeting Stone), a 1.92-metre megalith with crosses and Celtic circle symbols carved into it. Barefoot pilgrims who have crossed the Abar Dubh (Black Mud) from Tobar Cholmcille (Columba's Well) walk around the Cloch Aonach three times, praying constantly, then turn their backs on the stone and, arms outstretched, renounce Satan, the world and the body. Then they peer through the eyehole in the stone. If they are in a sufficient state of grace, they will be granted a vision of paradise.

I performed the ritual as prescribed, peered through and saw the verdant midsummer splendour of Gleann Cholm Cille (Glencolmcille), a magical world bounded by scarlet fuchsia, bracken ferns and flowering saffron whin bushes interspersed with brambles bursting into white flowers, soon to yield a bountiful crop of blackberries. A short time later, I sat with a creamy pint of Guinness stout and watched a spectacular sunset light up the headland at Sceilp Úna and illuminate the street of an Caiseal almost to midnight.

The fiery pink glow presaged a wondrous new day, which found me on the slopes of Sliabh Liag (Slieve League) looking down on Teileann (Teelin) Harbour and the expanse of Donegal Bay, at Sligo's majestic Knocknarea and as far as Nephin and Croagh Patrick in Mayo. I looked down on Reachlainn Uí Bhirn from the tallest sea cliffs in Europe at the summit above Bun Glas, with Donegal's coast winding off to the north. Finally, my gaze took in the breathtaking Trá Bán in Málainn Bhig, where cliff steps lead down to a beautiful lagoon and gentle waves lap the sandy shore. If a single glimpse of paradise is all that pilgrims are promised, then I must have been in a sufficient state of grace to warrant lasting impressions for the following 24 hours.

*Wednesday, 17 June 2009*

The Cloch Aonach is just one of a number of fascinating *stadanna* on the best-known pilgrimage route of Gleann Cholm Cille, an isolated Gaeltacht parish in the far reaches of south-west Donegal where folk traditions are still a proud, living and vital force. At the Oideas Gael college, director Liam Ó Cuinneagáin describes the pilgrimage that his own mother once explained for a world that was fast forgetting such traditions and rituals as the era of the Celtic Tiger dawned.[20]

'Now they start at the Church of Ireland, but once they started at our house further up the glen. People came to our house afterwards because [celebrated *seanchaí*] Micí Sheán Néill from Rann na Feirste would sit on telling stories for about two hours after it,' he recalls, adding that, in addition to such entertainment, the hardship of the *turas* was offset by the alternative of more rigorous penance. 'To do the pilgrimage five times during the month of June is the equivalent of doing Lough Derg. Most people back then would do it in bare feet and that was the real penance of the *turas*. Only a few people would do it barefoot now.'

While the season begins on the saint's feast, advance preparations are needed for the annual pilgrimage, according to Liam. 'Gaps [into fields] would be opened up by local farmers on that day. But some people would do the *turas* as soon as possible after midnight and they would be tramping down the reeds and briars for those coming behind them. Also there would be stepping-stones across the rivers and streams.' As for the prayers, 'It's three Our Fathers and three Hail Marys at most of the stations, but extra prayers are said at some.'

4.00 p.m.
I depart Oideas Gael with a small handbook that contains a detailed map of the *turas* route and lots more material to inform my pilgrim path.[21] The starting point is a kilometre or so away, and it is a glorious summer afternoon in Gleann Cholm Cille, far from forecasts of half a million unemployed and reports of a slump of 42 per cent in the net financial assets of Irish households.[22] As I walk, I read snatches of the booklet and study the map. The *turas* opens traditionally on 9 June because this is the feast day of Colmcille or Columba, the 'dove of the church', born at Gartan in north Donegal in AD 521. Alongside Patrick and Brigid, Colmcille is one of Ireland's three patron saints. He left an indelible a stamp on this place named in his honour, just as he did on Derry City (known in Irish as Doire Colmcille) or on the monastic island of Iona off the Scottish coast. In Gleann Cholm Cille, stories abound about the irascible saint, and visitors are pointed to places associated with these stories,

bearing physical traces that stretch back one and a half millennia. These are the stations of the pilgrimage. However, as with other pilgrimage trails, it is widely believed that many of these landmarks resonate with a pre-Christian spiritual force, harnessed and adapted to reinforce the message of triumph over evil and the promise of everlasting salvation in the Lord.

4.15 p.m.

The *turas* starts and ends at the Church of Ireland parish church named in the saint's honour on the small country road called an tSráid (the Street) and proceeds in a circular route of about 5.5 kilometres through 15 *stadanna*, beginning at a cairn, or pile of stones. This marks the spot where the 'dove of the church' is believed to have built the first place of worship in Gleann Cholm Cille after driving out the demons that his predecessor Patrick had banished here. An iconic megalith atop a rocky outcrop, less than 50 metres away, is the second *stad*. Pilgrims have traditionally moved through the stations barefoot over the course of about three hours. It is probably a blessing, therefore, that the route is mostly across fields and streams. It runs through Garbhrois and on to Séipéal Cholmcille (Colmcille's Chapel), up the steep slope of Sliabh Bhíofáin to the spectacular well called Tobar Cholmcille, and then back down through the Abar Dubh to the Cloch Aonach. Next comes a series of megaliths and cairns. The final standing stone, in the church graveyard, is surrounded by the resting places of the Musgraves – once landlords of the glen – and other local worthies.

4.45 p.m.

Down a small road bounded by luscious hedgerows and over a small bridge past the muddy estuary, I am now nearing the slopes of the promontory at Ceann Ghlinne. The *turas* is now recognised and accommodated as an integral part of the cultural tradition of the glen and, on 9 June, landowners are happy to open gates, fences and other passages for those making the stations to ensure that nothing impedes the procession of prayer. They also make similar accommodation each subsequent Sunday through the month to allow pilgrims to make the *turas* five times during June – possibly to avoid Lough Derg. Having actually been doing Lough Derg on 9 June, I have come on a weekday, yet landowners I meet along the way are still more than willing to let me visit stations that require such permission – so long as their gates are securely fastened on exit. That open access, along with friendly greetings along the pilgrim path, shows the warm hospitality of this still-isolated district. Celebrated American painter Rockwell Kent, who lived in Gleann Cholm Cille for a brief period during the 1920s, saw the glen as 'endless riven moors of grass and heather-grown turf and, if you like, God's presence – or more moving, Man's'. And of those places and people, he remarked:

> *There are the moors; and equal in their dignity, the people. And nothing, one might say of them, is there but innate goodness, kindness, charity and utterly unconscious pride; a pride that recognises no man to be better than themselves; a pride that is without envy; and being without envy, is content. And through contentment, happy.*[23]

5.30 p.m.

At the third station in a roadside field, I say my prayers and then pass a round stone around my body in a ritual of healing. The *turas* then moves quickly through the fourth, fifth and sixth stations, which are grouped together on an elevated area. The fourth station is a stone circle with another cairn at its heart, while the fifth is the ruined remains of a small building called Séipéal Cholmcille or Mullach na Croise. This is believed to be the site of the saint's first hermitage, and stones and clay from it have been taken away for their healing properties. A niche in the ruin is said to contain three stones known to have special healing properties. Beside the ruin is a line of three cairns with small standing stones and inside the rectangle is a stone square known as Leaba Cholmcille (Colmcille's Bed). The entire cluster is surrounded by the remains of a circular stone wall. This station requires the pilgrim to walk around the circle three times while praying, then enter and lie down on the stone 'bed', turn around on it three times, before circling each of the three cairns in prayer. From there, the path leads to station six, a large boulder with the trace of a circled cross carved into it; this can be felt if not seen. Pilgrims stand with their back to this stone, facing off towards the Atlantic Ocean, and make three wishes. Then back on the small road, around a sharp corner at a cluster of cottages and through a gate (which I hold open for a farmer on a small tractor before fastening it again to prevent sheep straying). The guide book and other sources suggest that the Turas Cholmcille takes between three and three and a half hours, yet I am already at the seventh station and have left the small, circuitous road that sweeps by Sceilp Úna and turns back up the glen. I march uphill to the seventh and eighth stations, the chair and the well.

6.00 p.m.

Liam Ó Cuinneagáin says: 'The chair is seen as halfway point and, on the way from the chapel and bed (*stad* five) to the well, pilgrims lift three stones. When they get to the well, they pray the Rosary while walking in a large circle around the perimeter and drop a stone at each turn.'

Testimony to this pilgrimage's popularity, therefore, is the huge cairn that sweeps in a long arc from the well, a crescent-shaped wall of loose stones piled two metres high and enclosing the well in a narrow space at the end of a path between high, rough-stone walls. In the heart of this alcove, the pilgrim now stoops below a small shelf festooned with votive offerings, including a small slab inscribed: 'Pray for Constanz Cherwinski lost at the Sturall' (a dramatically wild and remote headland north of Gleann Cholm Cille) and a variety of Marian statues. I scoop water from the small spring well, sipping and allowing three droplets to fall in honor of the Blessed Trinity. Standing sentinel over the supplicant pilgrims, meanwhile, is a white, primitive-looking but recently fashioned statue representing the saint. The narrow access to the well, along with the need for single-file progress elsewhere along the route, probably accounts for the generous time allowance for the pilgrimage.

6.15 p.m.

I emerge from the well to a spectacular view of the glen and the shoreline, where gusts are whipping waves against the rocks at Málainn Mhóir to the south. A short jaunt downhill, then to the chair for a traditional rest, avoiding the Demons' Rock, where heathen spirits were banished by Patrick before Colmcille expelled them forever. Then a brief walk downhill to the eighth station, comprising three cairns, each to be circled three times while praying. According to archaeologist Michael Herity, this completes the original *turas* of sixth-century sites associated with St Colmcille.[24] However, there is more to see and more praying to do. I set off along a long a wall enclosing sheep, past some old ruins and off to the ninth station, the Cloch Aonach, almost a kilometre away. After traversing the Abar Dubh, a brief pause at the stone basin called Umar na Glinne (the Font of the Glen) allows pilgrims to wash their feet before entering paradise.

7.00 p.m.
Making the pilgrimage alone can be confusing for the novice, since some of the metal markers have disappeared from the stations and, given the disparity of distances, others are not immediately apparent. So it was that, having had my first glimpse of paradise, I went on my way, searching for the tenth station at a staggered crossroads on the guide map between an Fhothair and an Droim Rua, off the road that leads to the top of the glen and on to Ardara. With nobody to guide me across the fields, I stick to the thoroughfare and pass a tethered white goat peering through a wooden fence. Maybe it puts a hex on me, because I fail to find the next megalith, which is hidden from the road by a dense hedge. However, I quickly locate the eleventh and twelfth stations because both are specially enclosed, marked and accessible from the road. The only other feature I identify is what appears to be a rough-looking cairn at the gable end of a house, with a wall built right up to the edge of it. After some hesitation while I compare this to other stations on the *turas*, I decide the mound of stones must be the tenth *stad*. So I make my station here, scrambling around the wall barrier to walk the traditional circle of prayer while ignoring stares from occupants of passing vehicles – including a car with a large and shaggy Old English sheepdog, which regards me from the front passenger seat like a disapproving aunt. It is a relief to move on to the enclosures of the eleventh and twelfth *stadanna.*

Having completed these, I set off back down the road to the thirteenth *stad*, across the street from the police station. On my way, I spot something through a gap in a hedge and double back. There, standing proudly in a field, is a large megalith with a smaller standing stone, a cairn of rocks and a sign that says 'Turas Cholmcille Stad 10'. I make my station and leave quietly, meeting the big sheep-dog in the car once more as I come back onto the road. The rest of the *turas* is uneventful in comparison. As I exit the churchyard after the fifteenth and final station, I revel in the fact that I have gone the extra mile, or at least the extra pile of stones. To heck with the begrudgers. Anyway, who is the big sheepdog going to tell?

10.30 p.m.

As sunset descends on paradise, I learn that the name of the townland with the elusive tenth station is Baile na nDeamhan (Town of the Demons). Local legend holds that Colmcille was viciously attacked by demons here. I take another sip from my pint and decide I know just how he felt.

*Tuesday, 23 June 2009*

4.30 p.m.

I arrive at Teileann Harbour expecting bawdy scenes of drunken licentiousness, but find instead a quiet cove basking in summer sunshine. My expectation is based on a reference in Oideas Gael's illustrated guide to Gleann Cholm Cille about 'another major *turas* to Tobar na mBan Naomh' (Well of the Holy Women). The guide points out that the Catholic clergy tried to suppress this pilgrimage because it encouraged 'excrescences of abuse, and especially drink and unseemly dancing', and it adds that pilgrims ignored the stricture. Yet, while the church was forced to retreat on this ancient practice even at the zenith of its power, the prevailing 'excrescences of abuse' in our new Ireland have dispatched it with barely a raised eyebrow.[25]

Today, the pilgrimage to Tobar na mBan Naomh is a distant memory for older inhabitants of Teileann and virtually unknown to outsiders. However, it was a central feature of a major study of Irish Catholic folk practices by Maynooth professor Lawrence J. Taylor as recently as the mid-1990s.[26] Although the *turas* was by then defunct, Professor Taylor records the testimony of local people who remember it well and also the common practice whereby mariners would lower their sails in salute as they passed by. The salute acknowledged the virtues made mortal in the form of the legendary holy women identified in another book as Ciall (Sense), Tuigse (Understanding) and Náire (Modesty).[27] Today, the harbour is virtually deserted and there is a languid air of midsummer indolence in a place that was once the greatest cod fishery in Ireland. According to the coastguard, after the pier was built at Lord Bradford's behest between 1881 and 1883, Teileann landed more fish from the teeming seas than nearby Killybegs.

Now the main port activity at the extended pier is the local sightseeing ferry, which takes visitors out to the spectacular cliffs at Bun Glas, towering almost 2,000 feet to the top of Sliabh Liag, which sits like a huge protective presence over Teileann and the surrounding parish of Gleann Cholm Cille. I ask a man beside the Nuala Star office about the well. It is as if he has been reminded of his childhood. He points to a small stone cross peeping from the crest of a nearby hill.

'That wee cross is one of the places where people used to pray on the *turas*,' he explains. 'Now it's not the well itself, but the well is off to the left of it down in a hollow among the bracken. If you go up to that cross, you should be able to find it. Yes, this would be the day all right for the *turas*; the 23rd of June was when people did it back years ago.' With his assurance that I am the first to make the *turas* today and a request to 'say a wee prayer' for him, I climb up to the ancient stone cross.

It is set in a small grotto with a tiny statue of Our Lady and a scattering of votive coinage, behind a stone marker with a carved circular pattern. I make the normal station prayers and then scramble through the undergrowth in search of the well, which I locate over a small, dry-stone wall. From most angles, Tobar na nBan Naomh is just a flat rock with a few knobs buried in the hillside. Two cups placed on top give it away. Moving to the front, the well is clearly visible beneath a canopy of concrete with a flat steel support. The protrusions on top are a stone roughly resembling a woman's shape, with a small round stone and the smaller top of a metal sphere nestling behind it. A few coins have been left by pilgrims here also, but their combined value is considerably less than those at the little grotto below – almost a sure sign that this well has run dry as a place of pilgrimage. And yet, as I descend the hill to the harbour I know that:

*somewhere a candle is being lit*
*to a saint*
*who may never have existed*
*rumour added to tale*
*a folkloric mix of hope*
*and hallucination in time of plague*
*who now*
*and where*
*are seekers of light …*[28]

5.30 p.m.

In the tiny public bar of Teileann's marvellous pub, the Rusty (certainly worth a pilgrimage in its own right for magnificent traditional music) I ask about the *turas* to Tobar na mBan Naomh. The younger customers shake their heads and say they don't know of it. Then an older man at the fireplace with an empty teacup beside him coughs, raises his voice and calls up memories. All ears tune in. He remembers doing the *turas* as a boy in the early 1950s and, as he warms to the subject, memories flood back of a local event that once ranked as a strictly observed annual rite in a seafaring community. It preceded and complemented the great bonfires that once lit up Sliabh Liag on this eve of St John's Day, he tells his small, enthralled audience. His memories evoke the lost magic of the midsummer observances that once appeased all the elemental forces of their world.

'I remember back then that the pilgrimage ended on the far shore,' he says. 'You could walk right across the sand then at low tide … but that was before the new part of the pier was built. They added that bit to the pier and the beach disappeared and then it appeared again across the harbour. You can't cross there now, so I don't know where the *turas* would end up now. It's a lot different now than it was back then.'

*Sunday, 28 June 2009*

11.00 a.m.

Newspaper coverage shows that hedonism thrives at the Curragh of Kildare as champagne is swilled and crisp €50 notes flutter in the sunshine – although the Derby Day crowd is 15 per cent thinner than last year at 23,500 and betting, as Johnny Murtagh rides Fame and Glory to win, is down by half a million euro. However, the horse race is not the only derby event of the weekend. Nearby, Punchestown Racecourse hosts an AC/DC concert at €76.50 a ticket and €30 for parking, while Gaelic-games stadium Croke Park is packed with Dubs watching their football side stuff Westmeath. Meanwhile, there is much talk of healing at Sunday Mass in an Charraig, where St Columba's Church is the main place of worship in Gleann Cholm Cille Parish. Fr Proinnsias Mac an tSaoir elaborates on the Gospel story of the woman who just wanted to touch the hem of Christ's garment. He tells his flock of more recent healing through divine intervention, and cites cases from the May edition of the *Sacred Heart Messenger* magazine. They included medical healing (of a spinal tumour), psychological healing (of anorexia) and spiritual healing (for a son-in-law who has started going to Mass again). A reader even found a cure for 'neighbours from hell'. But the thoughts of many at Sunday Mass are drifting off to the slopes of Sliabh Liag, which towers over the village. For in the parish bulletin and in the parish priest's post-Communion announcements are details of the *turas* this afternoon to the holy well up there. Indeed, the bulletin sells the event short, because this revival of an ancient pilgrimage encompasses no fewer than three holy wells – all of which, Fr Mac an tSaoir assures us, have 'real healing power'. They are within a small cluster of ruins on the summit dating back to the time of Aodh Mac Breac, the former bishop of Kildare, who spent his last years here as a hermit until his death some time between the years AD 589 and 595. The bulletin instructs pilgrims to congregate at the car park for a free bus to the pilgrim path in Teileann.

11.45 a.m.

The congregation files out into glorious sunshine, and an older man remarks to his younger neighbour, 'You'll sweat on your *turas* today.' Parishioners hurry home for an early Sunday dinner, passing the grave of Fr James MacDyer, a beloved radical pastor who spent more than 35 years ensuring that Gleann Cholm Cille was not wiped from public consciousness. Fr MacDyer became a beacon for other isolated communities, and among the traditions he promoted was the annual Sliabh Liag *turas*. Before his death in 1987, he was unable to make the climb and the pilgrimage fell by the wayside as an organised event. His successor, Fr Mac an tSaoir, is determined to revive it.

2.30 p.m.
Even after a picnic lunch, a leisurely stroll and a thorough perusal of the newspapers, there is lots of time to reflect on America's Miss Liberty, local girl Mary Cunningham, whose image once graced the dime and other coinage in the 'land of the free'. A tourism notice recalls outrage at her portrayal on the currency because she was merely an Irish domestic servant, but cheekily informs us that the artist was Irish also. The adjacent car park fronts the old national school where Miss Liberty once sat in her desk, perhaps dreaming of America. The deadline approaches, and a straggle of pilgrims emerges as the bus pulls in. There is a huddle as the priest climbs aboard. I settle into the vacant seat beside Fr Mac an tSaoir and note three men chatting outside. One is Bernard McHugh, who shot to public attention in the 1990s as a colourful contestant on Cilla Black's TV show *Blind Date*. Having until then worked as a fish gutter in a local processing plant, he became an instant celebrity, opening supermarkets and performing as a male stripper with his theme song, 'Delilah'. As his companions board the pilgrimage bus, Bernard slopes off towards the village shop with the air of a man with plenty

of time on his hands. A woman in spandex leisurewear and a straw Stetson-style hat climbs on board, calling out in a Belfast accent, 'Cad é mar atá sibh uilig?' ('How are you all?') Some children and another young woman follow her down the bus.

'There's the cowboys now,' says a woman's voice behind me.

'She's in good form for the *turas*,' another replies.

My attention turns to more spiritual matters as I start to chat with the pastor, a native of Fanad in Donegal's far north, who muses on the purpose of our *turas* and his hopes to revive official parish involvement in other ancient spiritual traditions of this Gaeltacht locality. He points out that there is great spiritual reward in the traditions observed by our ancestors and enthuses about the spiritual legacy of his new parish. He says he would greatly appreciate an archaeological assessment of the site we will visit today. We discuss other local holy places and I ask about Tobar Chiaráin, signposted on the road from Killybegs. Fr Mac an tSaoir says it is probably associated with Ciarán of Clonmacnoise (rather than Ciarán of Saighir) because his cult spread in the northwest of Ireland and over to Scotland, where there is still devotion to him, especially in Kintyre. While ministering in a Glasgow parish, Fr Mac an tSaoir had explored early monastic connections between the Celtic neighbours.

3.00 p.m.
With the final stragglers aboard we are off on the short winding road from an Charraig to Teileann. At the final sharp corner, a road sign points left towards the main route to the Bun Glas cliffs. The bus goes straight ahead on a minor road with painted-over directions for Sliabh Liag. Soon the engine is labouring up the start of a mountain

track as the wheels grind through loose gravel. Gates have been left open and a few pilgrims are walking. The bus rounds a hairpin bend, and several passengers wonder aloud if we'll make it at all; then it draws to a halt in a small car park, where a couple of picnic tables have been provided. We disembark and join others who have been waiting. The pastor remarks on the sturdy staff gripped by a man in old-fashioned hill-walking gear. The man laughs, 'Ach, a pilgrim needs a good stick for batin' the sarpents!' The man laughs, and off we set.

The pilgrim path winds around a sharp corner and into the big, sweeping bowl of Loch Chró Shléibhe, climbing around the edge towards another corner high up in the far distance. A fellow pilgrim explains that the lough is a shadow of its former self, and only two months ago it was abandoned as the local reservoir. In the 1800s, it covered seven acres and provided water for all the homes on the sheltered coastline below. Fr Mac an tSaoir says he heard that the lough had been affected by a lightning storm, which may have diverted one of the streams. The lake began to dry up and, with sheep grazing on the surrounding slopes, it was decided to source water elsewhere.

3.20 p.m.

We trudge up the pilgrim path to the first of a series of traffic resorts, where we pause to let the stragglers catch up. The man with the staff says this is a mistake – 'The idea is to keep going.' However, our pastoral leader explains that we need as many as possible to make the pilgrimage in a group so we can observe the rituals of prayer and preparation. A couple of quad motorbikes come up the path; a big stout man is on the first, and a young boy stands as he drives the second. They pull to a halt, and several youngsters clamber aboard. One child sits into a fishbox tied to the back of the man's quad, while two young boys squeeze onto the seat behind the boy. They phut phut off noisily as several remark that this is not really in the spirit of pilgrimage. A man on a tractor pulls up briefly and then drives through, followed by a couple of cars inching up the precarious path. We set off in their wake and, at each succeeding recess, we find cars parked by those determined to make this pilgrim path as easy as possible. Those of us who chose the traditional way pause for stragglers, our pace determined by the weakest so that no one is left behind.

3.50 p.m.
We run out of road where a tractor is parked, its driver gone on ahead on foot. Earlier a young man called Breandán had warned with a big smile that this is where the 'tough part' of the *turas* begins. He knows the mountain well, and I note that he is slowing down as I draw alongside. I ask if he is finding it tough, and he tells me he is because he now has only one functioning lung.

'I used to be up this mountain at least once a week. Then I got pneumonia and that developed into pleurisy and then I got the MRSA bug in one of my lungs. They had to collapse it, so now I only have the one lung,' he explains. This *turas* is his comeback to the mountain after a two-year illness and recuperation and he is mightily impressed by improvement work on the pilgrim path. Even at this juncture it is well marked, with newly created steps on particularly difficult parts. Here and there, rubber mats have been laid on boggy ground. One pilgrim points out that when grass and heather grow through the webbing they will still provide good footing. A young woman in the company says she and a few others did the *turas* last year, before the pastor decided to revive the pilgrimage tradition.

'We had to go through all the *clábar* then,' she remarks, scampering along now with delight. 'This is great,' she adds.

4.30 p.m.
Just ahead, the man in hill-walking garb draws to a halt alongside a couple of piles of rock gathered in loose cairns and signals for us to stop and wait for the priest and the other pilgrims. We admire the panoramic scenery until they arrive and, after a brief consultation as we gather around, Fr Mac an tSaoir addresses us.

'This is the start of our pilgrimage,' he says solemnly, pointing out that the cairns are believed to be the ruins of monastic cells. He reiterates his wish for a proper archaeological study of the Sliabh Liag monastic sites, then announces, 'We will now say a couple of decades of the Rosary here and I would ask you all to carry on from here in a proper spirit of pilgrimage. By this I mean that we should be silent to allow others to concentrate on their devotion.'

He draws out his beads and we recite the Rosary in Irish. On completion, we proceed in relative silence, although the Stetson-wearning Belfast mother occasionally has to rein in one of her charges, Dylan, who scampers ahead. Yet, slowly, with two additional pauses along the way for decades of the Rosary, we make our way to the summit. Each time we move on from a prayer spot, an older man drives a small metal stake into the ground so that these can be properly marked for next year's *turas*. This will ensure recognition of the designated places of prayer for all the years ahead when pilgrims will make their way up Sliabh Liag in the footsteps of Aodh Mac Breac.

4.50 p.m.
We surmount the summit and there ahead of us – at more than 600 metres above sea level – are the two quads and an

old Land Rover somebody has driven all the way up over the treacherous terrain. Daubs of yellow paint on rocks indicate the path to a spot where about two dozen others have gathered around the crumbling ruins. As we draw together, someone suggests that those already here aren't making the proper *turas* because they have missed the devotional aspects on the way up. Some hurry along to a cluster of stones around what turns out to be a murky well. A woman prostrates herself on a stone in front of it, lowers her face to the water and sips. Several others follow her example, including young Dylan, who baulks at sipping the water, then rises and lowers his dirty shoe into the water to wash it. His mother shouts, 'Don't!' and pulls him back but, next in line, I have already lowered myself into the designated attitude and I sip the water, which has been churned to a turbid murk. Rising, I note that the next and succeeding pilgrims simply dab the water with their fingers and make the Sign of the Cross.

5.00 p.m.

We gather at a spot near one of the other wells and the main cluster of rocks, where the priest is now in deep conversation with a man he soon identifies as local historian Eoghan Ó Corráin. Fr Mac an tSaoir addresses us, saying that our ceremony will consist of the Rosary and a blessing for pilgrims. He then gives an overview of the site where we are congregated, pointing out that this mountain-top well has never been known to run dry. He encourages us to use whatever containers we can find to take some of this blessed water, which has healing powers – for arthritis in particular, although he adds that its restorative powers will work for other ailments too. Our pastor then explains that while Aodh Mac Breac was a hermit, it was not unusual for such holy men to be joined by followers to dwell in a community of hermetic cells such as these clusters of rocks, all that now remains as evidence of their holy lives. He tells us that the church that once stood in the place of this main pile of rocks has the exact same dimensions as a church ruin in St Colmcille's birthplace of Gartan, even though it does not appear to have an altar like that site. He points out that Ireland is rich in the surviving remains of sites where these special followers of Christ once dwelt in prayer.

'They chose the mountains and other isolated places, but especially high places like this so that they could be nearer to heaven and more removed from other people to live in prayer.' Fr Mac an tSaoir then adds that, after the prayers and blessing, he will move around the site with Eoghan Ó Corráin so that people can ask about its various aspects.

The lay expert then gives a potted history of the site and its founder, Aodh (Hugh) Mac Breac: 'He was from the Westmeath area and he was one of three sons. As was the custom in those times, where there were a number of sons, one of them would be sent to an uncle or another relative to be reared. So Hugh was sent to an uncle in Kildare. While he was there, the father divided his land between the other two sons. When Hugh returned, he was very angry and he kidnapped the daughter of a local king to force his father to change his mind. But a monk was sent to talk to him and he convinced Hugh to enter the monastery.'

After that, Hugh rose quickly through the ranks and became bishop of Kildare, before turning his back on the world and coming to Donegal to end his days as a hermit. Others joined him and, as death approached, he told his companions that he did not wish to die alone. He asked one of them to die with him, but he refused.

'But then a man came to Hugh and he was a great sinner seeking absolution. On the very day that Hugh died, he died also,' says Eoghan Ó Corráin, who adds that there is a large body of folklore surrounding the life of this special saint. Some of the folklore also relates, of course, to the small recess in the rocks that has become known as the Wishing Place. After completing the pilgrimage, those who enter this tiny rock alcove and make a wish will have that wish come true, he says. To prove his point, he explains that a local man who completed the pilgrimage in his youth wished that he might have a long life, live in a big house and have a son become a priest. That man was Seán Ó hEochaidh, whom many of those present could have identified instantly as the renowned collector who made the largest contribution of material to the Irish Folklore Commission and subsequently to University College Dublin.

Eoghan Ó Corráin recounts one of the stories collected by Seán Ó hEochaidh about this very pilgrimage.

'There was an old man in Teelin who had great faith in Tobar Aoidh MacBreicne, and he did the *turas* to the top of Sliabh Liag twice in the one year. He was about a hundred years old at the time and he had a problem with arthritis. He went a third time to the *tobar* and, when he was tired praying, he shook his stick at the altar and said, "Be the livin', Aodh MacBreicne, if you don't cure me this time after me coming to you so often, I'll never come near you again!"'

A ripple of laughter runs through the gathering but quickly gives way to a buzz of enquiries about the location of the Wishing Place and its prospect of good fortune. But we have pilgrimage work to do before such frivolity, so we resume the Rosary in Irish, followed by a reading from the Gospel of St John that includes the well-known passage about being born again in Christ. The formalities conclude with a general blessing for the congregated pilgrims and fellow travellers on Sliabh Liag's summit.

5.20 p.m.
There is a general scattering around the site after prayers, and our pilgrim pastor almost takes a tumble while pointing out the stonework of what at first appears to be no more than a pile of rubble. A bigger gallery of spectators congregates, and soon we are all gathered for a group photograph. With others, I hand over my small camera to one of the two women taking photos and clamber back through the ruins to get into the group. I end up front and centre beside the priest, recorded for posterity in this image of the re-inauguration of the pilgrimage to the holy shrine on Sliabh Liag's summit. The congregation breaks up and queues form for the Wishing Place and at the well that may never run dry but is now churned to murky soup. I walk up the slight incline to where the mountain ends in a cliff precipice that plummets straight down into the seething abyss of the Atlantic Ocean. I have ascended Sliabh Liag before, via the signposted road to Bun Glas. That is a steep, narrow road running past Loch Mhín an Bhiolair on the right and then Cruachlann and an Carraigeán on the left, then turning on a hairpin bend perched around a chasm and finally ending at the upper car park beside Loch an Mhaolagáin. The walk leads from there to an Cheapach at the summit and the infamous, but actually not so treacherous, One Man's Pass over to the monastic ruins at the Eagle's Nest, where I now stand.

On that route, I was constantly aware of the ascent to Europe's highest sea cliffs, three times higher than County Clare's more popular Cliffs of Moher. On our pilgrim path (known as Cosán an Oilithrigh) around the bowl of Loch Chró Shléibhe, the mountain ahead conceals what lies beyond until suddenly there is nothing but the drop. Looking back, however, I see the picturesque harbour of Teileann with the wide sweep of Donegal Bay with Knocknarea and the Ox Mountains in the distance. Along its northern shore, the Bluestack Mountains roll like a great wave from Lough Derg's purgatorial sanctuary. Immediately beyond the ruins of Aodh Mac Breac's hermitage, the wave crests and crashes into the Atlantic waves with only the giant boulders of Bun Glas, twin rocky islands, peeking above the churning waves. From up here they seem like pebbles, and the pilgrim is aware that if the trek to Aodh Mac Breac's hermitage was like an ascent to the heavens, beyond is a reminder of the churning abyss beyond salvation. It is an awe-inspiring contrast made all the more poignant on this sun-kissed day by the presence off in the hazy distance of mighty Earagail to the north and the holy mountain of Croagh Patrick to the south, both revered as the homes of gods before the arrival of Christianity. I turn and rejoin some pilgrims at another cluster of stones, which are the ruins of monks' cells. Eoghan Ó Corráin is telling them how, in the late nineteenth century, a local landlord conducted a thriving business shipping Sliabh Liag stones from Teileann to Belfast, where they were used for the City Hall and other major buildings.

'The stones did not have to be cut, you see, because they came flat and ready to use,' says the local *seanchaí*, who launches from this anecdote into another, inspired by simply looking around him.

5.40 p.m.

The *turas* ends, and many pilgrims are already far below on the trek back along the pilgrim path. We move off in clusters or alone, no longer the strung-out group that paused for those needing more time. After the end of the rough terrain, the vehicles are heading down at slower speeds than their ascent, though maybe that is because the walkers are faster. The cars move gingerly along the rutted road, having to wait for those on foot to give way. There is a sense of high spirits among the walkers, however, with lots of chat about hunger, thirst and whether the bus will be waiting at the designated spot. We reach it in trickles, and there are phone calls and some confusion about when, and even whether, the bus is coming. Finally a voice says, 'Well, I think we should go down to the Rusty and wait there for the bus.' I and several others agree heartily; another call is made to advise others further back and we set off on foot again. Along the way, we lose pilgrims to lifts in cars but we soldier on to the final stage of our pilgrimage. Finally there are three pilgrims left. Both the others are local people. They tell me, to my utter astonishment, that this is the very first time they have scaled Sliabh Liag, which towers over their homes. They are excited by what they have achieved and our walk is animated by chat until we arrive at the Rusty. There, Breandán is already in place, offering to buy us all a drink. I decline his kind offer since it may be some time before I could return the favour.

Meanwhile, the barman provides news of the football championship as he pulls my pint of stout and we all repair to the tables outside. As several local people arrive, Breandán greets them with news of our *turas*. From his earlier estimate of about 90 pilgrims, he is now racking and stacking them by informing those who weren't there that there were a hundred of us at the summit. I suggest that by 10 o'clock tonight he will have doubled that number. Breandán laughs and replies, 'No, one hundred is a nice round number and that's what it will be.' He then tells us he first climbed Sliabh Liag when he was only five because both his parents were enthusiastic hill-walkers. Clearly after a two-year absence due to his health problem from a place he loves, today's trek was a major achievement. It must at least match the general success of reviving a pilgrimage carried on from time immemorial and only recently fallen by the wayside.

6.40 p.m.
A car pulls up beside the pub and informs us that the bus is waiting down at the corner. Nobody seems unduly perturbed as we continue to chat and sip our drinks. Five minutes later, the bus draws alongside, reverses and pulls up opposite. We climb aboard and I settle in beside Fr Mac an tSaoir again. He smiles when I inform him that we observed a 'final station' of our *turas* at the Rusty. We resume our earlier conversation about his plans for next year, when he hopes to organise properly the traditional Turas Cholmcille on 9 June and repeat the *turas* to Sliabh Liag. I ask about the pilgrimage to Tobar na mBan Naomh on 23 June, and he says that he will give some attention to reviving that as a parish event as well.

'It is important that we continue to observe these acts of devotion and go to our holy places,' he says quietly. 'These saints sought out isolated places to live their lives in prayer. They followed the example of Christ, who sought out similar places on mountains and in the wilderness to seek spiritual guidance. We all need that … especially now.'

As the bus pulls into an Charraig and I remark that his day's work is done, he adds urgently, 'It's all about prayer.' He repeats that phrase quietly a few more times before wishing me goodbye and safe home as we descend from the bus. Then, with numerous farewells from fellow pilgrims and an invitation to come back for the local walking festival and another trek over Sliabh Liag, I set off for home along the winding road on the north shore of Donegal Bay. I feel enveloped in an aura of goodwill and the grace of Naomh Aodh Mac Breac, the holy man who chose the harsh life of a hermit here in the mountains over the comforts of a lowland bishopric. I recall a remark I read by the American artist Rockwell Kent describing his sojurn in the sacred glen below Sliabh Liag: 'I've travelled north and south, east and west in search of mountain peaks but never until now have I found peaks whose summits reached so near to God as do you men of Donegal.'[29]

# Chapter 3

# Path of the Righteous

## Tóchar Phádraig

*Monday, 20 July 2009*

Mickey Mallon sits down beside me on one of the makeshift stalls at the summit of Croagh Patrick. Still gasping, he asks if he can have a piece of the peel from the orange I have just eaten.

'Just to get the juices flowing in my mouth,' he explains in his south Armagh accent. Telling me he set off from Murrisk at 6.15 p.m., he asks what time it is now. I tell him it's 7.15 p.m. 'Not bad for a man of 60,' he says proudly.

I tell him I set off at 9.45 a.m.

'So you've been up here all day then?'

'Well, no,' says I, 'I'm doing the Tóchar Phádraig from Ballintubber Abbey, the ancient pilgrim path.' He asks how long that is and I tell him it's 32 kilometres – almost a marathon with a mountain climb at the end.

'Well, good man yourself,' says Mickey, 'for I wouldn't have the patience to do the like of that.' So we sit for a while on our makeshift bench, shrouded in damp mountain-top mist, swap yarns and talk of people and places we know mutually. Then Mickey goes off to say his few prayers and I begin the descent with my left knee seizing up in pain.

The Tóchar Phádraig is the longest of the designated pilgrim paths supported by Heritage Ireland, and its preservation relies on a huge level of community support, particularly from landowners, who allow access to the ancient path for pilgrims formally registered at Ballintubber Abbey. It is a path of spectacular contrasts – across lush meadows and a few modern roads, along winding boreens and forest paths and through bogs and moorland, traversing several sections of flagstones and ancient timber straddles and finally ascending the winding path on the east side of Croagh Patrick to join the more commonly used trail to the spectacular summit. Finally, the path leads down to Murrisk, nestling on picturesque Clew Bay. Even without its spiritual resonance and history, the Tóchar Phádraig wends its way through a kaleidoscope of natural beauty that plunges the pilgrim deeper and deeper into a state of reflection, spiritual renewal and final exhilaration.

9.00 a.m.
Morning Mass in Ballintubber Abbey near Maura Walshe's excellent bed and breakfast, Radharc na Cruaiche. The beautiful old medieval church was founded in 1216 by Cathal O'Connor, king of Connacht, in gratitude for kindness shown to him in the locality before he gained the throne. The first reading is from the book of Exodus – the children of Israel are pursued into the desert by proud Pharaoh, yet trust in the god of Moses to lead the way. I am increasingly anxious to be off along the Causeway of Patrick to the holy mountain.

9.40 a.m.
I must look the part of a pilgrim because, as soon as I knock and open the door of the sacristy, Fr Frank Fahey

says, 'You're going walking the *tóchar.*' Or perhaps my hiking boots and shorts clue him in. Anyway, he soon has me officially registered and equipped with the laminated pilgrim map. We chat about the previous day's provincial football final victories for Tyrone in Ulster and Mayo in Connacht, then make our way through the abbey church, where he checks that I have lit a votive candle, and move along quickly to the Dancora (Bath of the Righteous), the starting point. Fr Fahey explains the characteristics that distinguish the 'pilgrim' from the mere 'tourist'. Pilgrims light a candle before setting out as a symbol of faith, much like the prayer they choose to say as they cross each stile along the way. The hardships along the way must be endured without complaint, but instead with the invocation, 'Thanks be to God.' If travelling in a group, cliques must be avoided by sharing the company of all the pilgrims at different stages. At designated stages, silence must be observed in prayer and pilgrims must share food, joy, love and care. Finally, what makes for a good pilgrimage is the 'change of heart'. To illustrate this, Fr Fahey bends down, lifts a small, rough pebble from beside the Dancora and hands it to me.

'Take that,' he instructs me, 'and when you get to the top of Croagh Patrick, leave it there and take up a smooth pebble to symbolise the change of heart you have had along the *tóchar*. You can then keep that pebble to remind you of what you have achieved.' So, with Fr Fahey's blessing, I set forth from the Dancora, where pilgrims once washed their feet in a stream that flowed over specially heated stones. Legend holds that it will flow again before the end of the world. Beyond the statue of Patrick, the first stile is a modest structure adorned by the small black cross symbol that will guide my way. I am off on the path of the righteous.

10.00 a.m.
I set out on a glorious summer morning across a meadow of sheep. This was once part of the abbey lands that encompassed 35,000 acres under the Augustinian canons before the dissolution of the monasteries by James I and a subsequent onslaught by Cromwell's army that tore apart Ballintubber Abbey. I progress from stile to stile across the first small road; then confusion. I walk one way, then another, looking for the waymarker. The map's linear pattern offers no clue. I see the fingerpost eventually and rush towards it, then repeat the exercise for the next waymarked stile. After several wrong turns and confused corrections, I come out on the main Castlebar to Ballinrobe road, where traffic whizzes by. I walk towards a service station, scanning the roadsides, then double back. Directly opposite where I emerged is the next stile, and I scurry across and over it. The pattern resumes as I scramble to find my way on the path less taken.

10.30 a.m.
Increasingly frustrated at the absence of clearer signage, I come to a fingerpost. A notice beside it says, 'No complaining; Thanks be to God. A Pilgrim does not complain.' My entire being relaxes with that invocation and I resolve that I will trust my instincts to find the way. It is as if I have been handed a homing device, a global positioning system, because now I turn each time into the path. Occasionally I am helped by subtle tell-tale signs of previous pilgrims, including cousins of Maura Walshe from the bed and breakfast, who came through on Friday and Saturday last. Home from America to take the cremated remains of their mother on a final pilgrimage along the *tóchar* before burial, they have left mildly disturbed grass at a few points and

occasional reassuring footprints in the soft earth. At other times I am guided by a magnetic sense that Croagh Patrick is ahead, perhaps beyond those hedges or the foothills of the Partry Mountains further along. It draws me along a route that once drew pilgrims to the sacred mountain of Cruachán Aigle on the eve of Lughnasa to pray for a plentiful harvest, and subsequently brought supplicants to the Christian god who replaced Lugh to the same mountain, renamed Croagh Patrick.[30] Today, as the faithful are forced to absorb the implications of the Ryan report on the abuse of children by church ministers, and as the losses of Irish banks are shored up by €73 billion of taxpayers' money, at the cost of some half a million jobs, the path is deserted but for this lone pilgrim.

11.00 a.m.

Reminders of the past dot the route, including Tobar na Cannúna or the Well of the Canons, reputed to have the cure of eye ailments. There are sites associated with the infamous priest-hunter Seán na Sagart, who terrorised the locality during penal times, when the dominance of the established Protestant Church was rigorously imposed. There are also strong reminders of the Great Hunger in village ruins, the site of a bully field (mass grave) for victims of want and destitution, and the road built by paupers paid with oatmeal, still known here as Stirabout Road. There are also reminders of the huge disparity of means brought about by colonisation and eviction, including the story that much of the land in this locality was won in a poker game between wealthy men. Helpful signage recounting the lore of the land is strategically placed beside the fingerposts and there is more information in a pilgrim's booklet that was provided at Ballintubber Abbey. It does not stint in recounting the pagan, Christian and secular story of a causeway built around 350 BC to allow passage of wheeled chariots between Cruachan, royal seat of Connacht, and the sacred mountain. At points along the way, parts of that ancient roadway survive in a foundation of gravel on which flagstones are laid under a layer of wooden planks. The largest flags are kept in place by kerbstones. At other points, the ancient legacy of pilgrims can be seen in the profusion of roadside plants – blackthorn bushes grown from the discarded pips of the sloes eaten along the way. There is also plentiful holly – whose name, of course, derives from 'holy'. The hazel copses yield nuts to sustain pilgrim wayfarers.

12.00 noon.
All is not plenty and plain sailing along the way, however. In the course of about half an hour, I almost sink into the oblivion of a marsh, escape the fangs of a dog called Rex and am struck by a falling boulder. The first of these trials comes beside the ruins of Teampleshaunaglasha (or Church of John of the Dykes) in the district of Bellabourke. A stile invites the pilgrim to cut through a field of long grass to the church, last used in 1562. I do so, only to find myself among marsh reeds and sinking fast. I pluck my boots from the mire and beat a hasty retreat to the safety of the wall, in panic-stricken trust that rapid movement will prevent further suction. Recovering, I reflect on the lesson that faith cannot be blind and close scrutiny of an intended path guards against unforeseen danger.

There is less danger of perishing in the encounter with Rex, but it risks serious bloodshed (my blood, of course). Again I am not following the signs in my path but looking at a fingerpost further ahead. So I pass a stile and walk into the 'street' of a private home, where the collie cross (and he is very cross) comes snarling and barking towards me, poised for attack. Having learned to extend an open palm slowly to instil trust in a dog, I begin to reach out. The woman of the house emerges, edging slowly towards us, warning me in a loud whisper, 'Don't put out your hand for he'll bite it.' She urges Rex to retire (not very convincingly, I regret) and she clearly fears he will bite her too – 'So we'll just chat here a while and see if that works.' So we chat and, although I know I am in danger of attack from this vicious dog, I am relatively calm. It is almost akin to an out-of-body experience. My remarks about Rex being a good guard-dog are brushed aside with, 'I don't know about that now,' and directions for the *tóchar* are given in furtive eye movements by a woman who clearly can't take her gaze off the snarling Rex.

Finally, I manage to back slowly towards the stile I've missed and I'm back on the trail. I feel immense relief in overcoming my second challenge. Perhaps I should have known the third would come before I am sanctified enough to continue on this particular path of righteousness. It arises at a stile that is missing the small inner tube that allows access when drawn to and fro into a bigger tube. The gap is plugged with stones, including a huge boulder on top. I try to move it aside before realising I will not be able to put it back. I decide to clamber over it but, as I do so, the whole thing comes crashing down, the boulder striking my left shin with a thud. First nothing, then intense pain as I watch a large bruise suddenly ooze blood. Mindful of the code of leaving things as found, even in my pain, I try to replace the stones. The best I can do is put back the smaller ones before hobbling off on my way.

12.30 p.m.

My trials have not ended, but subsequent brushes seem trifling in comparison. A sign warns pilgrims to be watchful for the 'mighty midget', the stoat, which pursues its prey relentlessly, paralyses it with a 'hypnotic fear' and then strikes, even killing animals much larger than itself. While I see no stoats, my encounter with a herd of Friesian cattle is like a scene from a cheap horror movie. As I enter the field, they come at me from all directions. Repeatedly, I drive them off by clapping, shouting and waving my laminated map as I rotate like a whirling dervish. Time and again, they shy off briefly, then close on me once more, their staring eyes like a herd of zombies with yellow ear-tags. Finally I make it to the next stile and forage for a stick to use in similar encounters. The opportunity arises shortly when a small herd of male Charolais cattle are equally drawn to me. I skirt along the side of the field, my flimsy stick at the ready, knowing it would have little chance of driving off a determined bull.

1.15 p.m.
Having avoided being gored in a land that once coveted the Brown Bull of Cooley, I cross the hill of Cloondacon (Meadow of the Two Hounds), where St Patrick quelled two attack dogs owned by a sceptical chieftain in his own brush with canine perils. I cross a stretch of bog where the *tóchar* is clearly visible in the flagstone causeway left undisturbed when the surrounding land was drained. I have almost finished the first half of the *tóchar*. Ahead I see the ancient village of Aghagower, a traditional place for rest, resuscitation and the sustenance of pilgrims. I have eschewed other rests along the way, including the fascinating site at Cranareen Well, where Patrick is said to have camped over two Sundays, baptising and instructing the converts who came by. Perhaps they had come for reasons other than the well, since right beside the well is the small hillock known

as Creaggaun a' Damhsa (the Hillock of Dancing), where the fairies are said to gather to cavort and enjoy themselves. A brief burst of rain blows away as the final stile takes me out onto the road. I step up my pace towards the ancient city, guided by a round tower that juts from the ruins of its monastic site.

Aghagower, now a small and remote but very picturesque village just south of Westport, was once the seat of the bishop of Umall from AD 460 to 1216. It had an episcopal church, a seminary, a convent and a large monastic school. I wonder if Rome's decision to make it part of the archdiocese of Tuam and remove its bishop was in any way connected to the establishment in that year of Ballintubber Abbey – or indeed, as I learned at the abbey, the fact that that was the year when St Dominic first promoted the Rosary as a form of devotional prayer. Reading through the literature about the *tóchar*, perhaps the Vatican's decision to eradicate the diocese of Umall was indeed related to the decision to install the Augustinian canons at Balltintubber and other actions that supplanted the power of the Celtic monastic religious establishment in those early years of the Anglo-Norman invasion of Ireland. When Patrick established his church at Aghagower, he installed a convert called Senach as its first bishop. Senach's daughter Mathona became a nun and founded the local convent; his son Oengus became a priest. Senach was promised that 'holy bishops of his seed would be there forever', according to the *Book of Armagh*, as recounted by renowned former archbishop of Tuam John Healy in a lecture, 'St Patrick in the Far West'.[31] While nepotism was rife elsewhere in the medieval church, one can only presume that Rome was determined to curb or even eradicate it at this point in the early years of the thirteenth century.

1.40 p.m.
Aghagower (Place of Springs) is a charming little place that overflows with monuments of its ecclesiastical past. There are the ruins of the old abbey church and the round tower, which now leans slightly towards the north, a couple of village-centre graveyards and a beautiful little riverside park with picnic tables for pilgrim wayfarers or other visitors. Then there are two holy wells and a place known as Leaba Phádraig (Patrick's Bed). There is also the large, modern graveyard on both sides of the Coach Road at the edge of the village and the modern church in its centre with two latter-day shrines – a crucifixion scene at the church gable and, across the street, a shrine to Our Lady of Lourdes established in the Marian year of 1954.

The last seems almost incongruous and alien in a place that has so much indigenous testimony to the faith of the locality. It is an imposed and almost contrived expression of religious faith in the form of a standardised, artificial shrine in a place of real spiritual value and resonance. But my main concern in Aghagower is lunch, including the flask of hot tea provided by Maura Walshe from the bed and breakfast to revive body and spirit. Afterwards, an exploration of the holy wells reveals that they have both been dry since drainage work was carried out in the area. Such is progress, I suppose, but it seems particularly unfortunate that the wells in the Place of Springs have run dry through human interference. For centuries and perhaps millennia before, Tobar na nDeachan (the Well of the Deacons) provided water for pilgrims, which they drank as part of the prescribed ritual of the *tóchar*. The other well, Dabhach Phádraig, seems to have performed a similar function to the Dancora at Ballintubber Abbey, as a place where pilgrims could wash their feet in the warmed water while making the *tóchar* to and from Croagh

Patrick. The waters of these two holy wells, which were connected by an underground stream, were said to have healing powers. Moreover, the clay from the base of a tree beside Dabhach Phádraig has traditionally been applied in poultice form for its curative value and has to be returned to the tree when the ailment heals. One piece of soil is said to have gone to America and come back safely.

2.15 p.m.

A group of men are digging a grave in part of the new cemetery as I walk towards the stile that will commence the second part of my *Tóchar* Phádraig pilgrimage. Equipped now with a traditional pilgrim's staff sent by Fr Fahey at Ballintubber Abbey, along with a lunch packed for me by the B&B, I am more conscious than ever that I walk in the footsteps of St Patrick, who left Aghagower with his friends Senach, Oengus and Mathona, on the Saturday before Lent in AD 441 to spend the season of fasting and prayer on the holy mountain that is now starkly and beautifully visible on the horizon, a cloud just brushing its summit in a day now bathed in golden, fresh sunlight. I salute the gravediggers in this popular place of Christian burial, climb the stile into a sheep meadow and follow the natural worn footpath that stretches out before me.

When Patrick set out on this route, we are told in the *Tóchar* Phádraig guide book, he was accompanied by a large retinue to reflect his new status as the designated papal missionary to Ireland – a mission bestowed upon him in that same year, according to the *Book of Armagh*. The guide book says that he undertook this part of the trek to Croagh Patrick on foot, leaving behind the chariots, caravans and other vehicles that so impressed the native population as he moved around the country. Yet he was still accompanied by his 'tradesmen, also a cook, a chamberlain, a brewer, a bell-ringer, a judge, a firewoodman, blacksmiths, scribes, embroideresses and charioteers. He also had bishops, nuns, priests and psalmists to aid him in converting the local people.'[32] They must have thronged the causeway, which grows quite narrow here as it changes from a chariot route to a narrow footpath that wends its way to Lankill and Stone Park beyond, with its multiplicity of ancient monuments. The park boasts a cist burial chamber dating from about 3000 BC; a Bronze-Age pillar standing 3 metres tall with pagan Celtic designs and a superimposed Christian cross etched into it; the ruins of an old monastery; St Brendan's Well, with a stone that is said to have curative powers; a penal Mass rock; and a graveyard dotted with flag tombstones.

2.45 p.m.

Back on a small country road, the *tóchar* comes to a corner that turns left at an almost 90-degree angle and starts to climb through wooded hinterland. The sign peeping out from the bushy roadside abundance beside the fingerpost identifies this as Lankill, and I realise that I have missed the landmark St Patrick's Well along the way. I consult the guide book to see if it is worth doubling back briefly and learn that this well – like Tobar na Cannúna back along the *tóchar* – has the cure of eye ailments. I've already taken care of that affliction, so I decide to press on up the incline, which grows steeper as it progresses. This is wooded countryside, but a mere shadow of its former abundance of beech and oak trees. The former were used to make clogs in a Westport factory, while the mighty oak trees were shipped off to England, where they were used in building the docks at Liverpool. One can only wonder how many clog-shod emigrants from these parts stepped onto those planks from home when they set off to seek their fortune or merely to survive.

Meanwhile, another roadside bulletin informs the pilgrim that road bowling is a tradition in Lankill, introduced by railway builders from the north and reinvigorated by workmen from Cork who cut down the oak trees. Past a homestead in which winter fuel logs have been neatly stacked in an open shed and some beautiful stone sheds opposite, the route from Lankill crests at a crossroads on the Tourmakeady Road towards Westport, 6 kilometres away, with Aghagower now 4 kilometres distant. A straggled group of holiday cyclists pedals past towards Westport as I sit on the low roadside wall to check my route. There is no fingerpost here to signify the route of the *tóchar* and I wonder if I have missed a stile somewhere after that last sharp turn in the lowlands. I did notice a stile that had been bricked up, rendering it impassable. Doubts creep in once more and Croagh Patrick remains invisible, but instinct and the experience of the trek so far suggest that the *tóchar* goes across the main road, rising again towards the heights of these Partry Hills. I trust that instinct and forge straight ahead.

3.15 p.m.
I have walked some more of the quiet road through countryside that is becoming more sparse and mountainous and, while I have noticed waymarker signs for a walking route, it is secular and does not bear the familiar pilgrim cross that has guided my way so far. I recall what Fr Fahey told me back at Ballintubber Abbey about the pilgrim's means of keeping to the path of the *tóchar*. As he handed me the laminated map of the route he showed me the fingerpost logo and the pilgrim-cross logo that would guide me on the path

of the righteous. The fourth means of following the *tóchar*, he said, was by asking those I meet along the way.

I determine to call to the house up ahead and ascertain whether or not I have strayed. It is a bungalow, set down a brief driveway from the road, with a huge Mayo GAA flag and a couple of cars out front. I knock on the glass door and a young woman opens it. By way of introduction I tell her I am following the *tóchar* to the Reek and ask if she could possibly fill my now-drained water bottle. She takes the bottle and heads off inside, leaving the front door ajar in an obvious gesture of trust in my pilgrim credentials. When she returns, she smiles kindly and hands me the brimming bottle. I ask her if I am still on the path of the *tóchar*. She confirms that I am, and asks if I'm walking all the way to Croagh Patrick. I say I am.

'You've still got a good bit to go then,' she remarks. I tell her that nothing could be more inviting than a good walk on such a beautiful day and that the scenery is getting more spectacular all the time. I then offer her my pilgrim's modest blessing of gratitude for the water and set off on the road that continues to climb to the heavens.

3.40 p.m.

Finally the road crests in a land of blanket bogland off a narrow country road fringed by beautiful flowering heather. Peeking over the near horizon, I see the now-familiar volcanic profile of Croagh Patrick. The woman in the house was right – it is still a long way off. Yet the road falls away from my footsteps now and I quicken my pace towards the lowlands below, where the Owenwee River flows. Down there, the road from Westport to Leenane forms the 'final frontier' of modernity before I begin my long ascent to the holy mountain. I am reassured along the way by the reappearance of *tóchar* signage, including the now-familiar incantation: 'No complaining; Thanks be to God. A Pilgrim does not complain.' Far from complaining, I feel my spirits lift with every footstep and I am exhilarated by the prospect of the climb ahead and the completion of my path.

4.05 p.m.

A right turn towards another hill and then a left turn at its base brings me back into wooded country, which seems to get more and more lush as I approach the main road. I seem to hear traffic off in the distance ahead. Then, as I round another corner bounded by verdant hedgerows with woods beyond, I see that the noise is actually coming from a huge mechanical digger being driven into a field by a large man. A Mayo flag wafts proudly from the back of the cab and the man stops just in the gateway and leans back to address me.

I gesture to ask if he wishes me to close the gate behind him, but he shakes his head and roars above the din of the engine, 'Are you for climbing the Reek?' I shout back that I am and he says, 'Well, fair play to you. How far have you come?'

'I've come from Tyrone,' says I, 'but I've only walked today from Ballintubber Abbey.'

'From Tyrone?' says he. 'Well, fair play to you.'

I nod at his Mayo flag then smile and shout out to him, 'Aye, and when I get to the top of the Reek I'll be saying a few prayers that we win another all-Ireland final and beat Mayo along the way.'

He nearly doubles over with laughter at that and I fear for a moment he could slip the digger into gear and take out the twin pillars of the gateway.

'Well, fair play to you and Tyrone,' says he, 'but there will be a lot more going up to pray the other way.'

I wave a good-humoured farewell at that and head off in the knowledge that not only does a pilgrim not complain, he also shares kind words and perhaps a laugh with those he meets along the path of the righteous.

4.20 p.m.
A little further on, past a sign on a gate reading, 'Beware of cross cow in field,' with only male cattle visible beyond, I come to a large, low building. It is succumbing to the ravages of neglect, and a *tóchar* fingerpost points the way through its grounds. The building is for sale and once housed some sort of archaeological centre. Around the side and tucked into a small space between the buildings on the site is one of the most fascinating features of the entire route – the Rock of Boheh. Scored with prehistoric art symbols including circles for the sun and a number of drilled holes that may have been for food sacrifice, the rock also bears the Christian cross to claim it for the new religion of Patrick. However, what is most remarkable about the Rock of Boheh is that it may have been used to divide the year into three. On other clear days, the sun from this vantage sets directly behind Croagh Patrick, a major reason for dedicating the peak to Lugh, Celtic god of the sun and one of the Tuatha Dé Danann, who were driven into the underworld after the battle of Moytura near Lough Corrib. However, a local man, Gerry Bracken, has detected that on only two days of the calendar – April 18 and August 24 – the setting sun seen from the Rock of Boheh rests on the summit of Croagh Patrick and then follows a diagonal path down the northern slope as if it is rolling down the mountainside. Even though this is not one of the designated dates – and I plan to be some distance from here, coming down from the summit, when the sun sets – I stand momentarily in awe of

the precision of supposedly primitive people at a time when science consisted in diligent observation and patient recording, with due deference to the sacred wonder of discovery.

4.45 p.m.

The final leg of the journey to Croagh Patrick is a long trek across blanket bog and seemingly endless stretches of deserted little roads with panoramic views of the holy mountain and the ever-widening vista behind. All that will remain will be the climb to the summit and the descent to Murrisk on the other side. From the wonders of Boheh, the *tóchar* re-emerges in the remains of its original flagstone causeway in sweeping bogland fields along the Owenwee River. I learn that the fields have names – Paircín na hAirne, Cnoc na Móna, Garraí na bhFuinseog – and I try to match them visually to those names.[33] The path, with an interruption to leap over a ditch, leads eventually to a small country road that crosses an attractive stone bridge in a slight detour, with the original ford crossing visible to the right. The dominance of the mountain ahead is pervasive and it is little wonder that it was worshipped as the dwelling place of gods in ancient times. Then, it was known as Cruachán Aigle, named for the son of Derg, who was killed by his uncle Cromderg in revenge for having killed Ciara. She was the daughter of Lugh, the god for whom the feast of Lughnasa and the month of August in the Irish language are named. As a representation of the sun, Lugh was honoured to ensure a good harvest. Little wonder, then, that St Patrick sought to incorporate this belief into the new religion he brought to the shores of Ireland rather than root it out or simply supplant it. By coming along this path to the Reek, he was on a mission to embrace the faith of the people and harness it for Christ. Indeed, baptising pagan monuments like the Rock of Boheh by simply inscribing them with the cross of Christianity ensured an easy and fervent transition to the new religion with no loss of face. For that reason, the Celtic cross, which is such an iconic symbol of Christianity in Ireland, incorporates the circle of the sun with the cross of Christ.

Yet the patron missionary was not ambivalent on where the new belief should rest. While embracing the sun, he did so in the name of Christ alone. In his *Confessio*, Patrick wrote:

> *This sun which we see rises daily at his command for our benefit, but it will never reign, nor will its brilliance endure. Those who worship it will be severely punished. We, on the other hand, believe in and worship Christ the true sun who will never perish, nor will anyone who does his will. We will remain forever as Christ remains forever, who reigns with God the Father Almighty and the Holy Spirit before time began and now and for all eternity.*[34]

Of course, another aspect of Patrick's decision to go to this the mountain was to follow a practice established by Moses, Elias and Christ himself – to seek out a high, desolate place and fast there for the season of Lent.

5.15 p.m.
I feel that I am about to begin the ascent and I can see the clear outline of the scree path that sweeps up to the summit. Yet the road stretches on, and there is no sign yet to indicate the path of the *tóchar*. I rest for a few moments in an alley-like shelter built of dry stones, eat some of the fruit I have brought along and drink from my water bottle. A cloud is now resting on the peak and I am aware that the forecast

for tomorrow is for rain and gales. I feel tired, but more determined than ever to press on for the final goal. Besides, I have absolutely no idea how I would give road directions for someone to come and pick me up. My only choice is to get to Murrisk – and that means going over the top.

5.45 p.m.
At last I am leaving the road and following the pilgrim path up the side of the mountain. It takes me around the back of the Portakabin buildings of the Mayo Mountain Rescue Team base and straight up to a trail that follows a diagonal course in what seems like the wrong direction, before turning right back on itself and launching off for the summit. Barely used compared to the path from Murrisk village on the other side, the ancient pilgrim path from Boleybrian is visible in some footprints and even the hoofprint of a donkey. Maura Walshe told me she had seen a donkey on Saturday ferrying bottles of water up to the stalls on the summit for Reek Sunday.

The *Tóchar* Phádraig path up the mountain begins with the final notice of the ancient pilgrim path before it merges with the normal route from Murrisk. The information notice tells of the Caorthannach, who was the devil's mother or the embodiment of the sin of pride. After a 40-day battle at the mountain top, Patrick banished the Caorthannach to the icy waters of Lough Corra, which can be seen from here in the wooded near distance, beyond some bogland, where work has been progressing on saving winter fuel. The Caorthannach, we are told, pestered Patrick throughout the 40 days of his Lenten sojourn, swooping down on him as flocks of hideous black birds. All he had to fight them off were prayers and psalms, which he chanted repeatedly from the mountain top. Finally, Patrick rang his bell loudly against them. When they began to give way to this symbol of his spiritual authority, he flung the blessed bell among them. That banished them in serpent form to the deeps of Lough Corra, where they remained for seven years before escaping to the Donegal waters of Lough Derg. There, Patrick had to do battle with the serpent once more. Eventually, he mortally wounded it, staining the lake waters red. His blessed bell, meanwhile, had been badly damaged in the initial battle on Croagh Patrick, when it rolled down the mountainside and a piece was broken out of it. However, an angel retrieved the bell and brought it back to Patrick. The sky was filled with white birds, who transformed the mountain top into a vision of paradise before Patrick was told to go back down to continue his work on the day before Easter Sunday. The legend tells us that on his deathbed, Patrick bestowed the bell to Brigid, who prized it. It was then known as Brigid's Gapling or Broken Bell.

6.30 p.m.
With a few brief pauses to take in the view below and scan the summit, now shrouded in a cloud, I reach the merging of the paths up Croagh Patrick near the Leacht Benain. This is the first station of the pilgrimage. It is a cairn of stones in a dip on the lower heights of the mountain; around which pilgrims must walk seven times, saying seven Our Fathers, seven Hail Marys and the Apostles' Creed. Helpfully, the notice on the Leacht Benain tells us that the second station is on the summit, so the slow ascent of the shale path to the mountain top begins. From here on, the pilgrim path is a series of frequent encounters. On this evening, the Monday before the vast annual ascent on Reek Sunday, pilgrims climb the penitential path from Murrisk in ones, twos or groups. As I scramble alone up the path of shale and sand, conversation with those coming down begins several paces

before the actual meeting and continues several paces afterwards. Seldom is there a pause for a close encounter, but the exchanges can range from simple words of encouragement or warning to lengthier information trading.

A couple of young boys, with Dad coming in their wake, tell me that I am about to reach the 'worst part'. I ask wryly if I should quit and give up and they urgently advise, 'No, it's well worth it.' An older couple make their way gingerly, helping each other down the treacherous path. He tells me that he once met a man on Station Island in Lough Derg who had walked there all the way from Omagh wearing only sandals. A young man from Cavan comes along breezily, using his rolled brolly as a walking cane and smiling broadly at his achievement. A group of young women and girls are coming down like crabs over the most difficult part. Yet invariably, there is an air of contentment prevailing among these descending as I scramble alone up the sliding path.

6.45 p.m.
A group of young men come down quickly, pausing only to allow me through a difficult part on the route that we have collectively identified as our preferred option. They tell me that I am less than 10 minutes from the summit, but ahead I see only a blanket of mist from the cloud that has enveloped our world. Below, I can see faintly in the distance the dot-like figures of people who have descended, some resting at the Leacht Benain to regroup with those coming behind. After my day of walking, the prospect of 10 minutes sounds like a path to paradise. Even at this height, I begin to notice the litter – which invariably consists of discarded plastic bottles that once contained water. I wonder again at the thoughtlessness of pilgrims who could not be bothered carrying away the almost weightless empty container they

manage to carry up full. Finally, as I surmount the lip of the summit with a huge rush of relief and joy, I see a public notice carved in stone: 'Keep Croagh Patrick clean. We appeal to pilgrims to take their litter back to bins provided in car park. Thank you.'

7.00 p.m.
I am finishing my prayers at the second station, on the summit, where the pilgrim kneels and says seven Our Fathers, seven Hail Marys and one Creed, when I notice a small pile of photographs pinned under a rock. I lift the congealing bundle gingerly; the photo on top shows a family scene. The young, bearded and proud father poses with his four children of varying ages under ten, the youngest a babe in his arms. The man wears a black-and-white striped windcheater and the children are smiling. Somehow, the family tableau with the lone parent seems incredibly familiar and poignant. Yet it is also frightening to think that this photo of family contentment and pride encapsulates a story that is probably such a huge tragedy that it prompted a pilgrim to struggle to the top of this holy mountain and pray. Tears well in my eyes and I feel several sobs heaving in my chest. I add a fervent prayer that this might not be all that remains of that family's happiness. I put the photos back without looking at the others, my mind conjuring an image of all the children 'who lie under the cairn'. The image is overpowering:

*Children lie under the cairn, unhallowed souls*
*Whose playground should be the duach and the dunes.*
*No higher than little children walking on tiptoe*
*Past SS guards at the selections in Terezín,*
*The cairn has become a scree, the scree a landslide,*
*And a raised beach the memorial to all of them.*[35]

For several moments after rising from my knees, my heart pounds with near panic in contemplating the stories of those whose images I am just too scared to view. For the rest of my lone pilgrimage on the summit, my mind races with thoughts of them as I recite the required pilgrimage prayers. Somehow the admonition to pray near the chapel for the pope's intentions seems a pointless distraction from what has now become the real focus of my pilgrimage along the *tóchar* to this place.

After walking around the chapel, reciting the prayers mantra-like, and then doing the same at Leaba Phádraig, I cast about briefly in search of the third and final station, Reilig Mhuire (Our Lady's Cemetery), also known as Garraí Mór (Big Garden), which I have read is a considerable distance down the western side of the mountain. By now, however, I am disorientated in the cloudy mist of the summit and my only reference point is the Oratory, which was built on the instructions of the Patrician scholar John Healy, archbishop of Tuam, when Croagh Patrick became an approved place of pilgrimage for the church at the beginning of the twentieth century. I walk around it once more, passing the makeshift structures of the stalls on top, their skeletal wooden frames over dry-stone walls waiting for the hordes to arrive on the coming Sunday, when the frames will be draped in tarpaulin and become the focus of fervent pilgrims buying tea and bottled water before, after and during the Masses that run continuously from just after dawn into the early afternoon. Yet I am all alone now on a deserted mountain top and I feel that I am truly in the shadow of Patrick, who wrestled with his demons and found peace here.

I wander back to the second-station cairn and drop the small, gnarled stone I have carried from Ballintubber Abbey there with another quiet prayer for the peace and repose of those depicted in the photos pinned at its base. I pick up a small replacement pebble. It is flat and smooth and it seems to shine with a radiance in my hand before I place it in my pocket. Then I sit on the low wall opposite, drink water from the home of the hospitable woman back along the *tóchar* and eat my orange, unknowingly saving the peel for Mickey Mallon. For just at that very moment, the pilgrim runner from south Armagh is bounding over the lip of the path to the summit, shaking me from my reveries and back into the world of people to meet and places to go.

8.15 p.m.
The descent is punctuated by more encounters; I move slowly because my left knee has frozen in pain. Each step is a reminder of the incredible suffering and sacrifice this holy mountain has inflicted and endured in the paths of pilgrims to its summit for thousands of years. Long since, Mickey and a young man in a Munster rugby shirt I met coming up on my way down have overtaken me on their rapid descent. Mickey paused only to remark that it is great to see young people climbing the Reek, but we still have to show them the way, before racing off at a bounding trot to meet his wife, who is 'bad on her feet' and still on her way up. Beyond the Leacht Benain, I follow the most popular pilgrim path for Murrisk, walking past the modern toilets constructed for the relief of pilgrims – where, I later learn, there are long queues for the ladies' on Reek Sunday. Down in a hollow, names have been written in white stones on the slopes around a small corrie lake. They include Polish names, testifying to the popularity of the Croagh Patrick pilgrimage among recent immigrants. Further on, the view of Clew Bay is breathtaking, as is the spit of Bertra Beach, the tombola of sand snaking out into the bay and claiming one of its reputed 365 islands.

8.30 p.m.
A final group of pilgrims from the traveller community comes along. These young women and a boy, all dressed in flimsy clothing and footwear, press ahead on the first stage of their ascent and ask how far it is to the 'flat bit' – the long plateau leading to Leacht Benain. I tell them it will take them about 15 minutes. The young boy asks if he can have my staff to help him get there. I tell him I need it to help me down. Nodding to my backpack, he then says, 'Give me a drink of that water then.' I tell him the bottle is empty and, when he asks to see, I pull it from its small side-pocket. He regards me as if I am not even half wise to be carrying an empty plastic bottle I could easily discard.

8.40 p.m.
Further on, I meet a young man and woman who turn out to be on holiday from the United States. They assure me they are not going to the top and only want to enjoy more of the 'incredible view' from a slightly higher vantage. I suggest they wait and do the entire trek to the top and they tell me they are returning home tomorrow.

'Maybe you should get here early when you come next time and climb the Reek,' I suggest encouragingly. 'It's certainly worth it.'

They smile and say they just might do that. With a word of concern for a young girl they met further down the slope, they head off happily. I then make my way down to the young girl, dressed in a light pink top and flip-flop sandals, who is slowly making her way down the path. She seems about twelve years old, but may well be younger, and she is from the traveller community too. She asks how it was up there and I tell her it was stunning and she should do it some time when she is dressed for the climb.

'I'd need a stick like you,' she says, 'and maybe a bottle of water.' I agree and suggest she also should have a pair of sturdy shoes or boots next time. As I press ahead around a turn, wondering if I should wait and help the young girl down the path, I meet a man coming up, who asks for her. It is her dad; I move on with a clear conscience, knowing that I have not left a child in distress.

9.00 p.m.
The final encounters of my *turas* come right at the base. A pair of young men are seated, looking at their two big bundles of sticks with unmistakable disdain. They are willow poles, just like my staff, which has been particularly useful in the descent with my wonky knee. I ask if they are selling them there and they tell me they are moving them up to a place just around the rocky corner above. They are obviously in no hurry to complete their task, telling me they have been preparing them to sell. I wish them good luck and say I am off for a pint. One of them grunts in disgust, saying, 'We'll not be having any pints till Sunday, depending on how many of these bloody things we sell.'

I move on and see a man in full climbing gear at the side of a brook. His red jacket identifies him as a member of the Mayo Mountain Rescue Team and he is speaking loudly into a hand-held radio, which crackles with static. I remark as I pass that he could get a more modern phone than that big clunker. He laughs and, pointing far up the slope, says, 'We're setting up a repeater station up there. We need it for radio contact with the other side of the mountain on Sunday because we'll have teams on both sides.'

I wish him luck and walk through the final gate, down the steps past the imposing statue of Patrick and meet a bunch of young men walking up. I warn them it is too late to attempt the summit. They laugh and say they have no intention of going any further than the steps. I hobble along with my bad knee and cut shin into the car park, where my partner, Delia, awaits. My boots are muddy and my clothes saturated with sweat but I beam at the thought of what I have accomplished since I left Ballintubber Abbey almost 12 hours ago. I pull on a fresh t-shirt and we head off to eat. As my body sinks into the car seat, I bask in a few moments of incredible warmth before I start to tell my pilgrim's tale of the *Tóchar* Phádraig.

*Wednesday, 22 July 2009*
After a day of rest and recreation, with a drive down to Killary Harbour and a visit to Westport House, I call with Fr Fahey at Ballintubber Abbey, where I receive my signed certificate for having completed the *Tóchar* Phádraig. He even lets me keep the pilgrim's staff as a memento. Then we set off for Ashford Castle on the pilgrimage of modern tourists who flock to Cong, the setting for the famous movie, *The Quiet Man*. My attention is caught by a notice for a boat trip to the ancient monastic island of Inchagoill on Lough Corrib and, as I read the advertisement inviting us to 'see where Irish Christianity began', the captain of the motor-launch ferry urges us to join him for the afternoon voyage.

2.30 p.m.
Armed with a marvellous roast-beef sandwich from the local butcher/deli in Cong, I come aboard, pay my monastic-pilgrimage fare of €20 and purchase a mug of tea for €2. Half an hour after the appointed time, we are setting off across the lough and I am sitting on the upper deck among a large group of German visitors. The outward and return journeys each take half an hour.

For much of that time, the public-address system on the small ferry plays the movie soundtrack of *The Quiet Man*. We gaze out across the waters to the shores of Lough Corrib and its islands and the Twelve Pins mountains of Connemara beyond. From his bridge, Captain Patrick tells us what to expect on our visit to the island, which will take just over half an hour. He does not stint in his description of what are billed as certainly among the most important archaeological sites in Ireland and, in the case of a standing stone inscribed in Gaelic, possibly in the entire world. This he can attest from his own studies in the field of archaeology. Unlike John Wayne's character in *The Quiet Man*, Captain Patrick is not selling himself short.

3.30 p.m.

We land and gather on the jetty, then in single file proceed in Patrick's footsteps along the short path to the promised wonders, now under the protection of the Irish government through the Office of Public Works and surrounded by state forestry maintained by Coillte. The first is the small and 'unique' stone with its simple inscription and a number of carved crosses. Beside it is the small Augustinian church called Teampall na Naomh (Church of the Saints), built by monks from the monastery of Cong in 1178; outside, a cairn marks the final resting place of an archbishop, we are told.

We gather in the chancel of the twelfth-century church ruins while a group of youngsters from the ferry that docked before us treat them as an adventure playground, squeezing through the narrow window opening behind the altar stone. Captain Patrick chivvies them out to give his talk. After this, we file across to the adjacent Teampall Phádraig, which, we have been told, was founded by St Patrick and his nephew

Lugna five years after they were banished to Inchagoill Island by the pagan druids of Cong in AD 445. The standing stone, we are informed, marks the burial place of Patrick's nephew and is in the shape of a boat's rudder because Lugna was the patron saint's navigator. Finally, we are left to our own thoughts and observations for about 10 minutes. We move from monument to ruin with the repeated warning that the ferry leaves at 4.15 p.m. and, if we don't make it, the next is at noon tomorrow. Before making my way back to the jetty, I pause to read the large public notice raised by the Office of Public Works, which makes more modest observations about the site than we have heard.

4.10 p.m.
Along the path, a man asks if I have ever visited the monastic ruins at Holy Island on Lough Derg. Momentary confusion over which Lough Derg he means (it turns out to be the one in County Clare) then leads to an absorbing and informative conversation about pilgrimage, archaeology, history, sport, culture, politics and much more that lasts all the way back to the Headford Castle shore. My encounter with Pat Sheedy, just retired as a history teacher at Roscrea Abbey to devote himself more fully to his cattle farm, golf and hurling, turns out to be the highlight of the day – a chance encounter from which I learn much of interest to take away. As for the cruise to Inchagoill Island to 'see where Irish Christianity began', the other pilgrims seem more than happy as they disembark at 4.45 p.m. Clearly there are few doubts that they have been given a glimpse of Ireland's hidden past, packaged neatly and delivered in two hours. If it whets any appetite for our rich pagan and Christian past and instils an interest in exploring further, well, isn't that great value for €20?

*Note: On 26 July 2009 an estimated 20,000 people made the Reek Sunday pilgrimage in rain and wind. Mayo Mountain Rescue Team and the Knights of Malta reported scores of injuries, including six children suffering from hypothermia because of inadequate clothing and footwear.*[36]

# Chapter 4

# Don't Knock It 'til You've Tried It

## Knock

*22 August 2009*

In truth, I am predisposed not to like Ireland's most popular place of pilgrimage – the shrine at Knock in County Mayo, dedicated 30 years ago by papal decree to Our Lady, queen of Ireland. I have not been to Knock since my one and only visit in 1981 and I confess to squirming uncomfortably every time I pass along the N17 Sligo to Galway road, miraculously transformed into a modern highway at this point. And who could fail to be impressed by the airport, plonked on raised moorland at Barnalyra, that brought me there in the first place?

On my last visit I witnessed this modern miracle, wrought at the hands of the almighty Mgr James Horan, creator of all that this tiny east Mayo village has become in a few decades. Before Mgr Horan's commercial approach to Catholic pilgrimage, Knock languished in the general decline of the west, despite the 1879 apparition of a succession of figures identified as the Virgin Mary, St Joseph, St John the Evangelist and the Lamb of God. In this pantheon of iconic revelation, Knock could surely stake its claim as Ground Zero for a galaxy of celestial beings. But back to my previous visit. The Republic of Ireland's general election in June 1981 brought sudden change in a tumultuous period centred on the H-block hunger strikes in the north. Fianna Fáil were ousted and replaced by another Fine Gael–Labour coalition led by Garret FitzGerald. One of the first things the new government did was suspend the costly Knock Airport project. This was seen as the beginning of the end for Mgr Horan's dream of making Knock a true contender for the high-flying pilgrim. But, despite their earthly power, Garret and his gang proved no match for Mgr Horan and his heavenly host.

As a senior reporter for the *Sunday Tribune*, I had a good working relationship with Fianna Fáil's outgoing transport minister, Albert Reynolds. It had most recently involved air-transport problems and another Marian shrine. On 2 May 1981, an Aer Lingus flight from Dublin to London Heathrow was hijacked by a former Trappist monk from Australia. Laurence James Downey boarded flight EI-164, doused himself in petrol and threatened to set himself alight before making his demands, the principal one being that the Vatican make public the 'Third Secret of Fátima'. The plane, with 113 passengers on board, landed at Le Touquet in northern France. I was covering the story at Dublin Airport and learned that a relief plane was being dispatched, carrying top-level negotiators, including Minister Reynolds, as well as senior police and military personnel. I pleaded with Government Press Secretary Frank Dunlop for a seat and, just before take-off, I got the nod from Albert

Reynolds himself. During our flight to Normandy, I chatted with the minister and also briefly with the security personnel. I learned that the plan was to inveigle the hijacker onto our plane on the grounds that the other plane did not have sufficient fuel to fly to Iran or Libya. The passengers would be out of danger and other measures could then be taken. I prepared myself for a flight to Tehran or Tripoli and wondered what I would do there with no passport, no credit cards and just a tenner in my wallet.

By the time we landed, the plan had changed and we were led to the control tower with me under strict instructions from the minister not to let the French know I was a journalist. So, posing as a government apparatchik, I had a front-seat vantage on negotiations that lured Downey into a false sense of security while French commandos secretly boarded the hijacked plane to overpower him. I interviewed the rescued passengers and commando captain. With the story wrapped, I then made frantic efforts to reach my newsdesk in Dublin on a fragile phone connection. Meanwhile, I was being urged to board the hijacked plane, because the EI-164 passengers had already left on our relief plane. However, my scoop would have to wait – it was after deadline and everyone had gone home. To make matters worse, as we landed at Heathrow for 'maintenance' on the homeward flight, the toilets passengers had been using all day overflowed and the contents poured down the plane's central aisle. Ah, the glamour of high-flying journalism. Next day, however, our paper had an exclusive photo of the hijacker and copious details of his quest, which he had obligingly left into the office before departure.

Perhaps it was that less-than-satisfactory outcome of my scoop in Le Touquet that prompted the ousted minister to respond positively to my request to accompany him to

Knock when the airport project was axed. So I travelled down to join Mr Reynolds at his breakfast table in Longford, and we set off for the west with his constituency handler Noel Hanlon, subsequently chairman of Aer Rianta, at the wheel. We almost flew there in Mr Hanlon's Merc and landed at the new basilica, where we were met by an ebullient monsignor, then whisked off down the road to Charlestown and up to Barnalyra and a huge expanse dug from blanket bog. The spot where Albert Reynolds had turned the ceremonial sod was now, the prophetic pastor told us, the runway he would complete – government or no government. Then it was back to his parochial house, where we were joined by local Fianna Fáil kingpin Pádraig Flynn, determined not to be denied the limelight in his own patch. Over a heaped plate of boiled mutton, carrots and spuds, Mr Flynn insisted that I accompany him to Castlebar, where he would reveal damning evidence about the new government's plan.

The day went downhill from there. Yet it was in the parochial house that I spotted a device that would colour my view of Knock forever more – a clocking-in machine for shrine workers. Why run a place of pilgrimage like a factory? I didn't wonder long, as Mgr Horan expounded on plans for developing Knock into a world-class shrine to rival league leaders Lourdes, Fátima and Guadalupe. It has been 28 years since then – and 23 since Mgr Horan died in Lourdes – and I am back to the future he outlined.

12.30 p.m.

This is pilgrimage on an industrial scale – acres of car park tucked away along access and exit routes, rows of stalls selling mass-produced plastic mementoes, trinkets and plastic bottles for holy water and even a shuttle service to move pilgrims with mobility problems across the wide expanses between the various shrine locations. The car park adjacent to the Knock International Hotel is filling up quickly on this, the 130th anniversary of the day of the apparitions and a family is having lunch out of the boot of their car – tea from a Thermos flask and individually wrapped sandwiches. I'd bet they are ham. At stalls along the route to the shrine, trolleys filled with colourful plastic flowers and other useful pilgrimage items await the arrival of holy hordes. I peruse the wares. Among them are plastic bottles in white and blue with screw-on tops, already labelled conveniently as 'Holy Water from Knock': five for €2 for the small ones, 60 cent each or two for €1 for the bigger ones. Around the corner on the main street are lines of more permanent shops selling similar goods and novelty items like linen tea-towels with 'comic letters' from a son who is 'writing slow' because the recipient 'can't read fast'. The names on the shops range from pious to exotic – St Anthony's, St Martin's, Golden Rose. On lamp-posts, advertising placards carry a triumphant message – 'Last Sunday 1.7 million people went to Mass … Now there's some good news.' Brought to us by *The Irish Catholic* – 'Your faith in your hands,' it does not say where the other 4.3 million Irish people went last Sunday. That would be of little interest to the gathering crowds in Knock, for whom Mass and observance of the prescribed rituals is clearly paramount.

12.45 p.m.

Back up the street and into the shrine area, where the original village church – at which the heavenly apparition manifested itself – is dwarfed in its surroundings. At the entrance, a man is handing out leaflets for the lobby group Cóir, urging a negative vote in the coming referendum on the Lisbon treaty for changes in the structures of the European Union. 'Good for them – bad for you,' it proclaims, going on to list a number of reasons for a negative vote. The crucial one, I suspect, warns of some 'EU court' dictating laws on 'abortion, raising children, marriage, euthanasia and more'.

A woman nearby is handing out densely typed pages outlining the benefit of the 'Brown Scapular of Our Lady of Mount Carmel'. It extols the virtues of this particular religious apparel, including the 'Sabbatine privilege' based on a papal bull of Pope John XXII from 1322, decreeing that those who wear the scapular and fulfil two other conditions made known to him in an apparition by the Blessed Virgin will be 'freed from Purgatory on the first Saturday after death'. Now, there's a promise to have you ticking off the days of eternity. With directives from heaven, miraculous testimonials and more, this monochrome literature seems as pertinent to the coming referendum as the Cóir message in colour.

12.55 p.m.

Past the small Church of the Apparition and the Shrine Information Office, a huge expanse opens up, with the papal cross and the basilica towering on the left and the crosses marking one of the Stations of the Cross on elevated land in the far distance to the south. In between, there are acres of paving and matching expanses of carefully manicured lawn, with people moving in all directions. A big information map welcomes me to Knock and I study it briefly, checking off those among the 50 listed features I might wish to visit. The Hill of the Crosses beckons, but I am intrigued by the entrance to a place that seems embedded in the hill, apart from a glass box on top with a cross on it. It is the Chapel of Reconciliation, where pilgrims come to confess their sins or to receive counselling, and the altar inside features a crucifixion scene bathed in natural light from the glass box above. With banks of confessionals along both walls and penitents – including a family with six children – waiting in the wings, the Chapel of Reconciliation is doing a steady trade, shriving the nation. Outside, meanwhile, a young woman sucks deeply on a cigarette while her mother does some business at one of the kiosks embedded in the wall.

On, then, to the Hill of the Crosses, where there are brightly coloured banners in the background, but a line of red-and-white tape and barriers precludes entrance. A young man and woman come through the gate – he with a large-lens camera and she with a reporter's spiral notebook held prominently in front as she advances on the shrine. God forbid she'd be mistaken for a pilgrim, I think, as I sidle past them and on to the old graveyard, one of the most natural features in the modern religious landscape of Knock. From there I walk around the side, past St Brigid's Hostel, which provides accommodation for shrine workers, and on to the museum, where a woman at the entrance asks where I'm from as she takes my €4 entrance fee. Then, for a survey she is conducting, she asks how I heard of the museum. From the big map up there, I tell her, pointing into the distance.

1.10 p.m.

The first exhibit features a collage of photos from different eras and a message: 'There are no strangers, only fellow pilgrims.' Other boards record fellow pilgrim Pope John Paul II being greeted by Mgr Horan in 1979 and Mother Teresa of Calcutta, who came in June 1993. In a glass case is the prie-dieu used for the papal knees. I move on through exhibits about Knock holy water, the Irish tradition of pilgrimage and the Children of Mary in sky-blue cloaks. Then it's Knock over four periods. The information is sketchy on the initial 50 years until the appearance of Archbishop Gilmartin of Tuam in 1929. Knock then becomes popular, and the first pilgrimage from the United States takes place in 1949. The shrine then enters its golden era, with Ráidio Éireann broadcasts in 1950 and the Marian Year of 1954, James Horan's arrival in 1963 and his appointment as parish priest four years later, pilgrimages for peace as the north erupts and the 1979 papal visit, with half a million pilgrims flocking to the new basilica. The post-papal era brings the miracle of the airport, completed in 1985 with the secular blessing of Fianna Fáil, by then back in power. Even against the competition of Lourdes, Fátima and newcomers like Medjugorje (where the Virgin appeared in 1981), Knock still holds its own.

But what of the humble beginnings enshrined in a museum exhibit about the legend of the capstone from the Church of John the Baptist in the parish of Cnoc Droma Chalraighe, built in 1828 under the direction of Revd P. O'Grady PP? It bears the aspiration from Matthew's Gospel (11:17), 'My house shall be called the house of prayer to all the nations …' I note the omission of the next part: '… but you have made it a den of robbers.' Then, from Psalm 118 (incorrectly identified in the exhibit as Psalm 117), the capstone has: 'This is the Gate of the Lord; the Just shall enter into it.' The manifestation of the initial inscription is evidenced in pilgrimages from England, the USA, Australia, South Africa, 'Rhodesia' and many other lands around the globe. It is followed immediately with two information blocks on Mgr Horan and his airport project and another on the Knock Shrine Society, founded in 1935 – a vast, unpaid, uniformed workforce of 1,200 'Stewards' and 'Handmaids', with an additional junior corps of recruits aged from 11 to 15.

But the claim to humility is elaborated in the next exhibit, introduced with the observation that 'The witnesses lived in houses like this', beside the facsimile of a thatched cottage with a mid-twentieth-century bicycle leaning against the wall. Inside is the familiar layout of the old Irish cottage of one bedroom and kitchen with open hearth and day settle, pristine with fresh whitewash and gleaming linen. There are religious pictures and crucifixes on every wall and other religious objects are strategically placed elsewhere. Secular adornment is confined to two porcelain dogs on the high mantel, just underneath a hunting rifle. The recreation of the environment in which the 1879 apparition is said to have taken place continues with a facsimile of a village forge, where the events were discussed in minute detail, and a collection of artefacts from other crafts and occupations. This is to portray the witnesses as ordinary people and the day as otherwise unremarkable:

> *In Knock, Thursday, 21st of August began in a very ordinary way. People made the most of the dry weather by working outdoors. They saved hay, brought turf from the bog, aired bedding and hung clothes out to dry. Once her work was done Mary McLoughlin, housekeeper for the parish priest, visited the Byrne family. They lived in a thatched cottage near the church. By evening the weather had changed and it started to rain heavily. Around eight o'clock she began to make her way home accompanied by Mary, eldest daughter of Mrs Byrne. As they approached the church, Mary Byrne cried out, 'Look at the beautiful figures.' Moving closer the two women saw a radiant figure and Mary Byrne exclaimed, 'It is the Blessed Virgin.' On either side stood St Joseph and St John the Evangelist and to the right an altar. On this altar stood a lamb surrounded by angels and behind it a large*

> *cross. Mary Byrne ran home to tell her family of the wonderful sight. Her mother Margaret, brother Dominick, sister Margaret and niece Catherine Murray all went out. They too saw the Apparition. Mary then hurried to tell the neighbours living near the church. Soon a small crowd had gathered at the gable. As they gazed at the Apparition they recited the Rosary and other prayers. The vision lasted about two hours from daylight to darkness. Rain saturated the witnesses but not a drop fell either on the gable wall or onto the vision.*

Adjacent to this explanation is an exhibit showing what the witnesses saw – the bent-over old-man figure of Joseph, the Virgin crowned, the mitred figure of John the Evangelist holding a book, which one of the witnesses said was like a statue she had seen near Westport, and the lamb and cross on the altar. To facilitate veneration by pilgrims, two kneelers are provided in front of the museum representation. Back outside in the concourse, meanwhile, details of papal recognition are listed: Pius XII's blessing in Rome of the Knock Shrine banner in the Marian year of 1954; 1957, when the church at Knock was affiliated to the Basilica of St Mary Major in Rome; 1960, when John XXIII (wrongly identified here as John Paul XXIII) recognised Knock as 'one of the most outstanding places of public devotion to the Blessed Virgin Mary'; 1964, when the bishops from the '24 most famous Marian Shrines in the world' concelebrated Mass with Pope Paul VI; and the visit of John Paul II in 1979.

Yet the value of a pilgrimage site is to be found in its witness for faith and healing, and the concourse of Knock's museum ends in a section devoted to miracles, portrayed most vividly in a large encased poster. This is one of a series of 12 commissioned by the Custodians of Knock Shrine and distributed to schools during the early 1970s, the decade that marked the end of an era when the Church Triumphant, as it were, ruled Ireland. The poster is remarkable for the figure of a smiling boy dressed in blue trousers and open-necked shirt, holding a crutch above his head, under the headline, 'The deaf hear and the lame walk.' For those familiar with the art of that time, the image is evocatively Maoist, strikingly reminiscent of Communist depictions of young boy soldiers holding AK47 rifles above their heads. The poster describes at length the belief in the miraculous properties of the gable wall where the apparitions were seen and the racks there for crutches discarded by those who are cured. It declares:

> *Cures have taken place at Knock down through the years to the present. They are not confined to any one type of believer. Many non-believers have been cured. They are not confined either to any particular age group or to one sex. Here the blind see. The dumb speak. The deaf hear. The lame walk. Sores and cancers are cleansed.*

The present tense and jubilant insistence on miraculous cures is dampened somewhat by the evidence presented. Central to that is the testimony of Marion Carroll in her book, *I Was Cured at Knock*, which details her miraculous recovery from multiple sclerosis while at Mass in the basilica in 1989. Apart from the uncorroborated testimony of those who give thanks for cures for various afflictions in the 1990s, such as 'unpaid tax resolved', 'threatened litigation avoided', 'suitable house found', aches, shakes and unexplained pains relieved, as well as cures granted after appropriate medical treatment, I find no evidence here that miracles are still happening at Knock, so I decide to go and see if the crutches are still being racked up at the gable of the apparitions.

1.40 p.m.
I make a quick visit to the basilica to familiarise myself with the layout before the penultimate Mass of the annual Knock novena. Across the beautifully presented lawns interspersed with flower-beds exuding an abundance of blossoms, the huge church stands sentinel. Walking past one of the flower-beds, I notice that at its centre is a post holding loudspeakers. I spot others in a flower-bed across the way. Then there are the bird-box Stations of the Cross, impaled on posts positioned higgledy-piggledy in the grass. The flags of Ireland, the Vatican and the EU fly over the great concourse where twin main entrances allow access into the cavernous interior of the basilica, with its central altar and a huge backdrop depicting the now-familiar elements of the Knock apparition. Pilgrims are coming and going and, in the central section facing the altar, a group of women is already ensconced front of stage. If I'm going to have a bite to eat and get seated for Mass at three o'clock, I had better do so now.

I make my way back across the huge expanse of paved concourse with the giant papal cross, where groups linger, greet each other and talk. Among them are several priests and clutches of earnest young men with black trousers, sweaters, white shirts and dark ties, whom I take to be clerical students. They chat and seem relaxed and comfortable with their surroundings as pilgrims make the Stations of the Cross and others do the rounds of the old church with Rosary beads. At the side of the old church, a woman in traditional Indian garb smiles as she poses for a photo at a giant sculpture of stone Rosary beads on the rendered wall. Nearby, what seems to be a stall painted in a Children of Mary blue and made up of sections on wheels is a movable shrine for lighted votive candles, advertised at €1.50 each and placed on banks that are building up rapidly and will soon spill into the next section to be wheeled along. The crowds mill around the Shrine Information Office as I pass out on to the street, where two women greet each other loudly.

'Did you get caught in that big shower earlier?'

'No, I was in at Mass. What about you?'

'Ah no, I was at my prayer group.'

Anything you can do, I can do better!

2.00 p.m.
Down the street, I cross over to the other side, where another large shrine bears the dedication:

> *To the memory of Captain Richard Jordan and James O'Malley who offered up their lives on the altar of their country in the year 1798, also Geoffery Cunniff and Tom Flatley, who paid the penalty of devotion to Ireland. May their actions tend to stimulate us to do something to throw off the yoke of the stranger.*

I make my way into a restaurant with a sign outside advertising Knock Shopping Arcade. A woman at the entrance asks if I am alone, then instructs me to sit at the first table, where a stern-looking diner is finishing her cup of tea. I order what seems to be the most expansive fare from the 'hot meals' menu – a variety of combinations involving chicken, sausages, bacon and eggs with chips, tea/coffee and bread. It comes in a few moments, a sparse, pre-processed offering for €12.95. I stock up on brown bread and tea; surrounded by statues of the BVM and other religious artefacts displayed for sale in their multitudes around the walls, and watch the comings and goings. Eventually a man is put directly in front of me. I greet him with a smile and a comment about the uncertain weather. He grunts gruffly. I finish up, pay at the till and leave.

2.30 p.m.
Inside the old church, pilgrims sit alone or kneel in groups in the pews facing the traditional-style altar and rails, with a stained-glass window enveloped by drapes. A sign to the right says, 'Our Lady of Knock pray for us.' Among the kneeling pilgrims is a young girl wearing a white lace mantilla; her mother's head is draped in a black scarf. There is silence, apart from the dragging feet of those coming and leaving. I join the pilgrims making the 'rounds' as they count their beads and shuffle along through the gathering visitors, past the huge glass wall that encases the gable, which has now been turned into yet another chapel, with replica statues of Mary, Joseph, John the Evangelist and the lamb and cross surrounded by a heavenly host of winged angels sculpted into the wall. There is a large gathering of people seated or kneeling inside the chapel, heads bowed or else gazing intently at the 'apparitions' before them. I note no evidence of racks for discarded crutches. To the right of the glass window on the holy spectacle a metal-framed square section of the wall is made up of stonework from the old gable. As praying pilgrims come along, they pause and touch it with reverence.

3.45 p.m.
I join the steady flow of pilgrims heading for the basilica, past Calvary and the papal cross, skirting the main entrance and moving to the second of the chapel entrances that allow direct access to the seating for the laity in each of the huge sections of the interior. I find a seat about 10 rows back, at

an angle of about 45 degrees to the main altar. The place is filling rapidly, a burble of low conversation pervading the room. Down at the front, the ushers – all men wearing green sashes proudly draped in diagonal fashion across the front of their suits – direct people to seats. The rows of linked and uncomfortable steel-rimmed chairs, set on the plain concrete floor and without the traditional kneelers, are soon filled up.

The basilica is a huge edifice, with poured concrete dividing walls closing off the individual chapel areas, which accommodate a combined 5,000 Mass-goers. The walls feature mock-Gothic-style window frames. A group pauses at the end of my row and, seeing that they require more than the two seats at the outside on my left, I move into the furthest vacant seat, two away on my right. This means I am sitting alongside a large woman, who glares to indicate that I am now invading her space. The man who leads his small group into the seats I have freed smiles almost furtively and then turns his head away abruptly, lest he seem overly familiar. I settle back and wait as the basilica fills – which it does, quickly, including the seats at the back of the altar in front of the giant fabric mural of the Knock apparition, which are clearly signposted 'Priests Only'. They are now filled by women in the white nun-like habits of the Handmaids of the Knock Shrine Society. Meanwhile, a local priest has come to the altar and is outlining the order of the afternoon's service, which will feature Archbishop Michael Neary of Tuam in the starring role of concelebrated Mass. He will deliver the homily on this auspicious day. For those who nod off, or who want a souvenir perhaps, a CD of the homily will be available to purchase in the bookshop outside immediately after the Mass and the Eucharistic Procession – which, because of the uncertain weather, will only take place around the covered walkway surrounding the basilica itself. Among other notifications is that the choir today comes from his own home town of Castlebar.

3.00 p.m.
The organ starts up and the choir starts singing a hymn that evokes all the triumphalist fervour of my Catholic youth:

> *Faith of our fathers living still,*
> *In spite of dungeon, fire and sword.*
> *Oh how our hearts beat high with joy,*
> *When e'er we hear those glorious words.*
> *Faith of our fathers, holy faith,*
> *We will be true to thee till death!*

All around me voices are raised in song – some in tune, most not – and here and there the words are sounded out in voices crackling with age. This is not the slow, gentle Protestant version, the tune composed by Henri F. Hemy to the same lyrics, but the strident Catholic anthem of my youth, belted out at the top of the lungs in a defiant declaration of Catholic righteousness:

> *Our fathers chained in prisons dark*
> *Were still in heart and conscience free;*
> *And blest would be their children's fate,*
> *If they, like them should die for thee.*
> *Faith of our fathers, holy faith,*
> *We will be true to thee till death!*

From the archway to the right of the Handmaids, the procession starts to enter solemnly, led by three men in the livery of Stewards of the Knock Shrine Society, smock-type tunics emblazoned with the knightly Maltese cross. They lead the way with a ceremonial crucifix and in their wake come rank upon rank of priests. They circle the central altar and then file up in twos on each side, kissing the altar cloth and proceeding to the rows of chairs arranged in an incomplete circle. I count a total of 40 priests in matching white ceremonial robes. Last, but certainly not least, comes the archbishop, who takes his place at the centre of the altar with four other senior clerics. Then the Mass begins with invocations and the congregation starts to sit down, except for an older man about two rows from the front. He refuses to rest like those around him and, for some minutes, he is the last man standing. When the gathered priests sit, so does he, as the Mass enters its preliminaries.

3.15 p.m.
'We are all challenged by the contemporary conditions of the prevailing culture,' Archbishop Neary intones from the altar. 'These profoundly affect the personal lives of all of us – lay faithful, religious and priests. There is nothing like a crisis to bring clarity. Now, in today's world, there is a crisis of hope, and yet there are very striking signs of hope in the church, where people are becoming actively involved in the mission of the church and working together with their priests as members of a team.'

The archbishop also sees hope in the close relationship of priest with the community at times of personal tragedy and pain, in the community's joy at an ordination to the priesthood, in the way a priest lives God's word. 'Ordained to bring hope and healing, sadly and shamefully, some have brought harm and hurt, resulting in brokenness, betrayal and disillusionment,' he adds. 'Today, the priest is summoned to be a herald of hope in the menacing desert of scepticism and cynicism.' He urges the values of those figures who appear in the Knock apparition as the virtues of priesthood, pointing out that the event occurred 'a hundred and thirty years ago on this very day, when the lifeblood seemed to be drained from the people through famine and emigration'.

He goes on: 'While in recent years, understandably, priests have experienced disorientation and alienation, now I feel is the time for movement to another situation. Having experienced loss and darkness, we search for the healing and peace that comes from knowing how deeply God acts in our lives. Without that peace we find it difficult to be present to anything other than our anxious concerns. The challenge will be for all church members, together with religious and priests, to find the heart to face the future without fear and with great trust, to surrender our spirit into God's hands and to pledge ourselves as bread that is broken and wine that is poured out for others. This transformation will only take place – can only take place – through prayer, reflection and the interaction of priests, religious and people who support and challenge each other. Through the grace, the power and the goodness of god, we as priests are seeking and discovering signs of a new future – one that is vital to the faith and well-being of every Catholic. Today, priesthood, when faithfully and intimately related to Jesus Christ in prayer, when reaching out to God's people in a compassionate, understanding and merciful manner, and when generously lived, has the potential to be a great source of transformation, inspiration and hope for all.'

The archbishop ends on a quote from the prophet Jeremiah, to polite applause from an audience that needs little convincing that the patriarchal church and its exclusively male leaders will make the decisions that 'promote dialogue and mutual reliance' because recovery of past esteem, certainty and position – not change – offers hope for the priesthood: 'The agenda for the priest is dictated by God's Word, and not by the various winds of change that happen to blow at a particular time.' While acknowledging that some priests have erred and sinned in not living the Gospel, the church and the 'lay faithful' gathered in Knock Basilica will forge ahead, convinced that they are fulfilling Christ's mission on earth in defiance of the scepticism and cynicism fostered by those who have fallen by the wayside.

3.50 p.m.
The healing ceremony is under way. Those who are 'genuinely' in need of the personal blessing are asked to raise their hands and the priests descend among them. The blessing is administered where they sit with hands upturned in supplication. In single file, the priests edge their way through the congregation, seeming to find several in every row of the vast basilica in need of a miracle. The demeanour of the church ministers is noteworthy, ranging from what seems like quiet exasperation to pious invocation. A very overweight priest shuffles along the rows, his breathing laboured and his brow beaded in sweat from the heavy ceremonial robes. Though he seems in need of a rest, he pushes on in what seems like a bid to administer the blessing to more people than his older competitors. Meanwhile, the faces of those receiving the blessing nearest me register looks of pain and earnest hope as the sometimes perfunctory ritual unfolds.

4.15 p.m.
We have arrived at the Communion, no thanks to the woman with the loud voice in the row behind me, who drags out each prayer and each response as if determined

to be heard clearly as the most earnest prayer in the entire basilica. Every single time, she comes in about three syllables behind the rest of the entire congregation, sounding like an echo chamber of pious righteousness. Perhaps it is as well that we were not invited to exchange the sign of peace in the traditional handshake with those nearest us.

When the distribution of Communion begins, we are asked to stay in our seats; the priests and other ministers of the Eucharist will come among us. Then, like a conveyor-belt assembly line, the 40 priests and a few Eucharistic ministers dressed as Handmaids of Knock collect their Communion hosts and spill into the throng, while a tenor soloist sings 'Panis Angelicus'. Conscious that I have a considerable journey ahead and not much time, I slip out of my seat and the row as the Communion wave passes by, walk to the rear, where there are many standing for Mass, and out into the fresh air once more.

Even with the main event in progress, there are still many pilgrims doing the rounds of the old church, touching the framed stonework, sitting and kneeling inside the huge window of the gable chapel of the apparition, making Stations of the Cross and generally soaking up the sights and miraculous wonders of the shrine. I take the exit nearest the old presbytery where Mgr Horan held court almost 30 years ago and see what appears to be a line of outdoor urinals. Above them a large polished-granite sign says, 'Uisce Coiscricthe/Holy Water'. A man and two women are busily filling bottles.

4.30 p.m.

Down by the car park, a group of travellers veers towards a big display outside one of the prefab shops proclaiming: 'Irish Souvenir Videos CDs etc. on Sale Here' and another sign identifying it as 'West Coast Craft for the best Irish Heritage Country and Irish DVDs and Videos'. The first sign is embellished with a little leprechaun figure smoking a long pipe, the second with a few big shamrock motifs. But sitting alone on a black-covered box in front is a vase holding a profuse display of artificial flowers. In the middle of this is a statue of Our Lady of Knock, gazing out on pilgrims to the shrine created and maintained in her honour.

4.55 p.m.
A diversion off the N17 at Barnalyra, where a huge scaffold on the hill just above the road marks the end of the runway, takes me up the hill and past a roadside sign showing a garish portrait of Christ, his shining heart radiating red and white light and the legend underneath: 'Jesus I trust in You.'

Knock International Airport claims to have the last laugh on its detractors in record levels of passenger traffic, reflecting poorly on 'secular' competitors. A sign at the entrance lists car-parking charges with effect from 1 March 2009. They range from €2 for under an hour, double that for two and treble for three, to €35 for a week, €99 for one month and one day, all the way up through €300 for six months and €650 for a year. Just in case of misinterpretation, it defines a day as 24 hours and a week as '7 x 24 hours'. Back at the roundabout, there is a spectacular view of north Connacht and the Ox Mountains of Sligo. It is blocked by a long and constant line of cars, parked on the hard shoulder to avoid charges.

7.40 p.m.
Families gather in clusters around the graves at Montiagh Chapel on the upland fringe of north-west Fermanagh, where it meets Donegal and Tyrone. In the centre of the

gathering, five representatives of local families bereaved in the past year lead successive decades of the Rosary. Fr Gallagher joins in the responses while sprinkling holy water from a black plastic bucket over the resting places of loved ones. The rain is just about holding off, having poured down while a Mass of commemoration was celebrated before an overflowing congregation. There are newborn babies in the arms of young first-time mothers, children, teenagers, young adults and elderly people who will soon be taking their eternal rest here themselves. I look at the gathering and the smiles and greetings exchanged with each glance. Here there is the comfort of recognition, an acknowledgement of community, pride of place and faith in a simple ceremony that goes to the core of belief and belonging. It strikes me that miraculous apparitions, elaborate shrines with vast commercial spin-offs and convoluted ceremonies undertaken on an industrial scale for stern, self-righteous pilgrims who look back to the cold, uncompromising Catholicism of the post-war era represent the faith of our fathers born of post-Famine shame. This is the religion that has failed us so miserably and left such hurt and pain among so many. It is no match for the expression of enduring faith that is there at the natural heart of our country.

# Chapter 5

# On the Great Road to the Sacred Heart

## An tSlí Mhór to Clonmacnoise

*Monday, 18 January 2010*
8.55 a.m.

To the cawing chorus of alarmed rooks and with the sweet incense of peat smoke in the bright winter air, I set off from the shrine of the pilgrim opposite Galvin's Corner House. Ballycumber's quiet village street is part of one of the oldest highways in the western world. One of six ancient roads that connected the kingdoms of Ireland, an tSlí Mhór (the Great Road) ran from Dublin Bay to Galway Bay along the Esker Riada ridge. For 1,400 years the Great Road brought pilgrims to Clonmacnoise, the monastic city of Ciarán Mac an tSaoir on a bend of the mighty River Shannon. There, one of the major centres of learning and devotion in the first millennium of Christianity drew pilgrims and those thirsting for peace and salvation. It also drew sinners intent on plundering Clonmacnoise's treasures of gold, silver and fine parchment, the work of devout monks, scholars and craftsmen.

My intentions are honourable on this beautiful winter morning. The low sun beams down on the flat land of raised peatland that stretches beyond the village into the vast inland sea of the Bog of Allen. In Ballycumber, cars on the school run and commuting workers glide by, while another lone pedestrian glances through his newspaper, homeward bound from the village shop. At the end of the long main street, the main road (to Ferbane) turns left, while at Flynn's of Grogan, an tSlí Mhór continues on the lesser of the two roads ahead. Flat and unwavering, it stretches into the far distance. Along one side, ivy has enveloped the telegraph poles, billowing out into huge green bushes over the road – nature reclaiming its own. Yet scant attention is paid to a lone hiker along this flat road that ends in a T-junction overlooked by a bungalow. Here the land begins to rise onto the Esker Riada, the great ridge of hills and hillocks of sand and gravel left behind as great ice sheets retreated north at the end of the last Ice Age.

To the left, I spot a pilgrim-path waymarker. The familiar yellow image of a cloaked figure with a staff has been dislodged and is lying back in the hedge growth. I study it for clues and note that arrows point both ways. I assume one leads to Leamonaghan, the island in the Great Bog of Clara where St Manchan built a church, while the other points up the hill, where I can see the bright yellow walls of the same saint's church at Boher. I opt for the latter and continue past a school, where children avail of last-minute playtime in the bright sunshine before class. In a cluster of trees, three little boys are having a heated exchange.

'So I'll be Indiana Jones,' one suggests. One of the others shakes his head, while the third says, 'No, I'll be Indiana Jones!'

It is a debate with as much chance of quick resolution as the current talks over the devolution of policing and justice in Northern Ireland.

9.30 a.m.
The doors of the church are locked, denying me a chance to see the Shrine of St Manchan. I try both sides, but the only unlocked door enters the sacristy. I refrain from entering for fear of being mistaken for a burglar. The adjoining presbytery is also in darkness, meanwhile, with no car in sight. I inspect the noticeboard and see that Mass times are listed for Tuesday through to Sunday, so I resolve to call back tomorrow. I take a cup of tea from the flask I filled after a hearty breakfast at the Riverside bed and breakfast in Clara. Fortified by that, I set out once more on an tSlí Mhór. Rounding a corner at the crest of the ridge, the view opens up to the north. In the near distance, I see the wooded hilltop of Bellair. I recall that when I called into Galvin's pub in Ballycumber the previous evening to enquire about taxis I was rescued from the annoying attention of a man who had over-imbibed. Learning of my pilgrimage plan, my rescuer described the route in great detail, noting that I would be able to see Bellair's wooded hill off to the right for the first half of my trek. He introduced himself as Gearóid from Glaslough, County Monaghan, who had 'come here for one woman and stayed for another'.

10.00 a.m.
A fingerpost announces my arrival at St Manchan's Well. It points the wrong way, but I spot the stile in the hedge opposite and see the well at the far side of a field, where a herd of young cattle are huddled. The well is surmounted by a small, recessed shrine with another statue of the same

hooded-monk figure as in Ballycumber. Smaller holy statues have been placed around his feet. At the base of the walled enclosure runs a serpentine rivulet, though much of this is caked into a block of ice. The solid rock down to the water is slippery underfoot, but I manage to scoop a handful to sip and bless myself with the sign of the cross. I recite another decade of the Rosary I have been praying quietly to myself along the way. In a small, stone-walled enclosure to the side, a large rectangular stone has been raised on smaller supporting stones, although there is nothing to indicate its purpose.

10.15 a.m.
A short distance from the well is Cappanalosset Crossroads, with one fingerpost indicating that it is 3 kilometres back to St Manchan's Shrine and another pointing to Clonmacnoise, 16 kilometres away. Devery's pub, now derelict, is an imposing building at this junction. Strong evidence suggests that a 'house of hospitality' stood hereabouts in ancient times to provide pilgrims on the Great Road to Clonmacnoise with rest and sustenance for the final leg of their trek.[37] But there is no rest for this pilgrim. I push on along the high ridge, past fields of grazing horses, cattle and sheep until the fields on the left give way to a broad expanse of bog with a long line of neat turf stacks near the fringe. From just ahead comes a loud rumbling, increasing in intensity and causing a slight tremor in the ground underfoot. I glance warily at the huge high-tension electricity pylon immediately ahead, expecting it to burst apart from the force of an infernal explosion and I pray for deliverance from this imminent threat. Then, suddenly, a tiny train engine emerges from under a road bridge, pulling 16 large rolling bins of peat mould. The bridge was dedicated in 2003 to Bord na Móna.

This semi-state enterprise, which harvests the peatland, owns a quarter of all the bogs in the midlands. The little train trundles off into the distance and the sound dies back to winter-day silence. I relax and spot a small herd of cattle regarding me with intense stares, while ignoring the noisy intruder, as if accusing me of having disturbed the peace.

10.45 a.m.
In a foolish bid for any news of the Belfast talks, I tune in to the radio on my mobile phone. Immediately, I realise my error and put it away, deciding to listen more intently to the day unfolding around me – to the sound of winter birdsong and the cawing of rooks perched in the bared branches of trees. The road meanders along the ridge between neatly trimmed hedges, with only very occasional traffic. One car with Clare number plates pulls up, and the passenger asks if they have missed the road to Moate. With the confidence of one who has studied the map intently, I tell them they have. They turn and go back, waving. With only the inquisitive attention of farm animals and occasional friendly waves from people, I am left with my thoughts on the pilgrim path of north Offaly, and I marvel at the attractiveness of a landscape I have never before considered.

11.00 a.m.
An tSlí Mhór sweeps down to a double junction where a small country shop faces the signposted road for Moate. A fingerpost pointing back tells me I am now 8 kilometres from St Manchan's Shrine and 12 kilometres from Clonmacnoise. I enter the shop and buy a bottle of water and an orange and sit at the picnic table outside to enjoy my snack in the winter sunshine. A huge sign opposite wishes 'all our customers a very merry Christmas and a

happy New Year' and adds that if 'Santa raids the fridge or forgets to leave batteries, please feel free to call on Christmas morning'. A nameplate at the entrance of the dwelling adjoining the shop says, 'Togher Wood House' and is adorned with the picture of a great bull. I regard the landscape around and see only a small copse of trees across the way with a decorative wheel in front. It is all that remains of the wood, and I reflect on the words of 'Cill Chais', the old Irish poem about the felling of the great forests in the seventeenth and eighteenth centuries: 'Cad a dhéanfaimid feasta gan adhmad? / Tá deireadh na gcoillte ar lár …'[38] Translated by Thomas Kinsella as: 'What shall we do for timber with the last of the woods laid low …[?]', this evokes an image in my mind of ancient times, when pilgrims moved along an tSlí Mhór through the great forest of this *tóchar*, perhaps having to contend with brigands, wolves and other predators on their sacred path to Clonmacnoise.

11.25 a.m.
From Togher, it is a very brief stroll to the second junction at the crossroads of Doon and I am halfway on my journey to the great city of Ciarán Mac an tSaoir. Doon Cross is dominated by three establishments – a pub, the ruins of a medieval castle, which was once the seat of the Mooney clan, and a long building proclaiming itself 'An Dún Transport and Heritage Museum'. A few cars are parked outside the museum and some men are busy with ladders, walking to and fro on the instructions of an older man wearing a navy jumper with a museum crest. The doors are open, so I enter and wander around briefly. The interior is full of cars of varying vintages, from an old 1920s model to vehicles that look as if they have just been parked

there for convenience between runs to and from the town. A shop window features a display of an old cottage kitchen with cute and cuddly dolls of an old man and woman relaxing by the open hearth. The man in the jumper comes along and I enquire about the museum and its opening hours.

His response is animated: 'I haven't opened the feckin' place this four years. If I did it would only feckin' cost me €3,700 for insurance and €1,600 for rates.' I notice the men with the ladder are keeping their distance. Would the county council not help keep the facility in operation? He declares furiously, 'Feck the help you'll get from them feckers, only to tax you for opening the feckin' doors!'

I later learn that his wife is a member of Offaly County Council.

11.30 a.m.

Fingerposts for Clonmacnoise at Doon Cross point in two directions – one across a bog road, the other towards Ballinahown, just across the county line in Westmeath. I opt for Ballinahown on the presumption that it most closely follows the route of an tSlí Mhór along the Esker Riada. The problem is that this road is the N62, a major artery linking Athlone with Thurles. The traffic is constant, and a roadside memorial headstone on the opposite side testifies to its danger. Wearing my high-visibility vest and hugging the side of the road, I set off gingerly, facing the oncoming traffic, while squeezing myself as far as possible into the verge. The problem is that the road is a better testimonial to the internal-combustion engine than the nearby museum. There is no provision for other road users as cars, lorries and vans whizz by. This section of the N62 does not have a hard shoulder, let alone a footpath for pilgrims, pedestrians or cyclists. Yet no money has been spared on an ultra-smooth asphalt surface, three lines of white and yellow lane markings and three rows of cats' eyes for night driving. It is a super speedway of peril for the unwary pilgrim; delivery vans in particular hurtle along without the slightest regard for non-motorised road users. As I turn sideways to avoid their extended side-mirrors, I feel the rushing wind of traffic.

The lack of provision is a huge pity, for there are several places of note along this part of the route, not least the substantial ruins of the Mooney clan's former seat on a bushy hill to my right and the entrance to the impressive Doon House on the other side. A fingerpost there informs me that the grounds are home to the Athlone Cricket Club and, further along, beyond a speed-limit sign reading 100 kilometres per hour, another sign nailed to a tree proclaims a facility for motocross racing – as if I need to be told. I squeeze behind a sign saying 'Welcome to Offaly' in another feint to avoid a van.

11.50 a.m.

As Ballinahown village looms ahead, the roadside is littered with traffic cones and an estate agent's 'For Sale' sign lurks beside a patch of overgrown bushes and marshy land with long rushes. In a brief lull in the traffic, I hear rustling sounds in the overgrowth. Then a dog – a border collie – darts out from the thicket and bounds right up to me, falling into step just a pace behind. I extend a hand guardedly to assure the dog I mean it no harm. It opens its maw and licks the hand furiously, then rears onto its hind legs and anxiously laps its tongue towards my face, its mucky paws drawing huge blots on my bright yellow vest. I move off and my new friend comes alongside, oblivious to the traffic as it guards my flank. This forces the cars and vans to slow down, signal and move out from the verge to avoid colliding with us. I know the drivers are cursing my lack of concern in having a dog – which they must presume from its relaxed gait is mine – on the road without a leash. So we continue for several hundred metres until, entering the village, the dog bounds through the gateway of a house opposite and I see it no more. At this point, a footpath begins on my side of the road. I pass by the neat grounds of St Colmcille's Church with its requisite Marian shrine and enter Ballinahown village.

12.10 p.m.
A car park has a display of information boards, welcoming visitors with lots of detail about the Westmeath village, whose 'origins and early existence are hidden in the mists of time'. We know, however, that in 1657 the Malone family moved their residence here from Kilgarvan. The Malones were *airchinnigh,* or lay abbots, of Clonmacnoise, who recovered their estates, which had been seized by Cromwell under the 1662 Act of Settlement. The unseen large house on the edge of the village is Ballinahown Court, built in 1746 by Edmond Malone. The information boards are the starting point for a sculpture trail around the village, which continues into a riverside trail, though I see little evidence of a river beyond the town's Irish name, Baile na hAbhann (Town of the River). A small pond feature beside the parish hall, however, has an impressive wooden sculpture of a wading bird atop a small decorative tree. An illustration on the information board shows me that the pond is actually a small fountain, but the jets are not working in January. The village seems to be festooned with other sculptures, including a Christmas crib and a small display beside the parish hall of a church, a high cross and the ruins of a round tower at the heart of concentric circles of stones.

Next door to the hall is Celtic Roots, a quality craft shop in the restored village schoolhouse, which has magnificent displays of sculptures carved from bogwood. The Meso range, I learn from a parchment sheet attached to a book, is 'inspired by Mesolithic woman'. It explains:

> *The first sighting of woman and man in Ireland dates to nine thousand years ago at Lough Boora, County Offaly, exactly where this ancient bog oak tree grew during this same period. This fragment of a living tree over five thousand years old has been lovingly carved and polished into a jewel – inscribed for you to treasure and wear knowing that it was created for you alone and captures the essence of who you are.*

Besides the jewellery, the display of figures sculpted from the rich, dark bogwood presents a glorious array of animal shapes, exultant human gestures, Celtic-art spirals and swirls and other immensely pleasing shapes released from the murky depths of peat bog, where they have languished for centuries and millennia. The display studio itself is an impressive celebration of high-end Irish craftsmanship – with prices to match. The welcoming and helpful assistant on duty explains that, while there are other crafts for sale here, the bogwood sculptures are produced by two artists in the Celtic Roots workshop at Ferbane.

If that wasn't enough to entice visitors from the N62 traffic corridor, across the street is Core, a shop of local crafts from Westmeath and Offaly. When I pop in, however, I'm informed that the café is closed for the winter. So, with a brief and welcome bathroom visit, I emerge again into the glorious sunshine, make my way to the main village junction, passing the two men with the ladder I had left behind in Doon, still carrying it, and find the second major sculpture of this pilgrim path – a gaunt medieval pilgrim, hewn from wood and pointing the way along an tSlí Mhór to Clonmacnoise. Unfortunately, in an act of official vandalism or mere ignorance, an ugly 'Stop' traffic sign has been placed directly in front of this wooden figure, effectively obscuring it from the view of most passers-by. With niggling annoyance at whoever decided to favour a functional sign over public art, I sit on a public bench, eat some fruit and finish the tea from my flask. A car draws up as I relax, heeding the road sign, and the young driver enquires by gesture if I need a lift. I indicate in the negative and watch as the men with the ladder place it against the building opposite and walk away.

12.45 p.m.
My road out of Ballinahown heads south-west to Clonmacnoise in a wide flourish, but right on the fringe of the village past the local school it narrows to enter Offaly once more. The school, I have learned from the information boards, has won a peace prize for its links with Wheatfield Primary School in Belfast. A car slows by my side and the driver asks if I want a lift. I tell him I am walking and he drives off, clearly perplexed at a pilgrim choosing to journey on foot through a land of cars.

The road rises gently ahead back onto the Esker Riada and I am well into the second half of my trek along an tSlí Mhór, enjoying the changing landscape as broad fields open up with views of grazing horses, cattle and sheep. A small distance beyond Ballinahown, however, the pastoral scene is broken by a large cluster of houses in what is almost another village. The only possible reason for this conurbation is that the residents favour living in Offaly over Westmeath; or maybe it is just an instance of crazy planning. Two men are chatting at the end of a driveway, and I enquire about the back road into Clonmacnoise. When I called to the visitors' centre there yesterday, Nicola, one of the very helpful staff, told me about this traditional path. The older man is eager to point me on my way.

'You see that hill way off there?' he asks, pointing along what appears to be an almost flat road with just a gentle rise in the distance.

'Is that what you call a hill?' I ask with a smile.

'No, not this hill here,' he continues, pointing to an even more insignificant bump in the near distance, 'the one on past it there. When you get to the top of that hill, the far one there, there's a road sign pointing off to Bloomhill and Ballyduff. Take that road and you go down a big hill and you go on that way until you come to a fork in the road. Take the left one, for the other will take you way off there,' he says, pointing in what I take to be the general direction of Athlone. 'That's what everyone about here calls the Old Pilgrim Road and it takes you all the way to Clonmacnoise.'

I thank him for his help and set off, comforted by the passage of all those pilgrims before me who are remembered still in the name of the road beyond the 'hill'. Ahead, I pass a house with a statue of the Virgin Mary facing it, standing guard with open arms on the lawn beside a small yellow shed. When I stop to get a closer look, a dog inside the house barks loudly. Obviously the owners rely on more than the Blessed Mother to keep a watchful eye on their home.

1.30 p.m.

I spot the road sign for Bloomhill and Ballyduff, almost enveloped in the thick hedge opposite a house covered in ivy with large monkey-puzzle trees peeping over its own thick hedges. The road sweeps down a decent incline and rises again to follow the crest of the Esker Riada. To the honking of a gaggle of geese grazing in a field, I feel myself relaxing as I leave the sparse traffic behind, crossing the road between the townlands of Clonderig and Lower Clonderig. Over the hedge to the left a short time later, I see a horse tethered outside a small house in what seems to be a makeshift quarry. It looks like a miniature post-apocalyptic scene, obscured from the view of passing motorists. A short distance away, the fork on the road points downhill to Bloomhill and the road for Ballyduff and Clonmacnoise sweeps up further on the pilgrim path to the left.

2.00 p.m.
The Old Pilgrim Road has settled firmly on the Esker Riada, which is now more apparent in the narrow ridge of sand and shale that frequently falls away to contrasting landscapes on both sides. Along it are many neat and picturesque farm cottages with adjoining sheds and awnings, neatly packed with stacks of turf bricks cut and saved from the surrounding bogs. Even this early in the new year there are signs of bloom on the gorse bushes facing into the strong rays of the sun. Some lone trees and bushes denuded of their leaves are enveloped and protected from the winter chill by thick vests of ivy, their branches the arms of sacred sentinels pointing to the heavens.

With my passage to Clonmacnoise reassured by occasional waymarker posts, the road follows a picturesque path up and down the inclines of the ridge, winding its way between bog and meadows, where some livestock are wintering out. The raised bogs have a uniform and linear appearance, with great swathes of dark-brown peat exposed by the harvesting machinery that can be seen off in the distance. At times, the contrasts in the view to left and right are marked – the one side featuring stripped bogland, the other a green blanket of fields with trees and modest homes. Further down the road, the scenes shift as the bogland and farmland trade sides. Occasionally, the countryside is remarkably pretty. Tiny green knolls cascade along between the trees and here and there are the traditional long and low farm cottages that have tucked themselves into the landscape, as modest and unassuming as many modern houses are garish show-offs. At other times along the Old Pilgrim Road, the geological and scenic integrity of the Esker Riada has been ravaged and destroyed by the gaping holes of sand quarries.

I search for a place to have a brief rest, but my quest is interrupted by a quartet of dogs – three at one house, including a pair of snarling bulldogs, and another baying viciously at its neighbour just up the road and eagerly awaiting my arrival. I curse myself for having forgotten to bring along my pilgrim's staff, recalling what my fellow pilgrim on Donegal's Sliabh Liag last summer said of its handiness for 'batin' sarpents'. I now know a good staff is essential for fending off too-eager guard-dogs who have not been tethered. In this case, I am saved by the woman of the second house, who responds to my alarmed look and wordless appeal through the kitchen window. She comes to the side door and calls the dog inside sharply and I continue on my way. Just a short distance off I find the crest of a hill, where there is a small green recess on the road with a ditch on the right. On the other side of this, the hill has been entirely removed by quarrying. This has left a gaping hole that has been only partly filled by huge bales of silage covered in shiny black plastic. I do a quick count – 115 big bales. In another part of the small quarry, bags of harvested turf have been built into a small hillock. Both silage and turf are hidden from the view of traffic along the road, although motorists who have presumably paused for the view have covered the soft grass verge of the recess in mucky tyre tracks. The crest of the half hill offers a wonderful view; as the land sweeps off into the far distance I believe I see my first glimpse of the mighty River Shannon in a bright thread on the north-west horizon.

2.30 p.m.

A tributary road from the left joins us in a fork on the pilgrim path and, almost immediately, a fingerpost with a waymarker beside it announces that it is 5 kilometres to Clonmacnoise. A level crossing in the road with a sign warns of 'Heavy Machinery Crossing' and a number of cars, probably belonging to Bord na Móna workers, are parked there. A little further on from that, a sign on a gate warns the unwary to 'Beware of the Bull' and, in an enclosed space, there is another sizeable cluster of big black-wrapped silage bales. Although there is no sign of the mighty and obviously hungry beast, an electric fence runs along the hedge for a considerable distance. I hurry along and marvel all the while at the little knolls that are the surviving evidence of the Esker Riada. We are now in the townland of Clonascra, translating as the 'meadow of the ridge'. From my small map I note other townlands in the district named as meadows, notably Clonfinlough, where a great carved stone with rather unusual designs has excited archaeological interest.[39] Incorporating Bronze-Age pagan and predominantly Christian-era carvings, the stone is noted for its motif consisting of a straight line intersecting with an oval, like the classical Greek letter phi. Interestingly, stones with similar motifs have been located in the north-western Spanish region of Galicia, where in medieval times the great pilgrimage trail of the Camino possibly competed with the Great Road to Clonmacnoise for pilgrims.[40] Of course, many Christians would have visited both the shrine in Santiago's great cathedral and the chapels and cathedral of the monastic city of Clonmacnoise.

2.50 p.m.
The landscape continues to undulate with every bend of the road, revealing more evidence of the near and distant past along the Old Pilgrim Road. In pagan and early Christian times, local custom and those in power who had settled along the thoroughfare would have guaranteed the safety of those travelling along an tSlí Mhór. These people lived in enclosed farmsteads with a view over the surrounding terrain for security, now evidenced in the many signs of ringforts atop the knolls of the Esker Riada. Today, the proof remains in the circular copses where trees and bushes grow. Landowners here, like practically every farmer in the land, would not dare cut down the remains of a 'fairy ring'. Then, suddenly rounding a corner, I can clearly see the Shannon flowing in a light-blue blanket just below me. By the time I reach a fingerpost indicating that it is 3 kilometres to my destination, at the forked junction of a road coming from the right this time, the mighty river has spread right across the landscape beyond. From here, it will accompany my passage at regular intervals on the pilgrim path to Clonmacnoise.

On the left, meanwhile, a red sign announces that the brown blanket of land just below is Mongan Bog Conservation Area. Designated by an Taisce, the national conservation trust, and Bord na Móna, the bog remains as living testimony to the landscape that would have extended over much of this area at the time when Ciarán established his monastery and sent Manchan out to spread the word. I look back at the way I have come. Suddenly, the vital importance of the Esker Riada for communication before the advent of modern engineering is starkly apparent. Below, the huge blanket of overgrowth conceals the ancient peatland, providing a home to all manner of wildlife. Over the neatly trimmed roadside hedge, I watch the furtive movements of water fowl, scurrying hither and yon amidst a scene that, even in winter, constantly seems to change hue – from orange to russet – over the bogland brush. The words of poet Patrick Kavanagh play in my head in a gush of exhilaration:

*Green, blue, yellow and red –*
*God is down in the swamps and marshes,*
*Sensational as April and almost incredible the flowering of our catharsis.*
*A humble scene in our backward place*
*Where no one important ever looked*
*The raving flowers looked up in the face*
*Of the One and the Endless, the Mind that has baulked*
*The profoundest of mortals. A primrose, a violet,*
*A violent wild iris – but mostly anonymous performers*
*Yet an important occasion as the Muse at her toilet*
*Prepared to inform the local farmers,*
*That beautiful, beautiful, beautiful God,*
*Was breathing His love by a cut-away bog.*[41]

A short distance along, a haughty piebald horse standing against the clear, blue winter sky on top of a knoll proudly surveys my passage through his terrain. I walk past green fields delineated by neat dry-stone walls and come across one remarkable balustrade, painstakingly built to hold up the esker beside a small country lane. It even has a fortified shelf for a lone bush, preserved out of absolute respect for the past, one suspects, as much as out of superstition. Eventually, the remarkable knolls recede and I am walking along the narrow road with its grassy centre line towards a line of trees to the side of the Shannon, which has spread beyond its normal course in winter flooding. At what turns out to be the final pilgrim-path waymarker, I suddenly catch my first glimpse of a round tower peeping above the trees beyond. Just then, a car pulls up beside me and the driver asks if she is on the right road to Clonascra. From my passage along the Old Pilgrim Road, I not only assure her that she is, but also tell her about the landmarks she will recognise on her arrival in that evocative townland.

3.00 p.m.

And so I arrive along the road that has brought countless generations to the monastic city founded by Ciarán Mac an tSaoir, another son of a simple carpenter, at the point where the Great Road of ancient Ireland crosses the Shannon. To my right are the Shannon Callows or floodplains, which are now largely part of the winter riverscape. To the left is a strong and prosperous-looking farmhouse set behind a line of trees, and immediately after this the monastic ruins begin in the impressive remains of what the official sign proclaims as the Nuns' Church or Teampall na gCailleach. As I study the ornate arched doorways of carved stone I ponder the translation of the church name and the use of the term *cailleach*, which I have come across only in reference to a hag or a witch. The church was built by Dervorgilla, wife of Tighearnán O'Rourke of Breffni, who was abducted by Dermot MacMurrough, an outrage that sparked war and caused MacMurrough to seek the aid of the Normans in Britain – in exchange for the hand of his own daughter, Aoife. Thus began the 800 years of Ireland's subjugation by those who ruled the neighbouring island. The abductor is remembered as Diarmaid na nGall or Dermot of the Foreigners. It is probable that Dervorgilla, the victim of the abduction, who retired to Clonmacnoise as a penitent in 1170, is remembered less kindly in the name of the Hags' Church. However, there is certainly nothing derogatory in its form or setting, a short distance from the main monastic site.

3.10 p.m.
Entry to the main enclosure of Clonmacnoise is through a modern graveyard, surrounded by the higgledy-piggledy graves favoured today by those who want the final resting places of their loved ones to stand out for eternity. While undoubtedly intended to show love and respect, the polished granite and garish mementoes jar in this particular setting, which show more than ever the tasteless look-at-me culture of modern Ireland and its inappropriate architecture. At the end of the Old Pilgrim Road and the entrance to a monastic site that has been a focal point since the earliest days of Christendom, they are even more of an eyesore. Yet not even this, nor the young man in black who walks ahead of me on my final approach, talking incessantly into the mobile phone clasped to his ear, can detract from the overwhelming emotion of walking the final few hundred metres of the Great Road to Clonmacnoise. Reciting the final decade of the Rosary I began about six hours ago back in Ballycumber, I pass through the final gateway and walk along the causeway on paving stones worn smooth by the bare feet of the

countless pilgrims who have preceded me. The landscape is transformed immediately into a haven of peace and tranquillity, with row upon row of modest memorials to those whose mortal remains repose in the blessed holy ground. These are marked by simple stone slabs, standing or flat, and the traditional Celtic crosses that incorporate the Christian cross and the circle representing the pagan sun. Picking a path through these sentinel memorials, the Old Pilgrim Road ascends the small incline to the original chapel of Ciarán, which marks the end of the traditional route to Clonmacnoise. During this quiet season, scaffolding encased in white plastic sheeting surrounds the smallest chapel of the seven places of worship on this ancient monastic site. Inside, restoration specialists are working to ensure that this sacred monument will survive more centuries and even millennia.

Turning back down towards the river to where Finghín's Chapel is adjoined by a magnificent round-tower belfry, complete with its conical stone cap, I wander among the sacred monuments of our past, concluding the final decade of my Rosary and soaking up the spiritual essence that hovers like an invisible blanket over this special place. I walk through Temple Connor, Temple Kelly, Temple Melaghlin, Temple Hurpan and Temple Dowling, past the North Cross and the South Cross and finally to the pivotal Cross of the Scriptures, before entering the magnificent remains of the cathedral that once stood proudly at Clonmacnoise until ravaged and suppressed by the English garrison from nearby Athlone during the Reformation. Finally, I wander over to the round tower, which, the annals record, was started by Ciarán himself before his untimely death at the age of 33. The work was carried on by his successor, Turlough O'Connor.

I smile to myself as I recall the story told at breakfast by Trudy, my landlady at the Riverside guesthouse in Clara. She had taken a visitor from Wales to see Clonmacnoise, and this round tower had particularly impressed him as they walked around it in the serenity and silence of a summer's day. Suddenly, an unseen loud voice broke the sanctified atmosphere: 'How did the feckers get into it? Sure there's no feckin' door!'

3.15 p.m.
I have reported to the reception desk, where Nicola offers to take my photo beside the statue by sculptor Jackie McKenna. It stands by the main entrance to the site from the car park. The crouched figure is Aedh, son of the king of Oriel, who is recorded as having died here while on pilgrimage in AD 606. Honoured thus as the first recorded pilgrim to Clonmacnoise, Aedh stands beside me – the latest pilgrim – and I feel proud to take my place among all those who have come here between his time and mine. Having phoned to arrange a taxi back to Ballycumber and my car which will take an hour to get here, , I wander back inside. Exempted from the admission fee as a pilgrim who has walked the ancient road, I settle down to watch the explanatory video and wander through the magnificent indoor exhibits, then head off once more to stand among the ancient buildings that were once the centre of a monastic city stretching over the adjacent hills. Clonmacnoise, then, was an important place of learning, a cradle of civilisation during the Dark Ages. It spread out here on the banks of the Shannon and drew those hungry for knowledge, spiritual solace and corporal healing to the special place of Ciarán. The monks, scholars and gifted craftsmen who once inhabited this spot are long gone, but Clonmacnoise is still a comforting core of spirituality, even in ruins.

5.30 p.m.
An hour after taking leave of Clonmacnoise, I am back in Ballycumber, where today's pilgrimage began, savouring a quiet pint in Galvin's Corner House and chatting with the owner, Paul. We talk of big modern houses that stick out like sore thumbs and have to be filled with 'stuff'; of people in fancy cars that whizz by on roads built for speed; of legal constraints on the traditional customers of quiet rural pubs; of town centres abandoned to unruly youth – young men blowing a week's wages on a single night out, girls fighting in the street with bellies full of vodka-based alco-pops. The village publican has discussed these matters with his former schoolmate Taoiseach Brian Cowan, but got little change from that. However, he holds out hope beyond the economic collapse.

'I manage the minor [GAA football] team here,' Paul points out, 'so I would know all the young lads. I'd know them all growing up and I can see a change since the economy has gone down. They never came in here much. They would be off in Tullamore or Moate for the big night out, but they can't do that now because they don't have the money for it. You know, between the taxi there and back and maybe a feed, they'd be out €30 or more before they'd even buy their first drink. Now they only have the €30, but they can come in here and have six pints for that. Some of them have told me they can't believe they have a better time now with less money. Maybe that's not such a bad thing, so!'

*Tuesday, 20 January 2010*
10.00 a.m.
After an evening of good craic in Carey's pub in Clara and another hearty breakfast at my guesthouse, I revisit Boher Church to see the Shrine of St Manchan. A disciple of Ciarán

at Clonmacnoise, Manchan was sent to found another monastery at Leamonaghan, a small island in the Great Bog just a few kilometres south of the church. The shrine, a gabled box of yew-tree wood, plated in gold with bright bronze ornamented figures, crosses and other embellishments, contains bones said to belong to the holy man who died during the great plague that swept through Ireland in the seventh century. The reliquary itself is dated from the twelfth century and it is notable for incorporating St Olaf of Norway, patron of the Viking people who once plundered Clonmacnoise and other Irish monasteries, among its original 50 representative figures. After the dissolution of the monasteries by the English monarchy, the shrine was guarded by the Buckley family, descended from the last recorded abbot of Leamonaghan, then at the thatched chapel of Millane in Cooldorrough. It was moved to the new church at Boher in 1860 and has been used to swear public oaths and as a source of cures. Standing alone and unguarded beyond a showcase with an electronic alarm, the shrine is a treasured link with the sacred past that glows under the beautiful stained-glass windows by Harry Clarke featuring representations of Ciarán and Manchan.

11.00 a.m.

Finally, I complete my pilgrimage at Leamonaghan, the small island in the vast flat sea of midlands bogland where Manchan founded his monastery. Only four days before other pilgrims make their way in annual homage to the site for Manchan's 'pattern day' on 24 January, I make my lone procession from the ancient graveyard with the ruins of a chapel down the side lane to the holy well and along the ancient *tóchar* causeway to St Mella's Cell.

At the holy well, an old tree is festooned with rags, beads and other tokens, the votive mementoes and offerings of those who have come seeking spiritual or physical cures from the holy waters, which are accessed down a set of stone steps with railings. A bag packed with the debris of offerings displaced or blown here in winter gales indicates that the annual clean-up of the site has commenced before the main pilgrimage. Yet the sanctity of this holy place is evoked most powerfully in the causeway of flagstones that leads off between hedgerows across the bog to a small walled enclosure. Here are the ruins of a small oratory, which offered reflective sanctuary in memory of St Mella, Manchan's mother. I climb the flagstone steps, enter through the low and narrow doorway and stand between the ancient stone walls. I raise my gaze to the grey winter sky and feel the Holy Spirit move within me as I pray within the sacred heart of Ireland.

# Chapter 6

# Searching for the Light

## St Brigid's Shrine

*Sunday, 31 January 2010*

The sign says 'Kilnasaggart Road', and I realise immediately that I have strayed from the path and crossed into a part of Ireland more renowned in recent times for sinners than saints. As if to emphasise my error, a dog that barked furiously only moments ago when I passed by races into the road and snaps angrily at my heels, creating a dreadful racket. In a final bid for deliverance, I bend to reassure the canine, even though I am in terror of being bitten. My desperate bid pays off. The dog yelps, wheels away and runs home. I hurry along to get out of a locality in south Armagh that has become infamous for 'explosive devices' placed under the Dublin-to-Belfast railway line. This is a place where strangers in the night arouse suspicions and the plight of a lost pilgrim might not be easily distinguished from the snooping of a spy. So I continue up the long incline to the summit.

On my left, I see the Poor Clare Monastery of the Light of Christ. Ahead and below the long hill of Faughart, the lights of Dundalk illuminate an arc around the bay.

It is my quest for the light that got me into trouble in the first place. A local newspaper reported that a candlelight procession would bring pilgrims from the Old Graveyard on Faughart Hill to St Brigid's Shrine for the blessing of the water on the eve of her feast day, February 1st. I got to the shrine at 7.30 p.m. and find several others waiting for the ceremonies, puzzled that it was so quiet. A man told me that the Old Graveyard was up at the top of the hill. I set off to find it, but missed the turn for the graveyard road and just kept walking, reassured by a bright glow ahead that I took to be the other pilgrims. It was only when I got to the brow of the hill that the source of light became apparent. It was an extraordinary rising of the moon behind Feede Mountain at the far side of Edenappa Road, which links Dundalk in the Republic with Jonesborough in the north. I then continued in the mistaken belief that the Old Graveyard, and other pilgrims, would be just around the next corner.

Now, returning to the shrine, I have spent the past hour tramping the dark winter roads around the birthplace of the patroness of Ireland, the bringer of light to the Gael, a saint who ranks up there with Patrick and Colmcille in the pantheon of top-drawer sainthood. Yet few facts seems to be known about Brigid of Faughart, even through her life was recounted by a monastic scribe within a hundred years of her death at the abbey she founded beside the Curragh of Kildare. Within the church, Brigid has been a pivotal figure, whose lifespan of 70 years or so bridged the transition between the missionary church of Patrick, who was still alive in her childhood, and the rise of the great Celtic church monasteries that began with Colmcille, who was a child in her later years.

Yet some renowned experts in the field of Celtic hagiography doubt that Brigid even existed.[42] Ian Bradley of Edinburgh University and others suspect she was invented in the document known as *Vitae Brigiti*, which is said to have been written by a Kildare monk called Cogitosus around AD 680. Cogitosus gives very little factual information about Brigid's birth and career. Instead, the document is merely an account of the successive miracles she performed, a ruse to elevate Brigid and assert the claim of Kildare as the primatial see of Ireland. It may also have been a ploy to Christianise the lingering devotion to Brigid, Ireland's pagan goddess of sun and fire, by ascribing to a Christian woman many of the same miracles believed to have been performed by the pagan deity. Today, Brigid's reinvention in the church as a feminist icon, the keeper of the flame, leading her believers to the dazzling sun when winter is banished, perhaps returns the cult of Brigid to the status it once occupied.

Those who flock to Faughart on her feast day, and again for a healing Mass in July, have absolutely no doubt about Brigid and her continuing intervention on behalf of her people. For them, the daughter of Dubhtach, a pagan chieftain who controlled the pivotal Gap of the North, and Broicsech, a slave described as a 'subordinate wife', who was later sold off to a Limerick man, ranks high in the Celtic celestial host of this early Christian period.

Dubbed 'Mary of the Gael', 'Spouse of Christ', and 'Friend of the Poor' in the litany of Irish saints, Brigid is extolled for her virginal purity among other traits.[43] Strange, therefore, that she shares her name with a Celtic goddess of fertility and light, whose annual celebration at the great turning day of the year, Imbolc, takes place on the Christian saint's feast day. With Bealtaine (May Day), Lughnasa (Lammas) and Samhain (Hallowe'en), Imbolc is one of the turning days of the calendar, portals to the seasons of spring, summer, harvest and winter.

Christian Brigid, we have been told, was as chaste as her pagan namesake was sexually licentious. Indeed, she even thwarted a suitor by plucking out her own eye. Notwithstanding that aversion to nuptials, the Irish form of the name by which she is known, Bríd, was adapted in Germany, where devotion to her was prevalent, as the title given by young men to the virginal young women they marry. The word came into English as 'bride'.[44]

Yet for a woman whose fame and celebrity have spread so far, accounts of Brigid are a jumble of contradictions. Hagiographer Daphne Pochin Mould discounts entirely the idea that Brigid was born in Faughart, claiming that her birthplace was between Rathangan and Monasterevin in County Kildare instead.[45] However, Pochin Mould's account does concede that Brigid was a highly prized political commodity. The story of her life staked her monastery's claim as the primatial see of Ireland and consequently ensured temporal pre-eminence for the kings of Leinster over the Uí Néill, as Faughart and the adjacent Gap of the North were central and pivotal to the Uí Néill realms of Ulster and Meath. Subsequent accounts of Brigid's life from the eighth and ninth centuries respectively, *Vita Prima* and *Bethu Brigte*, hint at a rapprochement between Armagh and Kildare in its descriptions of meetings between Brigid and Patrick.[46]

More recent scholarship has sifted through the political chaff and winnowed out some kernels of truth, as well as plausible explanations of why accounts of Brigid's life in these three sources incorporate clear elements that echo pagan beliefs and traditions in a Christian context. Rather than being deceptions designed to fool people into false belief, the merging of Christian interpretation with pagan tradition created a continuum in the expressions of the spiritual life of the people. Carole M. Cusack argues that Brigid is an ideal study for the transition from pagan to Christian Ireland because she is situated on the boundaries of those eras. The accounts of her life are clearly accounts of qualities that have been transferred from a pagan deity to a human, Christian saint.[47] Indeed, Cusack points out that *all* female Celtic deities may have been known as Brigid. She notes that the *Vita Prima* account of Brigid's birth, which was 'neither in the house nor outside the house', is a link to the idea that 'thresholds and places and times that were liminal (like dawn and dusk) were regarded as powerful in pagan Celtic belief'.[48] These places and times were portals where the supernatural and natural risked spilling into each other, thereby altering the normal laws governing space and time. These beliefs merge most notably with Christianity, perhaps, in the story in which Finn McCool's son Oisín returns from Tír na nÓg to find Patrick converting the people of Ireland. In the case of Brigid, however, the congruence of natural and supernatural is central to the fact that her feast day occurs at the time of the pagan celebration of Imbolc. That day is the threshold between the darkness of winter and the light of spring, and it is most marked in the tradition of hanging a St Brigid's cross on the lintel of doorways to protect people and livestock.

Modern examinations point to the fact that the miracles of Brigid correspond closely to the magic of druidic times – she hung her cloak on a sunbeam, turned water into milk and resurrected animals. They also agree, however, that the effect of these accounts is to represent the Christian qualities of faith, hope and charity. Another modern scholarly examination of the cult of Brigid points out the essential difference between the sexually licentious pagan goddess (or goddesses) and the Christian saint's virginal chastity and the Marian devotion in which it became entwined.[49] Moreover, the tradition of the followers of Brigid keeping alive the eternal flame has been compared to the Vestal virgins of pagan Rome. It is interesting that one of the early decrees after the Norman conquest began was in 1220, when the Anglo-Norman archbishop of Dublin, Henry de Loundres, ordered that the perpetual fire of Kildare be extinguished.[50] Breaking the links between pagan associations and Celtic Christianity must have had a profound impact on the now-subject natives of Ireland's Pale. However, devotion continued in the folk traditions. It is notable that the other duty of the Vestal virgins of Rome was to maintain a pure source of water. Perhaps this explains the dedication of so many holy wells throughout Ireland to Brigid.[51]

*Monday, 1 February 2010*
10.00 a.m.
The oratory at St Brigid's Shrine is filled to overflowing, with latecomers jostling for standing room in front of the plate-glass windows that surround all but a small area at the back of the altar. The choir has been enveloped by pilgrims, but the choristers respond marvellously to the pep-talk given by parish priest, Fr Christopher McElwee.

'Just pretend you're playing for Tyrone,' he urges them.

One of the women responds, 'Or Derry?' a reference to the priest's home county. Later, I learn that Tyrone GAA manager Mickey Harte gave a talk on the spiritual aspect of team preparation as part of Faughart's annual celebration of its star saint. But the theme of the day is new beginnings rather than past successes, and Fr McElwee proclaims this the 'first day of spring'. He notes the huge attendance of those whose devotion to Brigid testifies to her continuing intercession in so many Irish lives. Beside me, two tiny Indian nuns in Mother Teresa veils pray as fervently as the older Irish sister in front, who arrived late and was given a seat by a young bearded man, here with his wife and toddler child. As the mystery of the Mass unfolds in song and prayer, there is growing excitement in the congregation, almost a palpable sense that this is indeed a fresh beginning after a cruel winter – a time when light returns and life begins anew. We enjoy a clear view of the day outside as groups of schoolchildren scamper across the lawns towards the pilgrimage stations below. On the other side, a bus pulls up the road and a milk tanker edges by on its regular rounds. Inside, there is a relaxed atmosphere. This is a religious celebration with a warm family feeling.

11.00 a.m.
Fr McElwee ends the Mass with a general blessing of St Brigid as members of the congregation proffer religious objects – mostly the highly distinctive St Brigid's crosses, freshly woven from green rushes. Tradition dictates that each year a new blessed cross replaces the last on the lintel above the door of each home and animal shed, bestowing the saint's protection for another year. Several in the congregation also hold up bottles of water taken from the stream outside and its underground source, which is encompassed in the shrine. The parish priest then takes up the monstrance, which has sat on the altar throughout the Mass. It contains a relic of St Brigid. He carries it in procession through the congregation, which surges forward in the wake of the real presence of the saint among them. Outside, Fr McElwee stands with the relic and the worshippers line up in a loose but patient queue for individual blessings. The old, the sick,

the frail, the infirm, young mothers with infants and toddlers shuffle forward to the priest, each in turn seeking benediction for a new and better year.

The accents are local, predominantly those of north Louth, south Armagh and south Monaghan, with a sprinkling of more pronounced northern strains from Newry and beyond. Around the fringes, meanwhile, pilgrims buy their crosses and other holy keepsakes. I purchase my St Brigid's crosses (large €2, small €1) at a small table, where candles and bottles to be filled with holy water from the shrine are also on sale. The proceeds will aid Faughart National School and the victims of the Haiti earthquake.

The St Brigid's cross is a symbol almost as evocative of Ireland as the shamrock. Tradition says it was fashioned by the saint from green rushes on the floor to instruct a dying pagan chieftain in the one true faith. Down the years it has been a powerful and potent symbol in the custom and practice of Irish people, who used to gather supplies of rushes and place them outside the door on January 31 each year. After a special evening meal in honour of Brigid, a girl in the family went outside, knocked on the door and called out in Irish, 'Go on your knees. Let the door be opened. Let Brigid in.'[52] She then carried in the rushes, which the family used to make new crosses to protect family and livestock and bring a new year of peace and plenty. Today, the folk tradition still exists in Faughart, where the crosses are being made by schoolchildren under adult supervision, a happy little workshop on a day out from the classroom that conveys all the joys of the first day of spring. But, as if to remind us of the darkest days so we can bask in the light of the future, I notice a brass plaque set in a window of the oratory beside the stall. It says:

*Perpetual light, in memory of Omagh Bomb Victims and all who suffered from violence in Ireland. Lit by 16 year old James Hughes at St Brigid's Shrine, Faughart, on 25th August 1998. Please pray for the dead and bereaved.*

11.30 a.m.
Access to the shrine is through heavy cast-iron gates erected by members of an Garda Síochána, the Irish police force. Beyond, a quartet of saintly figures – Oliver Plunkett, Malachy, Patrick and Colmcille – stand guard over steps leading up to the path and then to a small, glass-encased altar surmounted by a statue of Brigid, dressed in blue and holding a bishop's crozier. Underneath is written, 'A Naomh Bhríd, guigh orainn' ('St Brigid, pray for us') in old Gaelic script. Inside the glass is a representation of Christ laid out in his tomb, under an altar on which stands a smaller statue of Brigid. In front, a painted grey concrete altar rail with kneeler is scuffed and worn down by pilgrim knees and elbows. A small group kneels now in silent prayer, before moving on to begin the pilgrimage tour with an Our Father, a Hail Mary and a Glory Be on the near bank of the small fountain that sets a tiny stream running down the hill. The same prayers are said on the far bank, on the flat stone in the centre, and each time the pilgrim makes the 10 circuits of a cross set in a cairn or mound. The pilgrim then moves off downhill beside the small stream through a beautiful copse of beech trees, stopping at the Stations of the Cross along the way to repeat the three prayers. I pause momentarily at a small Fátima-style grotto erected by the Pioneer and Total Abstinence Society from Dundalk. Added to the familiar iconography of statues is a framed picture of Pope John Paul II.

Moving on, the pilgrim path and the Stations of the Cross lead to another gate, with access across a narrow road to the lower area of the shrine. As I walk that way, I am greeted with a huge smile by one of the little Indian sisters who prayed beside me at Mass. Another path-side plaque at the entrance to the lower area of the shrine informs me that a restoration was funded in 1997 by the Ladies Auxiliary to the Ancient Order of Hibernians in America to 'honour their patroness'. Strikingly different from the upper area, there is a noticeable absence of trees in this larger open space. The stream runs down through lawns with picnic tables and toilets on the far side. A small, roofed structure in the shape of a covered well has been built over the stream at one point, its stone walls circling unnecessarily over the course of water and its slated roof gable bearing the carved representation of a St Brigid's cross.

But the focus now is on the busy bottom end of the parkland, along an old dry-stone wall where the stream turns sharply to the right. The first thing the pilgrim notices here is the sheep-wire fencing on top of the wall, festooned with shoelaces, hankies, Rosary beads and other supplicant offerings. A larger stone in the wall has a circular cavity, outlined in white against its grey colour. Into this indent kneeling pilgrims insert the crown of their head, resting against the stone in prayer. It is in this corner, one realises, that the traditional stations of the pilgrimage are made. It was these rituals that the countless generations who came here each February 1st down through the centuries made, before the main shrine in all its Roman Catholic glory was opened in the 1930s.

Here and there, novice pilgrims like me (or forgetful pilgrims, perhaps) quietly discuss how the stations should be observed. Those who know explain the procedure for each of the large stones, pointing out the order of prayer. First is an Our Father, a Hail Mary and a Creed on the near bank of the stream; then this is repeated at the 'hoof-marked stone', the 'knee-marked stone', and the 'waist-marked stone'; next come 10 circuits of the 'eye-marked stone', made while reciting a decade of the Rosary, and finally a single Hail Mary, said kneeling at the 'head-marked stone'. Frankly, it is difficult to distinguish one stone from the other, apart from the head and knee stones, but a safe formula is to just follow the pilgrim in front and repeat the familiar prayers. The far end of this passage, moreover, has a large stone at the foot of a Calvary-style shrine in the shape of a reclining chair. That is precisely how it is being used by pilgrims, who come along and sink into it, resting their backs against the stone for a prayer or a photo or both, while holding on firmly to their new St Brigid's crosses. Around them is a group of children, some playing, others praying. I sink into the stone and a woman kindly offers to take a photo with my camera. It is difficult to pray while staring into the lens, but it is another welcome reminder of how friendly and helpful my fellow pilgrims are on this glorious day, as the sun beams down on those who come to honour Brigid, the bringer of light.

Then it's back up towards the oratory, where the simple crosses are still being fashioned, to smiles and friendly acknowledgement. A horsebox has drawn up just outside one of the gates. Inside, a woman is teaching a boy to weave the rushes from a pile on the floor. They smile happily as they work, the woman explaining patiently the sacred folk craft. A lorry squeezes around the corner, a man on a tractor busily cuts a hedge and horses graze in the bright light of a new year as I set off on foot for the Old Graveyard of Faughart Hill.

12.00 noon.

In stark contrast to the manicured lawns at the shrine, Faughart Old Graveyard guards its ancient history in a wild profusion of growth. It is a jumble of old and modern headstones – some shattered, many with inscriptions worn away – flat slabs, the crumbling ruins of a chapel almost totally obscured by thick ivy and a big yew tree, billowing out to envelop surrounding graves. That is my first impression of a designated national-monument site that survives in the splendour of age and decay beside a relatively large and well maintained car park for pilgrims. A simple worn path through the tangled growth and headstones leads to another burst of rhododendron greenery and a narrow passage along a dry-stone wall covered in weeds. Here the branches are bedecked with the tell-tale rags all the way to the cut-stone steps down to St Brigid's Well, which is surmounted by a sizeable obelisk. At its base is a narrow doorway and a few more steps down to the blessed water.

As I descend, a woman coming up says she has filled the ladle with water and asks could I do likewise. Indeed, the long-handled cup has enough to fill my half-litre bottle. I squeeze into the narrow gap and step down gingerly to replenish it. The atmosphere here is dark and dank. I emerge with the ladle and hang it up in a recess as a man comes down. The woman pilgrim is still there when I ascend and we talk briefly and gaze out over the beautiful countryside. I ask her the whereabouts of Edward Bruce's grave. The woman seems puzzled but the man who is ascending from the well offers to show me. And so Peter Daly, as he introduces himself, leads me past his own family burial plot to the tumbledown chapel with the huge yew tree beside it.

Parting the unkempt lower branches, Peter points to the flat slab.

'That's it – the grave of Edward Bruce,' he says matter-of-factly. 'There used to be writing on it but it's worn off.'

I regard the grave with a mixture of bewilderment and awe. For here, in a small, nondescript plot obscured by overgrowth, is the grave of a man who fought alongside his brother King Robert I of Scotland when they defeated England's King Edward I (Longshanks) at Bannockburn in 1314 and 'sent him homeward', as the popular Scottish song recommends, 'to think again'. Here is the lord of Carrick, who wrested control of almost all Ireland from the English, laying waste to the stronghold Norman garrisons of Carrickfergus, Dundalk and Trim; the Gaelic champion who drove the Anglo-Norman conquerors right back into Dublin and across the Irish Sea to plead for help at the court of Edward II.[53] Here is a chieftain in the line of the Uí Néill, crowned by the Irish clans in 1316, invited to Ireland by the kings of Meath and Ulster. Here lies a hero of the combined ancient Gaelic realms of Scotland and Ireland, determined to halt the annihilation of his civilisation, whose entitlement to be recognised as *de jure* high king of Ireland was pleaded to Pope John XXII in 1317. Here was a man commended to the Vatican as 'pious and prudent, humble and chaste, exceedingly temperate, in all things sedate and moderate, and possessing power (God on high be praised) to snatch us mightily from the house of bondage with the help of God and our own justice, and very willing to render to everyone what is due to him of right.'[54] In modern Ireland, where it is possible to take a *Braveheart* tour of locations used by Mel Gibson for his 1995 movie about William Wallace, who helped the Bruces assert Scotland's independence, the remains of Edward the Bruce languish in this lonely graveyard.

Of course, you can always find a contrary opinion in Ireland. Because Edward the Bruce's campaign of terror against the Anglo-Normans coincided with a great medieval famine that swept through western Europe, caused by a sudden climate cooling that prevented crops from ripening in the years 1315 to 1317, he was blamed for its consequences in folk memory. Thus, a century or more later, the *Annals of Ulster* named 'Edward de Brus' as 'the destroyer of Ireland' because during his three and a half years here there came horrific 'death and loss'. The annalist adds that 'people undoubtedly used to eat each other throughout Ireland.'[55] Notwithstanding the fact that the same calamity swept through England and the rest of Europe north of the Alps, as far as Poland and beyond, with tales of mass starvation, infanticide and cannibalism rife, the blame fell on Edward Bruce. When his debilitated Scots-Irish army was finally defeated at the battle of Faughart in October 1318, Edward was executed and buried in the cemetery beside St Brigid's Well. As all of western Europe sank into despair, remorse and recrimination, which in turn would exacerbate the Black Death, instigate the wanton cruelty of the Hundred Years' War and undermine the church in a wave of corruption and apostasy that resulted in the Reformation, the hero of the Gael became the villain of the piece and was left here to rot.

Back in the Old Graveyard of Faughart, I discuss briefly the exact whereabouts and importance of the Gap of the North with my friendly guide Peter Daly, before he hurries off home to tend to the cattle on his farm in the adjacent parish of Dromintee, County Armagh. With a few remarks about the McKenna Cup Gaelic-football tournament, Tyrone manager Mickey Harte's contribution to the St Brigid's Triduum and the continued devotion that brings pilgrims to Faughart on February 1, he wishes me well for the candlelight procession.

'I don't think I'll be able to come tonight because I'll be working with the cattle,' he says. 'I always say my cattle come first, my family second and I come last.' With a smile and a wave, he climbs over a broken-down part of the wall beside the locked main gate and sets off home in his pick-up truck. I am left to ponder the hidden mysteries of Faughart Old Graveyard and I spot an official plaque with a bilingual notice erected by Bord Fáilte, the Irish tourism board, almost totally hidden by the ivy on the ruined walls of the old chapel. This notes:

> *Brigid, Ireland's most famous abbess, is said to have been born here. Tradition says that she lived here for some time before going to Kildare. A fragment of a cross-base is one of the few remains of the Early Christian monastery on the site. The western end of the medieval church is older than the western* [*sic*] *portion. Nearby there is a Holy Well dedicated to Brigid. The graveyard also contains the grave of King Edward Bruce who was killed in 1318.*

How the mighty have fallen from favour, even when the latest figures show that visitor numbers from Britain, our most important tourism market, fell by 16 per cent in 2009, with declines of 6 per cent in numbers of tourists from North America and 10 per cent in numbers from mainland Europe.[56] Yet, wandering around the Old Graveyard and the adjoining car park, I am struck once more by the captivating beauty of the Gap of the North, once guarded by Moyry Castle, which fell to the Bruce. Below, a small country road branches off into south Armagh. Brooding over the land to the north is the bulk of Slieve Gullion, the squat mountain once worshipped as a goddess by the ancient people who settled here, before being christened and made holier by a disciple of Brigid, St Monenna. With hours to spare, I decide to head off in that direction, thereby following the path of the modern, secular pilgrims who flock to Newry for its bargains.

1.00 p.m.
By the time I join the main traffic on the M1 motorway that speeds shoppers from Dublin to Newry, I have meandered through the back roads of south Armagh's Ring of Gullion. It is a magical land that resonates with mystic associations. It is the land of Monenna, a disciple of Brigid, who was joined by 150 Virgins of Christ in her foundation at Faughart before they relocated to escape the noise and bustle of Dundalk. I have previously written of the marvellous Monenna and how the other sisters followed her to Killeavy on the slopes of Slieve Gullion.[57] A lone sister stayed to watch over the Faughart cloisters after Monenna performed what must rank as one of the strangest miracles ever ascribed to a saint. The sister pleaded with Monenna not to be left behind, fearing that her beauty would tempt men. So Monenna turned a young beauty into an ugly old hag. I prefer her later miracle: during a visit by Bishop Finbarr, the water drawn from the well at Killeavy was transformed into the finest beer, prompting Finbarr to caution his retainers not to drink too much. It's hardly a wonder that the well still draws many pilgrims.

Newry, on the other hand, draws even more to its retail shrines, much to the dismay of Dublin government ministers. They accuse cross-border shoppers of 'unpatriotism'. Not long ago, the same ministers extolled the huge benefits of an 'all-island economy', while lining up Newry and Belfast as 'back-shop' locations for their wondrous financial-services sector. Today, the legacy of the Celtic-Tiger 'miracle' is in the aisles of Sainsbury's supermarket, where shoppers with Dublin accents relay the price tags in the liquor section into phones clasped to their ears. Even on a Monday, the adjoining car park is full of cars with southern plates, through which people pick their way with overladen shopping trolleys.

Elsewhere, however, the new city is relatively quiet, so I buy a sandwich and coffee at a deli on the canal bank, retrieve my car and head out the road towards Carlingford across the border, to enjoy a picnic with my back to the Cooley Mountains and the captivating Mournes sweeping down to the sea across the lough.

7.30 p.m.
Back at St Brigid's Shrine, a man in a high-visibility jacket waves us into the car park, even though it seems packed to capacity already. Another man signals me into a new, improvised centre aisle, but a car pulls out near the exit gate and I slip into its spot. Other drivers are squeezing their vehicles onto both verges of the small country roads as pilgrims disgorge and head off up the hill on foot. Accompanied by Michael, an old friend I chanced upon in Carlingford, who asked to accompany me on the final part of my St Brigid's Day pilgrimage, we stride off up Faughart Hill. Others in front of us have torches to light their passage through the gloom. Already there is a sense of something sanctified on our raggle-taggle route to the ancient holy place where the procession will begin. When we turn right where I mistakenly went straight ahead last night, other walkers from the south-Armagh side join us. By the time we reach the Old Graveyard, we are a throng. Wrapped for warmth in the chill night air, we are searching for the light and a spring of hope on this dark and wintry evening.

8.00 p.m.
There is a buzz of excitement among the happy pilgrims gathered in clusters in the car park and along the road. Up on the wall of the Old Graveyard, in an alcove above a bricked-up hearth that now forms part of the car-park boundary, a

bonfire is lit. A local man beside us in the crowd explains that this convenience for cars and buses was actually built on the site of the old monastic ruins. The open fire is a dramatic harbinger of the light of spring and its flame is spread among the pilgrims, who first light their candles from it and then pass it on to others in turn. A young woman selling candles and St Brigid's crosses at the gate is still doing a steady trade for the local school and the Haitian earthquake victims. Fr McElwee takes his position beside the fire up on the wall as if he were on a pulpit. Wearing his priestly stole, but also a baseball cap, he leads prayers of benediction for our pilgrimage before calling out the order of procession. The crosses and flags borne by local men will lead; then will come the relic of St Brigid in its monstrance, followed by the candle bearers. A van with a public-address system will follow, leading the Rosary and hymns, and the general group of pilgrims will walk in its wake. Fully equipped with our lit candles, Michael hustles me forward, saying that we are not mere followers, but the vanguard. So we make our way through the general horde, past the van with speakers jutting from its rooftop taxi sign, and take our place among those who will light the way to St Brigid's Shrine.

8.30 p.m.
Through absolute darkness we move along the road. The other candle bearers are mostly women and girls, with just a few young men, all wrapped against the chill. Several hold leashes, with their dogs ambling along in the pilgrim procession. Men in high-visibility jackets stand sentinel at the entrances to houses. A man in front wears a woolly hat with the logo and name of a bank and I wonder if he is here praying for forgiveness or deliverance from the financial quagmire. Then we come around a bend and suddenly

Dundalk town provides a great arc of light from below. The light draws us on our descent of Faughart Hill, around the last corner and down to the shrine, where another large crowd awaits our arrival. Among them, a group of six stands above us at the shrine, three pairs of mothers and daughters. All of them are cradling lit candles that light up their faces and all are dressed in warm winter jackets, but one of the girls is wearing a pair of bright-pink pyjama bottoms. Through the Garda Síochána gates, up the steps guarded by the saintly quartet, and our procession ends as pilgrims gather closely around the shrine.

9.00 p.m.
Fr McElwee stands behind the altar rail on which the saintly relics now rest. From a printed order of service, he leads us in invoking the blessings of Brigid on the new year heralded by this rite of spring. Then we pray for help and succour in a 'time of great trouble and distress' and reflect on the huge depth of goodwill, generosity and gratitude evident in this simple procession of faith. The flag bearers form a guard of honour and I note that the pole-top cross that has led our way on the pilgrim path is a cross of St Brigid. On the shrine roof, lit by a single spotlight, Brigid welcomes us to her Faughart birthplace. And finally, the ceremonies close with the other pilgrims singing out the words they all seem to know:

*High above enthroned in glory,*
*Sweetest saint of Erin's Isle,*
*See thy children kneel before thee,*
*Turn on us a mother's smile.*

*Sancta mater, hear our pleading,*
*Faith and hope and holy love,*

*Sweet Saint Brigid, Spouse of Jesus,*
*Sent to us from heaven above.*

*Dear Saint Brigid, Erin's children*
*Far and near o'er land and sea*
*In the world and in the cloister*
*Fondly turn with love to thee.*

9.15 p.m.
We make our way quickly back to the car park, exit and are soon winding our way down the great hill and speeding off towards the M1 motorway below. Although the gloom still prevails, I sense a chink of light ahead, courtesy of Brigid, harbinger of hope and herald of the spring.

# Chapter 7

# A Walk in the Garden

## To Glendalough

*24 February 2010*
1.00 p.m.

Colette at the Hollywood Inn warns me that there will be no mobile phone coverage once I head up into the Wicklow Gap. The friendly bartender with the American accent – who also happens to teach forensic chemistry at Dublin City University and who worked as a crime-scene investigator in Washington DC – immediately adds that she only mentions this because she is constantly reminded of the fact.

'I live in Greystones and I travel that road all the time,' she explains, 'and people says it's risky because I wouldn't be able to call anyone if I had a breakdown.' Explanation concluded, we agree that the absence of mobile phone networks is probably one of the most attractive features of any remote district in a modern world that expects and demands instant communication. Colette recalls that we managed adequately before mobile phones: if you said you would be somewhere at a given time, you made sure you were there.

For one embarking on a once hugely popular medieval pilgrimage route, the talk of mobile phones seems inappropriate. It seems perfectly appropriate that I estimate my time of arrival at Glendalough and inform somebody of the route I am walking in case anything should happen. The pleasure and spiritual benefit of a walking pilgrimage is enhanced by the absence of distractions. Colette then mentions that she has been listening to Gerry Ryan's 2FM radio show and there was a discussion of how little we are informed of the huge number of excellent hiking trails in Ireland. As I pay for my bacon-and-cabbage lunch, she wishes me well on my walk; I wish her better in her trek back to the United States to testify in a retrial linked to a case she worked on four years ago.

9.00 p.m.
The young man ordering pints of Guinness for his quartet in the public bar of the Glendalough Hotel has walked the Wicklow Way from Dublin, but they have 'an equipment problem'. Two of the party had inadequate rain gear.

'We knew it would rain, but not this much,' he says, 'and this Irish rain just seems to soak through everything.' He adds that it was a relief when they encountered some snow because they did not get so wet. Tomorrow they plan to do local walking trails around Glendalough. 'At home in the Netherlands we do not even have hills, so this is marvellous. And now we have found the right pub, so even the rain can be forgotten.'

*Thursday, 25 February 2010*
8.10 a.m.
The traffic report on RTÉ Radio 1 says that both the Sally Gap and the Wicklow Gap are 'impassable'. As I hear this, I am actually in the middle of the Wicklow Gap, heading

west and shrouded in thick fog as I sluice my way through slushy snow and ice. I drive gingerly along the unfamiliar road while reviewing the plans I drew up during field explorations yesterday, when the weather forecast predicted no more than rain showers in the morning and a dry afternoon with occasional sunny spells. My plan was to leave my car in Hollywood, get an early start on the 30-kilometre route and then, in the absence of bus services or other transportation, get a taxi back to retrieve the car that evening. Indeed, even the forecast of rain seemed too pessimistic only minutes ago when I left the Glendalough Hotel, and it seemed to be shaping up to be a dull but dry day after yesterday's persistent showers. Ahead of me, the road seemed to rise into the summit shrouded by a low cloud, but I expected that to drift off as the day unfolded. Then, at the brow of the Glendasan Valley, where the road reached a height of 400 metres above sea level, the fog began and immediately the snow enclosed me in a wintry desert landscape. Visibility was down to about 20 metres.

For our Celtic ancestors, fog had the ability to confound and thwart the senses of mere mortals, and the *ceo draíochta* (magic fog) that descended on the court of Cormac MacAirt lulled the warriors of Ulster into a coma and left Cú Chulainn alone to defend the northern province and save the Brown Bull of Cooley in the most famous saga of ancient Ireland. While there is no bull at stake now, I conjure up the image of being lost and befuddled in this unfamiliar and harsh landscape:

*Ceo draíochta i gcoim oíche do sheol mé*
*Trí thíorthaibh mar óinmhid ar strae,*
*Gan príomhcharaid díograis im chóngar*
*'s mé i gcríochaibh tar m'eolas i gcéin.*[58]

8.30 a.m.
Parking outside the Catholic church in Hollywood, I don my outer rain gear, take up my pilgrim's staff and walk over to the waymarked stile beside the village post office at the start of St Kevin's Road. The stile is barricaded and a big notice on the adjoining gate warns that this is private property and access is prohibited. I walk down to the big information map outlining the route further along the road, but there is another, similar notice on the gate beside it. Back at the car, other vehicles are pulling up alongside and people are filing into the church. I decide this is a sign that I should attend Mass now and ask somebody afterwards about public access to the pilgrimage route.

9.00 a.m.
The celebrant welcomes the Lenten Mass-goers to St Kevin's Church, thanks God for 'warm hearts' on this cold and snowy morning and asks us to pray for the forgiveness of those whose hearts remain cold to others. There is a sizeable congregation of about 60 present, including a group of schoolchildren, who file up to the three overhead galleries in this beautiful little chapel of ease. It is built in three gable ends, with the altar at the centre of the long wall. Each gable has its own overhead accommodation. The design creates a feeling of closeness, which adds to the reverence of ritual here in this tiny Wicklow village, part of the parish of Ballymore Eustace, where St Kevin is believed to have been born. In Irish, the village is Cillín Chaoimhín, meaning Kevin's Little Church; it probably acquired its Hollywood title in deference to its role as the starting point for the ancient pilgrimage road to Kevin's monastic retreat at Glendalough. One of the four great pilgrimages of Ireland, which drew supplicants and penitents from throughout Christendom, it was acknowledged

that completing the pilgrimage seven times was equivalent to a full pilgrimage to Rome. Into medieval times and beyond, the faithful gathered from the great fertile plains to the west and made the sacred trek into the barren heights around and beyond the Wicklow Gap to the monastic city in the valley of two lakes and seven churches.

9.30 a.m.
A friendly older couple who greeted me on the way into Mass confirm that the stile across the way is the starting point of the pilgrimage road. They walked part of it some years back. I return, read the notice, which is as abruptly categoric as the barricaded stile, and then consult the big map once more. It shows the route bubbling out around Quarry Hill past the Motte, St Kevin's Bed and St Kevin's Chair and circling back around to join the main road for the Wicklow Gap further on. Deprived of the start, I decide that I had better just walk along the main road and rejoin the route at that point. However, I pay a visit to the second St Kevin's Church in the village, a beautiful old Church of Ireland place of worship, sitting atop a little knoll surrounded by a cemetery. This was probably the site of the original Little Church of Kevin, when the saint came to minister here after serving in Kilnamanagh in the present-day Dublin suburb of Tallaght.

As I close the gate firmly I read the service times and note that one can worship here at 10.30 a.m. on every 'fifth Sunday or as announced'. I recall the story of the staunch Ulster Protestant living in Canada whose travel agent could not convince him that he could not book a holiday flight home for the 'Twelfth Week' in July, because the month only had four weeks.

Out on the road again, I set off up the hill, walking on the right to face oncoming traffic. A van drives by, followed by two cars and a small truck. Each vehicle ploughs up a huge splurge of slush, which comes cascading onto me. And still the snow falls. By this time I have only walked about 200 metres and I decide that, even with my rain gear and high-visibility vest, I am as much a road hazard to these vehicles that veer out to pass me on the narrow road as they are a nuisance to me. I walk back into the village and once more pause at the big map. It is only then I notice the familiar pilgrim-path waymarker post that has already guided me through unknown terrain in Donegal, Mayo and Offaly. It may have been obscured by the snow but, now revealed, it offers two starting phases for the walk. I can go either around Quarry Hill, along the path that is strictly prohibited, or straight ahead, down a gorge between that hill and Dragonhill.

I choose the latter, and enter land that also has a public notice posted on the gate, but this one is less authoritarian than the one down the way. This one really just absolves the landowner from any 'duty of care' to me as I pass along on my pilgrim path. Since I don't even know the landowner, I have no expectations of any such care. So I set off along a firm but rutted path that runs by marshy ground, while a flock of sheep forages in the slush on the side of the hill. Some distance along, a loud caw from a herring gull draws my attention to the hilltop cross, where the bird perches on an arm. This obviously marks St Kevin's Bed. As I offer up a prayer for a good pilgrimage, the bird reminds me of the story of Kevin's novitiate in Wales. The saint went off into the wilderness to pray at the start of Lent. As he stood with arms outstretched in prayer, a blackbird built a nest in his palm. Kevin stood there throughout the Lenten season, while the bird hatched her eggs, brooded and raised her nestlings before flying off. Only then did Kevin return to the monastery.

10.30 a.m.
The pilgrim path has turned sharply left, through a gate which again has a public notice absolving the landowner of his duty of care. A short distance ahead is the main N81 road from Dublin to Baltinglass and places beyond. Over a stile, however, the path sets off along a small country road and the sound of traffic recedes completely. The snow is fresher here, with less disturbance. A post-office van pulls out from a road to the left and the female driver waves a greeting before I turn into the road she has emerged from. The climb now starts in earnest as the road ascends towards a succession of corners. Apart from the birdsong and the occasional plop of slush from branches, there is silence between the high, moss-covered banks of this ancient road. I follow it up through the townland of Dunboyke, then into the Scalp, which cuts a path along the lower slopes of Slievecorragh, towards the rising sun.

11.00 a.m.
I pause for a brief standing break, eat an orange and sip coffee from the cup of the thermos flask I filled at the hotel. A car glides by, a big four-wheel-drive vehicle with an Armagh registration. The woman driver waves and I set off once more along the lee of the hillside. Below in the valley a dog barks furiously in response to its own echo, sounding far off against the hills. Yet, apart from the snow-covered slopes immediately around me, I can see little of the local terrain, even when the high banks and hedges are interrupted to allow a wider vista. On a slope opposite, the forestry begins and disappears up into the fog, the visible conifers hugged closely inside a blanket of snow. Further along, great gantry-like pylons appear and I can see them ascending the slopes opposite. As I pass underneath one

of them I hear a crackling noise, which I take to be the intense current moving along the high-tension wires. I wonder if this is a normal feature or merely one confined to slushy days. A car pulls out from a roadside house; the older couple inside wave and drive off around a corner. I follow and, almost immediately, find myself back on the road for the Wicklow Gap, which by now is fairly clear of the slush.

I weigh my options. I'm already well behind my schedule for the day and, with approximately 25 kilometres to go across the fog-bound Wicklow Gap and uncertain of the weather, I decide on an alternative strategy. I will walk those parts of the route that are off the main road. That means returning to get my car. I set off on the 3-kilometre hike on the road that slices its way between Slievecorragh and Broughills Hill, arriving down the hillside towards the two St Kevin's Churches on the flatter land that stretches off into the fertile plains beyond. As I return to my starting point, the voice of Kevin Conneff of the Chieftains is sounding in my head. I'm remembering him performing a ditty about his home village in Wicklow at the Singers Club in Slattery's of Capel Street, Dublin, many years ago:

*In Hollywood I long to be,*
*Now, not the place across the sea*
*But in County Wicklow, Ireland's lovely garden,*
*Where no pretenders will you find*
*But decent people, warm and kind,*
*And flocks of friendly sheep into the bargain.*[59]

As I arrive at my parked car, the Angelus bell peals out its call to prayer. I recite as much as I can recall and take my leave of Hollywood at last.

1.30 p.m.
About a kilometre on past where my trek through the Scalp rejoined the main road (R756), St Kevin's Way traverses the first of a few bridges and veers off through Coonmore on the south side of the King's River. It follows this ancient route for about 10 kilometres more, then rejoins the main road and the pilgrim route spur from Valleymount on a long spit of the Blessington Lakes or Pollaphuca Reservoir at Ballinagee Bridge. I am back into the valley of the big power pylons. Two great arches of high-voltage lines traverse Leeraghs Bog on my right and the land and the main road veering off into the higher country of Lockstown Upper and Granabeg on my left. Further along, the entrance to a quarry on the left offers the first suitable place for parking so I can resume my walk, but a huge, roughly written notice warns firmly against it, adding in large letters: 'No exceptions'.

I drive on, looking for somewhere more hospitable for a pilgrim wayfarer, and find it under the brow of Knocknaboley and Corriebracks, where a small rivulet springs from the rocks just above the roadway on my right. On either side of a pilgrim waymarker post, two seats have been carved from solid rock, inviting a pause. The spring water flows through a culvert and gushes from an old-fashioned pump in a garden on the other side of the road. From there, its course takes it along another channel into a large pond, turning a small mill-wheel on its way before providing a sanctuary for a large and happy gathering of wild and domestic waterfowl. The ducks, geese and other fowl frolic and cavort happily in their wayside haven under the gaze of a big studio window of the adjoining house. I take another coffee break before setting off on foot once more.

After a while, the road begins to rise again, up onto a shelf course that sweeps along the lower slopes of

Loughanlee and Knocknadroose, over all the little brooks that flow down the slopes into the Kings River. I have settled into a steady gait, when suddenly the road takes me through a rather unkempt farmyard and the paving ends. The road now becomes a lane and follows a course over a rough track. About a hundred metres on, I encounter a huge puddle that fills the entire roadway, without any means of skirting it on the edge. Further along, I see a similar pothole of indeterminate depth. Again, I decide that retreat is the better part of valour and walk quickly back to the car, making sure by seeking out the waymarker posts that I have not strayed from the path of St Kevin's Way. Car retrieved, I then head back to where I left the main road at Coonmore, turn right and begin the steady climb to the Wicklow Gap through Granabeg and Knockalt to where the routes converge, as St Kevin's Way emerges from the gated exit through a cultivated forest. The major ascent to the gap commences just below the 817-metre peak of Tonelagee (whose name in Irish means Arse to the Wind). It proves every bit as hospitable as its name suggests and the thick fog envelops it once more, the sleet resuming over a frozen landscape. At the second of the designated car parks placed in quick succession at the summit of the gap, I pull in to survey the land, crunching over the icy snow of late February. An observation deck is barely discernible on the south side. I find an information board there and manage to scrape it clear of freezing slush just long enough to read it before it is covered again. From it I learn that the ancient pilgrim road is 'visible' just 50 metres from where I stand in the direction of the Turlough Hill Reservoir and Hydropower Station and Lough Nahanagan. All I see is a thick blanket of icy mist, so I repair to my car and begin the slow descent.

2.00 p.m.
A short distance below the summit of the Wicklow Gap, however, the fog lifts completely and the surrounding landscape takes on a friendlier demeanour. A roadside fingerpost points to where St Kevin's Road resumes its off-road course. Further ahead, there is parking at a lay-by viewpoint for the old lead mines at the top of the Glendasan Vale. I pull in, don my walking gear again, take up my pilgrim's staff and set off on foot back up the road to resume the trail at the part where it becomes accessible nearest the gap. It is a marvellous reintroduction to the old pilgrim road and, even with the enforced intrusions on my trek, I begin to sense the exhilaration that a medieval pilgrim might have sensed as he set off down the final part of the trail.

The route from here is dominated by the other attraction of the district – the rich industrial legacy of the old mine works. Founded in the 1790s when Thomas Weaver, manager of the Avoca mines further south in Wicklow, discovered a rich vein of lead and zinc in Glendalough and adjoining Glendasan.[60] With fluctuating fortunes through boom, bust, famine and fatality, the lead mines continued to operate until their final closure in 1957, at one time employing more than 200 miners and supporting a community of about a thousand on the relatively inhospitable mountainside with their own school and other facilities. Today, all that remains are the ruins of the old works – stone walls and cobbled floors and huge piles of shale and rocks, extracted and worked for their hidden wealth. Yet the memory also survives in this tourist lay-by and in the obvious pride of a local community – which becomes apparent later, in conversation with a small group of local men in the Glendalough Tavern. They recall the final fatality, on 22 January 1957, when two miners struck a piece of dynamite while drilling. Jim Mernagh, married with two young children, died instantly in the explosion, while co-worker Robbie Carter was seriously injured. The Canadian Mining Company, which had taken over the mines the year before in misplaced hopes of locating more lead, finally closed the operation less than six months after the accident, leaving little more than a legacy of lung and other chest problems.[61] However, it also left one of the finest vantage points of the trail, atop a big pile of mine refuse.

Below, the trail snakes along the south bank of the Glendasan River, which trickles through the rocks to open out below, where the vale becomes rich and wooded. I look towards the distance and a thought strikes me, in the words of another popular Irish folk song, which I recall in the gravelly voice of Ronnie Drew of the Dubliners:

*In Glendalough lived an oul' saint*
*Renowned for his learning and piety*
*His manner was curious and quaint*
*And he looked upon girls with disparity.*[62]

The song recounts the story of the saint who reacts to the wooing of 'Kathleen from over the way' by hurling her into the icy depths of the upper lough of Glendalough, below the spot where Van Diemen's Mine would later be sunk. It is a comic take on a lingering reputation of the saint who loved birds, cattle and otters but eschewed the fairer sex to an extent that must make him the patron of misogynists as much as silversmiths and the archdiocese of Dublin. Yet, standing here at the top of Glendasan, the vista reveals what may be a type of optical illusion brought on by the *ceo draíochta* through which I have passed. The high mountain ridges of Camaderry on my right and Brockagh Mountain, where the road traffic snakes down on my left, take on the shape of two giant thighs meeting far below in the wooded glade where the glens come together. Just beyond, the slopes of Trooperstown Hill or Maoilín have the gentle rotund shape of a pregnant belly. I regard the scene, which cannot be detected from the R756, and surmise that this is the very view that drew Kevin to his hermitage in the saintly bower almost 1,500 years ago, and that brought countless disciples and pilgrims after him. To the man who shunned female company and all the countless supplicants who have walked the trail in his honour before me, this final part of their pilgrim path must have seemed like a return to the comfort of the womb. Bolstered by the discovery, I begin the path of my descent with relish.

2.15 p.m.

From a waymarker pilgrim-path post just below the main group of ruins from the old mine works, the route staggers down the slope along causeways of shale, a variety of stone steps and bridges of old railway sleepers, which provide an excellent and varied path over marshy places and rivulets feeding the Glendasan River. The river, in the words of poet Patrick Kavanagh, roars 'niagarously' over the rocks and boulders and splashes its course down to the calm below. Soon my path has dipped below the level of the road, which hugs the shelf on the side of Brockagh to the left and then takes a more graded downward path. Then, just before the mountainous descent levels out at the point where the Wicklow Mountains National Park ends and the huge forest looms, there is a small concrete bothy in the shade of a lonesome pine. It is a shelter used by man – and beast – to escape the inclement weather. I take a cursory glance inside and am shocked to see a goat, white with brown patches, lying on its side, its eyes open but glazed in death. There is no particularly strong smell and the carcass seems relatively fresh. I move along, wondering whom I should inform.

A few hundred metres beyond I come on the imposing grey house that is Teach Chaoimhín, a retreat centre operated by Catholic Youth Care. I check and find that it is deserted, as is Teach Lorcáin, a similar retreat centre a short distance away. A substantial stone structure is crumbling further along the path, where mountainside gives way to thick forestry and cultivation and the river now takes a more leisurely pace through the Glendasan Vale. The ruins of what must have been semi-detached homes are being enveloped in the trees planted by the state agency Coillte. Yet it is the removal of the lintels over the doors and windows that give them a spectacular look, as if some Incredible Hulk in panic-stricken flight has burst out from within.

2.45 p.m.

The river flows gently past a group of houses on the far shore and stepping-stones, big and placed cheek by jowl, invite a crossing. Large notices at both ends don't: 'Private Property, Access Limited to B&B' says one, while the other identifies the bed and breakfast by name. Further along, other houses have stepping-stones too, but no prohibition notices. Then, just about a hundred metres past the strong metal gate guarding the entrance to the Catholic Youth Care facilities and Coillte, the river takes on the aspect of a canal, slow moving and deep, before passing a platform on the bank overlooking a weir dam. The platform provides a great vantage as the water cascades over the barrier onto the rocks below. A big public notice, however, fends off casual investigation, warning of dangers 'including but not restricted to' sharp drops to rocks below, deep waters, slippery sharp rocks and other surfaces and submerged rocks. If that isn't enough to strike terror into an explorer's heart, it warns, 'Do Not Enter'. The 'occupier' also notifies the passer-by that he has also excluded 'any duty of care' in accordance with the Occupiers' Liability Act 1995. Yet the platform and the little causeway bridge leading to it are very sturdy and they have been covered in a mesh-wire safety-grip surface to ensure the safety of those who ignore the large red-letter warning: 'Keep Away'. I don't, and while sitting on the wall over a caged sluice area of the structure I watch the water glide gently by and cascade over the edge.

3.10 p.m.
St Kevin's Road continues for a short way along the gravel lane to a bend at a tidy green cottage, then past the entrance to a large red-brick house signposted simply as 'The Cottage'. Here it meets another road leading to the car park for the upper lough at Glendalough and, all of a sudden, the iconic round tower of the monastic city is right in front of me and the pilgrim path has ended. My hotel room and a hot shower beckon, but I turn right into the impressive arched entrance and begin to explore the medieval wonders that adorn the site.

Here, Kevin turned his back on the world and came to live the life of a humble hermit. Yet the reputation of the monk spread. He was a scion of the noble Dál Messe Corb people who once ruled Leinster. He had been baptised by St Crónán of Roscrea, educated by St Petroc of Cornwall and lived a monastic life from the age of 12, while he studied with St Eoghan and made the acquaintance of Sts Comgall, Cannich and Ciarán of Clonmacnoise.[63] As he lay in his remote cave, perched high above the upper lough in his hermetic retreat, dressed in skins and living on a diet of nettles, herbs and the fish brought to him by a wild otter, others began to move to his Wicklow hideaway in hopes of learning. Eventually a monastery was established and he was inveigled into becoming its first abbot. Kevin's plan to build was thwarted by the local pagan king, who happened to have an ailing pet goose. Kevin suggested that he should be granted as much land as the goose could fly over and the pagan agreed, confident that the dying bird could barely flap its wings. However, Kevin miraculously cured the goose, which then flew over the entire valley. For his part, Kevin lived to the venerable old age of 120.

4.00 p.m.
A leisurely stroll through the monastic city that surrounds Ireland's best-preserved round tower takes in the cathedral and a couple of the seven churches for which the glen is famous. Most of the monastic buildings date from the eleventh and twelfth centuries, the heyday of the European pilgrimage.[64] A footbridge over to the road that goes along the south of the valley is closed, so I double back and set off on the road for the upper lough, past the hostel, before gaining access to the pedestrian path that crosses the marshy ground in a studded wooden walkway. The sweep of the near shore at the upper lough is well developed, with a car park and a cluster of buildings, which are closed for the season – except (thankfully) the public toilets.

Here and there, people walk along the shore of the lake, but there is no access to the lonely hermitage of Kevin, in a cave perched high on a crag further along the shore of the lake. Called St Kevin's Bed, it was from here that the saintly misogynist is said to have hurled the seductive maiden identified by the Dubliners song as 'Kathleen from over the way' into the rock-strewn waters below, in his determination to preserve his chastity even at the expense of her life. Indeed, the patron of Ireland's most populous archdiocese comes across as an irascible and antisocial individual who shunned society and is mostly identified with animals and wild birds. Legends about his miraculous exchanges with these creatures portray him as the St Francis of Assisi of Ireland, although he falls far short of the Italian in social graces. Yet the legacy of the holy place he founded in Glendalough is a lasting shrine and draws more visitors than any other sacred site on the Island of Saints and Scholars. As I wend my way back from the upper lough, many of these out-of-season visitors are congregating on the boardwalk, taking pictures of a couple of deer that have wandered out from the brush.

4.30 p.m.

Declining once more the attractions of a hot shower and nap before dinner, I pass the hotel and set off back up the road. A pilgrim's staff lies discarded at a wall alongside the river and I place it on top for use by another as I stride off back along the pilgrim path on which I arrived. Up the glen, a car is parked outside Teach Chaoimhín, the Catholic Youth Care retreat centre, so I knock and inform the man inside about the dead goat in the bothy up the way. In case any children from the centre should come upon it and be upset, I tell him. Then, retracing my steps up the causeway, I head back up into the wilderness of the Wicklow Gap, along the rough mountain path of St Kevin's Road to where my car is parked. In doing so I am making some amends for having not walked the central part of this heritage route. With the stretch in the day on a fine spring evening, I should be back at the hotel down below in plenty of time, and without the added concern of having to retrieve my car. Meanwhile, I am drawn back to the high vantage point that looks down into Glendasan Vale, the view that might have drawn Kevin to Glendalough. It shimmers in the dull light as the day recedes and the words of W.B. Yeats seem most appropriate:

*What motion of the sun or stream*
*Or eyelid shot the gleam*
*That pierced my body through?*
*What made me live like those that seem*
*Self-born, born anew?*[65]

# CHAPTER 8

# IN THE FOOTSTEPS OF PATRICK

## The Slemish pilgrimage

*Wednesday, 17 March 2010*

On St Patrick's Day each year, pilgrims flock to the Ulster-Scots heartland of north Antrim. Just beyond Broughshane, to the east of Ballymena, they walk in a steady procession that starts early and finishes in the late afternoon. They walk in the footsteps of a boy slave taken in captivity and exiled far from home among people who did not share his faith. From the age of 16, as Patrick himself recounts in his *Confessio*, he herded pigs and prayed for deliverance. Here on the slopes of Slemish, the annual trek on 17 March is a modern procession of families, couples, friends, schoolchildren and lone pilgrims. They come without any formal organisation in a spontaneous act of devotion to Ireland's patron saint, or simply for a healthy ramble to mark the day that's in it. Since I first undertook the ascent of Slemish – for the second reason – about 10 years ago, its popularity has revived considerably and the peripheral organisation has improved a lot. Yet the inherent sanctity of the Slemish pilgrimage is rooted in its lack of formality and the huge sense of enjoyment and fun experienced by the participants. But it also brings a stark reminder of a boy who endured extreme hardship before his escape, yet who overcame any residual grievance to come again among the people who had treated him so cruelly and offer them the hope of eternal salvation in Christ.

On a glorious early morning drive through Tyrone's Glenelly Valley in the heart of the Sperrin Mountains, through south Derry and across the Bann, past the huge Cistercian Monastery of Portglenone, I come into Paisley country and am struck by the glaring contrast between the residual simple faith of pilgrimage and organised religion. The radio is dominated by the fallout from revelations that Cardinal Seán Brady, primate of all Ireland, administered oaths of secrecy 35 years ago to two young victims of child sex predator Brendan Smyth, who continued his criminal abuse as a Catholic priest for two decades. Radio host Pat Kenny tells me that Cardinal Brady has been greeted by spontaneous applause at Mass in the cathedral of Patrician Armagh and I feel a pang of despair that a wrongdoing against innocent children is exonerated by blind obedience. On air, I hear the strident condemnation by Mary Doherty, founder of the lobby group Renew, of those who would dare to question the church or its leaders. Then, in contrast, I am heartened by the humble homily of the cardinal, who admits that he has failed. From such repentance, atonement may have a chance. The lengthy radio segment ends as I drive up the final approach to Slemish. I am directed from a small checkpoint to parking facilities nearby.

11.00 a.m.
I slip into the packed car park at Buckna Presbyterian Church just as the traffic marshal hauls the gates closed; the cars still arriving are now being directed to park on the other side. I slip into a space beside crush barriers that provide an access passage to the front of the church, where £1.50 tickets are dispensed for the return bus trip to the mountain. A friendly marshal tells me they expect up to four thousand to climb the mountain today and advises me that complimentary tea and refreshments are available in the church hall. When he tells me that long queues built up for the shuttle bus last year, I decide to forgo the tea for now. Within minutes, I am travelling along the small country roads from the townland of Ballyligpatrick to Carnstroan, with Slemish straight ahead. A squat peak of about 400 metres high, Slemish rises above the Antrim plateau rather like Uluru in central Australia. Rather than parched desert, however, it is in a yellowed early spring landscape that is beginning to don its mantle of green. Formed about 350 million years ago of a rock called dolerite, Slemish is a volcanic plug that cooled much more slowly than the basalt surrounding it, leaving it alone and stark in the landscape. Ancient people might have assumed an otherworldly presence on Slemish because of its dominance. More than other Irish hills and mountains, it seems to invite spontaneous climbers. It was here, we have been told, that the boy Patrick was taken as a captive slave to herd pigs for Milchu.

Our small bus packed with pilgrims passes along narrow roads bounded by dry-stone walls, bounding fields to the right with an ancient rath and a patch of ground known locally as the Swine Craes, in memory of the pigs tended by the boy saint below the brow of Slemish. Patrick failed to specify the place of his captivity in his own writing, giving rise to claims that it may have been in Mayo. However, both of his earliest biographers, Muirchú and Tíreachán, writing independently in the seventh century, named Slemish as the place. As renowned Patrician scholar Bishop Joseph Duffy comments:

> *...there is no reason why they should have mistaken or falsified a place-name which would have impressed itself on Patrick's converts and had no other significance, either for the prestige of the church of Armagh or as a pagan place of worship like Croagh Patrick.*[66]

He is said to have tended sheep or goats on the slopes of Slemish, sheltering from the icy winds of winter in the caves to the south-west, yet rising daily to worship God in a zealous conversion to the faith he had previously neglected before and during his early captivity.

11.30 a.m.

The zeal of conversion is still a moving force at Slemish Visitor Centre, where pilgrims disembark from the shuttlebus services from Buckna and from the ECOS Centre in Ballymena. Just beyond the facilities pavilion and a big fast-food vending van called Philadelphia, a divided walkway leads to the entrance and exit of the slopes. Two men guard the far end of this channel, handing leaflets to those going through. One document is a small booklet by Dick Keogh called 'St Patrick: the Shamrock, the Snakes, the Sacrifice'. It is published by the Cherith Gospel Outreach Trust with an address in Thurles, County Tipperary. The other is an invitation to the Special Spring Gospel Mission at Ballymena Free Presbyterian Church on Lord's Day, 11 April. It is wrapped around another leaflet from the Free Presbyterian Church, published by the Revival Movement Association: 'In a world without direction, certainty, hope, consider Christ, only saviour now and forever.' The man with the Free Presbyterian leaflets greets me warmly as I come through, bearing my pilgrim's staff.

'You're well geared up for it,' he remarks warmly, 'with your stick and all.'

From the portal to the base of the mountain, we move in a steady stream across the uneven ground, helped here and there by the rough steps. Then the climb begins and, unlike Croagh Patrick and most other Irish mountains, which have a reasonably gentle gradient to start, Slemish is a real climb virtually the entire way up. The 'path' is more like a challenging stairway to heaven, with footholds spaced far apart. It is an almost vertical ascent. Yet those of us who are climbing do so in a hugely congenial atmosphere. People encourage each other; men gallantly boost those less able and offer a hand to pull others up the most difficult parts. At various points, the heather and bracken provide the only aid. Pilgrims grab it in clumps to haul their bodies up over another precipice. Here and there, people pause for breath and take in the increasingly impressive views back out over the land below, well beyond Ballymena town, about eight miles distant. On a small outcrop just above me, a woman admires this view with enthusiasm. Her male companion, still climbing, calls up, 'Aye, we should build a house here, Donna.'

The frequent pauses while others negotiate difficult bits means that the pace is reasonable and each small section of the climb has a bonus payoff in a wider vista and closer proximity to the summit. Two smiling men are holding a big yellow banner, while another cradles a guitar. The banner says, 'John 3:7'

'Know what it means?' one of them calls to me.

'Aye – "You must be born again …"' I reply, impressed by my own recall.

'You believe it?' he shouts back.

'Of course – it's why I'm here,' I assert as I stride off above them and out of hearing.

The banter is friendly, often in the musical accent of north Antrim and Derry and an array of GAA and rugby tops is on display. A young girl in a sweatshirt identifying St Paul's Primary School wears a huge green top hat in honour of the day and enjoys the admiration of people she passes along the way. A group of young male students strides along at the centre of attention. Two are dressed as St Patrick, in flowing green robes and lime-coloured bishop's mitre hats. Both are barefoot and grinning as they pose here and there for photos.

11.40 a.m.

The entire ascent has taken just over half an hour, and the summit of Slemish offers great views, although nothing compared to those of a clear summer's day. One of several marshals on duty up here for Ballymena Borough Council says, 'On a really clear day you can see Scotland off there and the Antrim coast.' He points to the east and north. 'And down that way,' he continues, sweeping around to the west and south, 'you can see the Mournes, and across Lough Neagh beyond the Sperrins to the hills of Donegal.' Even with a limited range today, clusters of pilgrims take in the views at various rocky outcrops as the steady stream of new arrivals comes over the crest. A man and woman arrive; he heads straight for two marshals, smiles and calls out to them in a Belfast accent, 'So where's our certificates for making it up here?'

There is a lot of good-humoured banter in the glow of achievement. Pilgrims scurry from one vantage point to another in the formidable breeze, pose for photos and enjoy snacks before regrouping with their belongings and heading off along the flat summit, where metal stakes with red-and-white tape ribbons have been driven into the heather. At the southern end, another marshal directs us down the path. It is an eminently sensible system, introduced since my last time up here, when those descending had to negotiate their way around the climbers. But even with the one-way traffic, the way down is almost as challenging as the ascent – a steep path of footholds just wide enough to jam a boot into. Already the soft boggy earth between the crags is well churned, adding to the treachery of slippery patches. Just below the summit, I step into such a patch below me and end up in a sitting position. I grab a clump of heather to rise again. Ahead of me, the young girl in the green top hat takes a practical approach, advising her mother how to negotiate a particularly difficult bit: 'Get down on your bum,' she calls out happily. 'It's the only way to do it – right down in the muck.' Her mother skirts around, looking for an alternative, as I pick my own way gingerly past them. Finally, the slope bottoms out and, with a running bound, I am back on earth, noting that the people around me are much the same group as those who accompanied me on the climb. I wonder if any of them have been touched by the benign God who spoke to Patrick on the summit of Slemish, where he went to pray many times during the day, 'even in times of snow, frost or rain'. As he did so, he wrote, 'More and more [his] love of God and reverence for Him began to increase.'[67]

12.00 noon.

The descent takes exactly half the time of the climb and we filter in a raggle-taggle procession back to the Slemish Visitor Centre, where hordes of new pilgrims are arriving and moving towards the hill. A group of teenage boys is cavorting around the rocky path. One takes a headlong dash at a rocky promontory, then jumps and somersaults before landing on a patch of grass between boulders. His onlookers express cool applause, then lope off in case they might be expected to match the move. I am struck by the notion that they are about the age Patrick was when he was brought here as a slave. He turned to prayer to sustain him during the five years he spent working on the slopes of Slemish for Milchu, but perhaps he had his moments of madcap amusement as he chased stray livestock.

12.20 p.m.

Pilgrim visitors, including a group from Kildare who had been on the summit an hour ago, study the big information boards in the small, modern Slemish Visitor Centre. Outside, family groups sit at picnic tables eating snacks from the van and there is a constant flow to and from the small mountain. I answer queries from a young man with a clipboard, carrying out a survey for Ballymena Borough Council; then a young woman comes along with a similar questionnaire as I wait for the shuttle bus. They want to know if I could suggest any improvements to the site. I urge as little development as possible to retain the integrity of Slemish, but I suspect somebody will be looking for commercial return from tourism. I chat to a middle-aged couple from Toome as we board the bus and on the journey back to Buckna. They do the climb together every St Patrick's Day.

'It's a tradition and I hope we can keep doing it for a long time yet,' she remarks.

We disembark at the Presbyterian Church, where a big queue of over a hundred people waits to scale Slemish in honour of a boy slave who became a saint. It's a tradition, you see.

1.40 p.m.
On a 90-minute drive south through Ballyclare, Belfast and Saintfield, news comes through of St Patrick's Day celebrations throughout the world. I reflect on the Irish experience of emigration. For a nation that has been subject to so much enforced exile, it is almost exclusively those who remained, or those who took a few years overseas then returned home to settle down, who most often and vocally articulate our understanding of emigration. Having lived for more than a decade in Canada, I know the pain of realising that there is no going back. I know that this day marks a brief interlude in the year when we celebrate our Irishness together – even in Toronto, where St Patrick's Day celebrations were prohibited by a city by-law inspired by the Orange Lodge until the year after I moved there in 1987. That was the legacy of the Belfast of North America, as it was dubbed. As I drive through the original Belfast, I muse that we have moved a huge distance from the days when the 17th of March was just another workday in a Protestant state for a Protestant people. My drive brings me to the ancient cathedral town of Downpatrick, where huge crowds are gathering for the annual St Patrick's Day parade. I skirt the town centre, however, and take a diversion for Saul and the hamlet of Raholp beyond. Here a huge statue of Patrick, said to be the biggest in the world, dominates the drumlin landscape from the highest hill, called Slievepatrick. I am guided by frequent and clear signage for the St Patrick's Day walk and end up in the expansive but almost packed car park. This is the cusp of the very heartland of Patrician Ireland, a place that was once renowned for pilgrimage from all over Christendom, and today it is the very start of St Patrick's Way, an 18-kilometre hike. The more widely promoted St Patrick's Trail is a driving route of almost 148 kilometres. It also starts here and follows

a waymarked road through Downpatrick and south-west through Castlewellan, before entering the mighty Mournes and continuing down to Newry, then sweeping back up to the cathedral city of Armagh, the primatial see established by the patron saint.

Patrick's remains lie in the grounds of Down Cathedral, where those of Brigid and Colmcille are also reputed to be. It was here that Patrick began his mission among the Irish, and it was here that it ended. While in captivity, Patrick had a vision from God telling him to escape. After some travails, he made it home among his own people.[68] But, he tells us, he had further visions of the people of Ireland calling him to come among them once more. So, after rudimentary training at Auxerre in Gaul, he was ordained as a deacon and as a bishop not long after, possibly when news came of the death of Palladius, who had been sent by the pope to convert the Irish in AD 432. Patrick would be his successor; he was quickly elevated by St Germanus, who had himself been consecrated bishop directly from the laity in AD 418.[69]

Now in his mid-thirties, in the footsteps of Palladius, but with more than a rudimentary knowledge of the Irish and their tongue, Patrick embarked on his mission. It is believed that he first landed at the mouth of the River Vartry in Wicklow, but sailed off again, trying to get to Antrim. His ship sailed north along the coast but was driven by high winds and currents into Strangford Lough. Patrick sailed up the Slaney River and landed at Raholp.

2.15 p.m.

Today's walk, organised by Down District Council and the local Lecale Ramblers walking club, offers a magnificently signposted main route that totals all of 23.35 kilometres, according to the registration advisory material. For beginners and novices there are shortcuts and diversions, making the walk as short as 6.85 kilometres. Unfortunately, registration has closed for the walks that officially started at 10.30 a.m. and many who have already completed the route are clambering into cars and heading for home. I notice cars from Dublin and Westmeath. Undaunted, I decide to set out on my own. A man I ask for directions hands me his route map with detailed instructions, telling me that I am now at point 1 and point 30, the start and finish. I should go that way, he says, pointing down the hill. So off I go, against the flow of weary walkers. I notice most are wearing hiking gear, unlike most of those who clambered up Slemish earlier, who wore everything from town shoes to wellingtons. I set a brisk pace in a bid to finish as much of the walk as possible while daylight lasts, which should give me about four and a half hours. On the map, I notice a section where I can take a handy shortcut along Ballyhornan Road and cut out about 4 kilometres of the route. As I trudge down along St Patrick's Road into Raholp, I receive friendly greetings from those completing the route.

'You're going the wrong way!' they call out to me helpfully, one after the other. I smile and tell them I'm just being contrary.

2.40 p.m.

The route takes off to the left along a small narrow laneway opposite Roneystown Road, turning right, then left, going over a stile, along the side of a field to the brow of a hill, where it picks up a waymarked trail again leading to a stile and out onto and across Strangford Road. From there, it follows Myra Road for a short distance before branching off again to the left into another small lane, where we meet the narrow Slaney River, then through a farmyard and onto the shore of Strangford Lough. Legend has it that when Patrick landed here, he was spotted by a slave boy, who summoned his master, a chieftain called Dichu. Dichu rushed with hound and sword to challenge the interloper. Patrick calmed Dichu's hound by chanting a psalm and converted the master, who was suitably impressed.[70]

3.20 p.m.

Along the foreshore and a mucky laneway, the route skirts a swamp and a couple of inlets separated by low hills, until we come to Castle Island; the castle in ruins and the island joined to the mainland. Here we meet the Castle Island Road, which takes us down to Lisboy Road, at the end of which we re-cross Strangford Road into Saul Mills Road. A short distance further along we cross the busier Mearne Road and move up the brae to the arched entrance of St Patrick's Memorial Church, the most ancient Christian ecclesiastical site in Ireland. I now realise that, while negotiating the Mearne Road, I have missed the short diversion to the well in a private garden there. This is where, legend has it, Patrick produced a fountain out of the earth through prayer, and it was here that the earliest baptisms were conducted. The very first was that of the daughter of Dichu, who then donated his barn for a place of worship. The barn stood on the very spot where the church was built, a 1933 reconstruction of a small stone church with a round-tower belfry, , designed by Henry Seaver of Belfast and built to mark the 1,500th anniversary of Patrick's arrival.

The church's setting is tranquil and resonates with the sanctity of its ancient origins, bathed in a gentle light from the stained-glass window carrying a representation of the Apostle of Ireland. Outside, where the only cross of St Patrick flag I have seen all day flies proudly for his feast day, the grounds are packed with graves and remnants of the great abbey that once stood here. A notable feature is the small stone cell with a vaulted roof, similar to structures found at other ancient Irish monastic sites. Another, similar cell here has been rendered with plaster.

There are excellent information boards in the church entrance hall. I am particularly struck by the salutation and blessing for those who visit:

> *Go forth, traveller, in the Name which is above every name: be of good courage; hold fast that which is good; render to no man evil for evil; strengthen the faint-hearted; support the weak; help the afflicted; honour all men; love and serve the Lord, rejoicing in the power of the Holy Spirit. And may the blessing of the eternal God – the Father, the Son and the Holy Spirit – be upon you in your going out and your coming in.*

Fortified by that, I set off again in the footsteps of the patron.

4.15 p.m.
From the first church in Saul, the pilgrimage route goes along Slievegrane Hill for a couple of kilometres, before turning sharply right onto busy Ballyhornan Road. The traffic on this small country road seems to be comprised solely of big cars. With roadside hedges trimmed neatly in time for spring growth, there is also a profusion of litter, a far cry from typical Ulster admiration of 'Protestant hedges'. I note the waning of that civic propriety, or the on-the-spot fines, that once kept roads and streets here relatively litter-free compared to further south. The concentration of litter from a particular fast-food outlet, moreover, would make this a suitable site

– with others throughout the country – for a study of how long a brand-name burger lasts before car occupants pitch the wrapping out of the car window. Luckily, the route veers into a side road with no litter and I come upon a more idyllic pastoral scene, with farmers on both sides of the road winnowing ploughed fields in the spring sunshine promise of a harvest in time. A short distance along, the trail turns into a well-paved side road, running past a handsome country house and a sign for Struell Wells.

If Saul's atmospheric church invoked the spirit of Patrick, this idyllic haven more than complements it. Struell's four holy wells are set in a neatly walled enclosure between craggy hills and surrounded by trees. An open area leads the pilgrim past a paved apron and the foundation walls of a church that was never completed. The first well inside a beehive stone structure is accessed from the rear, through it has now been closed off by a secure grilled gate. Beside it, windows from a medieval church have been encased in the stone wall, like small confessional portals. This well is known simply as the Healing Well, though all four at Struell are said to have strong healing powers. A stile gate in the wall takes the pilgrim into a considerable expanse of lawn with park seats and, right in the middle, another stone-encased well with a beehive-style roof. This is the Eye Well; again, it has since been secured with an iron-grille gate.

The setting is ideal for a snack, and I drain my flask as a couple stroll around with an older woman in their wake.

'It's very interesting, isn't it?' the older woman remarks as she passes to join the others outside the enclosure.

'Yes, and very serene,' I add.

I pick up my belongings and stroll over to the concentration of buildings on the far side. These are the bathhouses where pilgrims bathed in the blessed waters that were sanctified by Patrick himself. Tradition says that the Struell Wells – the name derived from an tSruthail (the Stream) – were already places of pilgrimage in pre-Christian times. On his arrival in this district, once known as Lecale, Patrick spent nights chanting psalms before bathing in the waters, thereby channelling all the spiritual properties associated with the wells to the honour and glory of the one true God.

Written accounts of pilgrimage here date only from medieval times. There are several records of great crowds gathering here for the ritual pilgrimages from 1306 until the nineteenth century. The penitential ritual of the pilgrims to Struell Wells involved circling all the wells and cairns and the Penitential Ring, seven times on the knees, sometimes carrying a large stone.[71] The penitent then sits on the Chair of St Patrick, a natural feature in the craggy outcrop looming over the enclosure, where St Patrick is said to have spent nights between his prayers. The pilgrim turns three times, being careful to turn from left to right, and follows this with prayers at the altar on the south side-wall of the ancient chapel, before concluding the pilgrimage by bathing in the wells. In the mid nineteenth century, thousands of pilgrims flocked to the wells at a time when the Irish Roman Catholic Church was clamping down on traditional pilgrimages that incorporated many pagan practices. God, in the guise of his minister on this part of the earth, was affronted by the fact that the male and female pilgrims who flocked to Struell Wells bathed in the same facility. Even though the pilgrims were not cavorting in a communal bath, the local priest prevailed on Protestant grandee Lady Cromwell to build a second and much larger bathhouse for the men, with a sunken bath, allowing full immersion. The women were consigned to the back of the block for changing and their bath, or shower, was taken under the original stream, gushing from a hole about a metre up the wall. While modesty was thus preserved, clerical interference caused pilgrim numbers to plummet. They continued to decline as the Church Triumphant took control of all aspects of spiritual worship and public behaviour.

4.30 p.m.
As I make some last-minute notes about Struell Well, I meet one of the organisers of the St Patrick's Day walk. John Quinn, secretary of the Lecale Ramblers, expresses his concern when he finds out that I am taking up the rearguard. When I assure him that I plan to complete as much of the route as possible, we consult the map. He cautions against my plan to double back to the Ballyhornan Road, pointing to a note on the map printed in bright red: 'Short-circuiting the Walk between points 15 and 22 is NOT RECOMMENDED due to the Danger posed by Fast Traffic, Blind Bends and Lack of Verges.' As a compromise, I take up his offer of a lift to Ballyalton, thereby cutting off a circuit that would have brought me nearer the town centre of Downpatrick and the Magh Innis (Island of the Plain) of Lecale, where Patrick carried out much of his ministry. John assures me I will still experience 'a marvellous part of the route'. Having spent months preparing the waymarkers and signage, he should know. So between stops for signs, which are bundled into the back seat, he tells me that the March 17 walk has been taking place for 20 years through this locality, steeped in the lore of Patrick and sought out by pilgrims for centuries. He leaves me off at the designated spot and I wish him happy trails as I climb over a stile and set off along the path of Patrick once more.

As I step along a small lane bounded by hedges and dry-stone walls, it is obvious that this indeed is the crowning glory of the St Patrick's Way. There is Slievenagriddle to my right, with its Neolithic chambered grave, and far off to my left and ahead is the huge statue of Patrick with his hand raised in blessing. Almost a kilometre along the route, the road forks and, mindful of John's warning to resist the temptation of going straight ahead towards Slievepatrick, I veer to the right and continue on my way over a couple of stiles towards Ballystokes.

5.30 p.m.
Having come through a farmyard and past a few houses, the trail swings down the lower southern slopes of Slievepatrick to the beautiful shores of Lough Money, a reservoir with a small building perched out on an island reached by a causeway. The road to the island is blocked off by a gate, but the trail leads on to the north shore, with trees to the left and the higher ground of Carrowvanny to the right. A short diversion here, I learn from my map, will bring me to another chambered-grave site and the Long Stone; this is included in the featured St Patrick's Way. However, anxious to complete the route at its highest point before the daylight fades, I press on through a number of gates and the Hamptons farm, then along another walking trail between high dry-stone walls with the roots of ancient trees growing up from the pavement, until it opens up into Roneystown and thence into St Patrick's Road in Raholp once more, just opposite where I headed down to the shoreline earlier. A right turn down the hill and up the far side would bring me to Bannaghan and the ruins of the church that marks the spot where St Tassach administered the last rites to his friend and mentor Patrick on this day just shy of 1,600 years ago.

Legend has it that when Patrick died he left instructions that his corpse was to be sent off in a car drawn by two unbroken oxen. The beasts were taken from Clogher, on the Strangford shore just beyond Castle Island, and bore the saint's mortal remains until they stopped in Magh Innis. That is where Patrick was buried. Occupying that spot, the magnificent Church of Ireland cathedral, where the remains of Brigid and Colmcille were also taken for their eternal rest, now presides over the town.

6.15 p.m.
Up the hill in Raholp, past the old school and the GAA club's grounds, the entrance to Slievepatrick has a small car park and a lodge painted white with green and saffron trimmings. Inside the gate, the pedestrian way begins with a notice that the erection of this monument marked the 1,500$^{th}$ anniversary of Patrick's landing at Saul on foot of a suggestion by local men Joe Smyth, William Taggart and Bill McMullan. The 10-acre site was 'freely' given by T.J. Hampton. At the time it was called Slievewilliam. It was renamed and consecrated Slievepatrick on 17 March 1932.

Just beyond this, the path to the top features the first of a series of simple wooden crosses, marking a symbolic road to Calvary. Up through a narrow channel of parkland bounded by trees, across a footbridge over a small country road, and then opening up into a wider expanse with a Fátima grotto to the left (put there for some bizarre reason as a 'millennium project' in 2000), a crucifixion scene nestles in a hollow. Above it is the uncultivated higher mount on which the giant statue of the patron presides, his left hand gripping his crozier and his right raised in benediction. At 10 metres high, the statue is an imposing presence up close. Its pedestal offers a magnificent view over the surrounding terrain and the route I have just walked. To the north, the coast of Strangford Lough is still clearly visible in the fading light; to the east and south, the drumlin hills stretch off into the distance, with the waters of Lough Money just visible in the foreground. To the west, meanwhile, lie the outskirts of Downpatrick and closer still the round tower of the reconstructed first church at Saul. Just below it is a pub called Paddy's Barn, named in honour of the barn donated by Dichu for the first church.

As I wend my way back down Slievepatrick, I am amused at the thought that the modern celebration of Ireland's patron saint, who landed here in AD 432 to quench a thirst for eternal salvation, is conducted around the world in places like Paddy's Barn.

9.00 p.m.
After a brief courtesy visit to Down Cathedral, where a huge boulder marks the otherwise simple grave of Patrick and his fellow saints, I make my way through the streets of the town still recovering from its big parade. The pubs are heaving with revellers as family groups head home in a snarl of traffic, past a deserted shopfront named the Room of Prayer. Out on the road, I follow the designated St Patrick's Trail south and west through Clough and Castlewellan and into the Mournes. Near the Long Island Reservoir in Slievenalargy, someone has set fire to the brush on Tullynasoo Mountain. It burns in the evening dusk like Patrick's fire on the Hill of Slane gone out of control. I travel through Hilltown and Mayobridge, skirting Newry and on to the ecclesiastical centre of Irish Christianity, which poet John Montague in his 1993 collection, *Time in Armagh*, called a 'maimed capital, a damaged pearl'.[72]

The small city is also in the aftermath of another of today's countless parades, hyped events where pride in Patrick is expressed with inflatable shillelaghs and grotesque Mardi Gras masks. It has become a patched-up hooley modelled on New York and Rio de Janeiro, barely recognisable from the desultory cavalcades of my childhood, when parades were for Protestants and we squirmed in embarrassment for the Americans who came in shiny green jerkins to 'see the original'. They ended up, if they were lucky, watching their own high-school bands high-stepping past Dublin's GPO as we made our way to Croke Park for the Railway Cup football final and an expected Ulster victory.

The church holiday has virtually disappeared in the excess of secular celebrations, which always seemed more appropriate when conducted abroad. Yet the thirst for the annual piss-up seems unquenchable, with St Patrick's festivals lasting a week or more. In cities, towns and villages, 'traditional' celebrations are built on the template of a new, secular Ireland and even our ageing emigrants, who once were the focus of attention, slip into the shadows of another 'me-too' event.

Further along my road, past the ancient mound of Eamhain Mhacha (Navan Fort), the small Armagh village of Killylea celebrates with an evening parade of 40 loyalist bands. This is a recent attempt by Ulster Protestantism to stake a claim to the missionary from Britain who brought the message of Christianity to our shores. I head on for west Tyrone and wonder what next – the Presbyterians of north Antrim treating us to tea and traybakes after a healthy hike up Slemish?

# CHAPTER 9

# FIRST STEPS IN THE NAME OF CHRIST

## St Declan's Way

Emerging from the Fountain bed and breakfast in the heart of Ardmore village on a bright morning in early April, I barely make it across the street before I have my first pilgrimage encounter. A man greets me and enquires if I am 'off walking'. I tell him I am setting off on St Declan's Road. 'All the way to Cashel?' he enquires. I explain that I am doing the Heritage Council route as far as Lismore, still a good day's hike of 30 kilometres. My new acquaintance then informs me that I will be passing by the very door of his home place near the banks of the River Lickey. His great-great-grandfather settled there when he moved down from Cavan to pick potatoes around the time of the Great Famine and I will recognise the house from its distinctive gates. 'In my family we always made our own gates and our own headstones,' Micheál Ó Rathaille informs me proudly. As I turn for the road ahead I reflect that, even though they moved far from Cavan, his family lost none of their instinct for building strong gates to hold onto what wealth they amassed and ensure it wasn't frittered away on fancy headstones at the latter end.

The ancient pilgrimage path of St Declan's Way has the notable distinction of traversing the first district in Ireland to embrace the message of Christ. Into this ancient district of the south coast, known as the Déise, Declan brought the news of eternal salvation through the Gospel in AD 415, long before Patrick's mission began in the far north-east. What he lacked, obviously, was a good public-relations campaign and strong political lobbyists. Otherwise we would be parading hither and yon for St Declan's Day on July 24 and there would hardly be a peep on March 17 for the foreign interloper.

For Declan was of one of the great noble families of ancient Ireland, a scion of Eochaidh Feidhleach, who claimed the high kingship of Ireland for a period of 12 years and was followed by 'one hundred and seven kings of their race and kindred', according to the *Betha Decclain*, the ancient account of Declan's life. This records his father as Erc Mac Trein and asserts that Declan was sanctified in the womb and 'was given by God as a prophet to the pagans for the conversion of multitudes of them from heathenism and the misery of unbelief to the worship of Christ and to the Catholic faith.'[73] Baptised by Colman, he was carefully schooled from an early age, spending a long time with Díoma in preparation for his mission. He then went to Rome, where he was consecrated a bishop by Pope Hilarius and sent home to Ireland to preach the Gospel. On his way back across the continent with a retinue of disciples, who included Runan, son of the king of Rome, Declan met Patrick. The latter was going to Rome, where he too would be consecrated bishop, this time by the new pope, Celestine, and also sent to preach to the Irish. The two men 'made a league and bond of mutual fraternity and kissed in token of peace.'

On his arrival in Ireland, Declan became one of four 'holy bishops' who preached the word of God before Patrick's arrival. The others were Ailbhe, Ciarán and Ibar. Declan brought his mission to his own people in the Déise, where he was:

> *...wise like a serpent and gentle like a dove and industrious like the bee, for as the bee gathers honey and avoids the poisonous herbs so did Declan, for he gathered the sweet sap of grace and Holy Scripture till he was filled therewith.*[74]

Yet none of these early missionaries has the renown of Patrick, who was the first to 'turn chiefs and kings of Ireland to the way of baptism, faith and sacrifice and everlasting judgment.'[75] To illustrate the point, the *Betha Decclain* recounts the story of Declan's visit to Aongus MacNatfrich, the king of Cashel. While allowing the missionary to preach the Gospel, the king declined to accept the faith on the grounds that Declan was of the Déise, rivals of his people, the Eóghanacht. However, when Patrick arrived in Munster, Aongus 'went from his own city of Cashel to meet him, professed Christianity and was immediately baptized.'[76] Aongus clearly saw no problem with conversion by Patrick, 'a man who was of British race against which the Irish cherished no hate.' However, before leaving Munster, Patrick bestowed his blessing on his brother bishops by naming 'Humble Ailbhe the Patrick of Munster, greater than any saying, [and] Declan, Patrick of the Déise – the Déise to Declan for ever.'[77]

Declan's life then centred on the monastic city that grew near his *díseart* or hermitage, comprising his first oratory and cell beside a holy well on the cliffs of Ardmore. It was on this scenic headland, which legend holds had been an island before Declan rolled back the waves, that his mission began. The place had been indicated by the landing place of a rock that had carried Declan's miraculous bell from Wales after a follower had omitted to take it on board their ship. It is here that the devotion to the Patrick of the Déise has continued down the centuries. Reverend Professor Power notes in his introduction to the translation of the *Betha Decclain* that Declan is honoured with a pattern week of devotions, rather than the traditional pattern day accorded to other Irish saints.

The nature of the devotions and festivities surrounding St Declan has changed as much as they have ebbed and flowed down the years. According to an excellent booklet, produced in 1979 by local teacher, historian and enthusiast Siobhán Lincoln, there is a gathering at the well at midnight on 23 July and the 'rounds' are done, but the principal gathering is on Pattern Sunday, the Sunday nearest to 24 July.[78] Pilgrims continue to come throughout the following week, but not at all to the extent that they did in former days. However, the booklet also quotes at length from a first-hand account of the pattern celebrations in Ardmore by 'a gentleman of high attainments and undoubted veracity', which had been given to Mr and Mrs L.C. Hall, who toured Ireland in 1838 and 1840:

> *The crowd then formed a long line winding up the narrow path that leads along the mountain's brow to St Declan's Chapel … The scenery was beautiful as we looked over the precipitous cliffs across the Bay of Ardmore. On the*

> *brink stands the remnants of a chapel, said to be the first built in Ireland. On entering the gate, on your right side is the well St Declan blessed; a narrow doorway leads to it … they knelt down to the well and said their prayers … at twenty different periods I counted the people as they passed; they averaged fifty-five a minute, which gives a total of 12,000 or 15,000 persons.*[79]

Meanwhile, down in the village:

> *…the tens, sixty-four in number are now complete. Eating, drinking, dancing occupy the multitude. One figure is walking about with a boiled leg of mutton and salt in one hand, a big knife in the other, vociferating 'a cut for a penny, a cut for a penny!' Here cheese and fish are selling, some tents contain gaming tables.*[80]

And later on:

> *…all now appears confusion, every man is drunk and every woman is holding a man back from the deadly combat; bloody knees from devotion and bloody heads from fighting are not uncommon … 25 July – Tents nearly struck; a few of the most devout remain to complete their devotions. Seven o'clock – all is still again and Ardmore is again a mere secluded village.*[81]

Siobhán Lincoln's booklet also notes: 'By 1831 numbers attending the Ardmore Pattern are said to have fallen greatly, due to the efforts of Fr McGrath, the local priest.'[82]

According to James T. Quain, the current St Declan's Church in the village was built while Fr Patrick McGrath was parish priest from 1836 to 1846. It is described as 'of the plain, spacious and substantial type characteristic of country churches of the second quarter of the last century.'[83] So, while he was suppressing the traditional pattern, Fr McGrath was hauling Catholic worship into line with the practices that would come to dominate a more puritanical expression of faith in the dark ages of the late nineteenth and twentieth centuries. However, the pattern continued to draw large numbers of pilgrims to Ardmore, as attested in 1914 by Revd Dr Power, who commented:

> *It is hardly too much to say that the Declan tradition in Waterford and Cork is a spiritual actuality, extraordinary and unique, even in a land which till recently paid special honour to its local saints.*[84]

Writing in the 1960s, Daphne Pochin Mould reported, 'Since 1951, the spectacular revival of interest in Declan's well at Toor has shown that this very early saint is still a force in the contemporary sense.'[85] At that time, Ardmore was celebrating a 'a whole Pattern Week, with a variety of events, whilst in the church, the Forty Hours devotions are held, beginning or ending on St Declan's Day.' A reason for this revived devotion, Pochin Mould explained, may be connected to the 'plenary indulgence' attached to the 'Ardmore festival at the request of Doctor Sheehan, bishop of Waterford (1891–1915) and the then parish priest of Ardmore, Jon Walsh (1884–1901).'[86]

Whatever the draw then, one suspects that the crowds that flock to the Ardmore Pattern Festival today are not drawn entirely by the prospect of a plenary indulgence, but rather by the mighty craic surrounding the weekend event, which in 2010 will run from 23 to 25 July. According to the festival publicity, it will offer a feast of mostly free events ranging from open-air concerts to fireworks, sandcastles, fancy-dress competitions, art events, puppet shows, traditional storytelling, guided historical tours, discos, football blitzes, a flower festival, a busking competition, powerboat racing, kayaking, live music sessions, golf, a treasure hunt, teddy bears' picnics and much more. The modern festival was established in 2007 to revive the pattern, and has gained strength since as a family-based festival, with events organised by local community groups and organisations. So, almost 200 years after Fr McGrath tried to haul his parish into line with the new strictures of Irish Catholicism, they are still up for the craic along with the pattern prayers down in Ardmore.

*Wednesday, 7 April 2010*

The glorious sunshine of this Easter week notwithstanding, Ardmore's tourist office is closed until the season kicks off officially, so I call in to the tea shop at the bottom of the main street to ask about a map for the ancient pilgrimage route of Declan to Lismore. As the tea-shop owner goes off to look for a walking brochure, one of a couple of female customers says she knows precisely what I am looking for. She is fairly sure she has one she can let me borrow for my trek. Soon we are up at her home, where she rifles through leaflets and books, until she turns up the superb pilgrim map produced in the early 1990s by the Ardmore Co-operative Group.

'Now, I'll give you a loan of this,' Mary Moloney emphasises once more, 'but I do want it back because this is like gold dust.'

The walking guide has five trail maps with extensive annotation and other advice for the walking pilgrim. Mary tells me that her son used it as a leader of the group of local Boy Scouts who carried out a trek to relaunch the route almost 20 years ago. Not only that, but her husband, Jim Moloney, supervised the Waterford County Council crew that carried out preparatory work on the trail in this district. And as if to cap the trio of happy coincidences that I might not have found out about if the tourist-information office had been open, she runs a bed-and-breakfast guesthouse here. I am soon booked in for a couple of nights.

Within an hour, I am seated with Jim Moloney, who recounts in great detail his memories of the trail I will walk. He advises me on where to be careful and even mentions a particular part to avoid – he has been informed reliably in recent days that it is impassable because of the recent poor weather. The retired council foreman is also able to give a potted history of the route's revival, paying particular tribute to former county engineer J.D. Halley, whose enthusiasm overcame the reservations of many local landowners and sceptics. For Jim Moloney, the assertion of public rights of way is of paramount importance in preserving heritage and ensuring that the ancient path of Declan is open to pilgrims of the future.

'When J.D. Halley was the engineer, I used to have to inspect those rights of way on a regular basis to make sure they weren't interfered with,' Jim says. 'Anything like that should be reported to the authorities immediately.'

With an assurance that I would let him know of any impediments along the way, I receive his blessing, his son's map and a great breakfast from his wife to set me off on the ancient heritage route to the very first Christian settlement in the land.

*Thursday, 8 April 2010*
9.00 a.m.
After my initial encounter with Micheál Ó Rathaille as I set off on St Declan's Road, I crest the summit of the Bóthar Ard (High Road) and the land falls away gently from the townland

of Ballinamertina to Clais na Muc. In the far distance, the land rises again to the route of the N25 Cork-to-Waterford road, where I can already hear the morning traffic speeding along with cares and concerns far removed from the Christian mission that prompted Declan to leave his coastal redoubt for the heart of the Déise. Looking back, I see the sandy coastline and the headland punctuated by the ancient round tower that rises proudly from the monastic city, now a sea-side village resort. My borrowed map tells me that the road I have taken through the small coastal plain, below which I passed the local sports grounds of St Declan's GAA club and in an adjacent field saw men bent to the backbreaking task of planting carrots, is Bóthar na Trinse (Trench Road). The use of Irish is a worthy reminder that this district, close to Ring on Helvick Head, was still a vibrant Gaeltacht area until modern times. Its college instructed such august alumni as Maud Gonne MacBride and Éamon de Valera, not to mention generations of teachers who came to prepare for Ceard Teastas Gaeilge examinations of competency in the state's first official language. Peeping over the far side of Ardmore Headland is Youghal Bay, where the Blackwater flows into the Celtic Sea. I see a ship at anchor there, or is it moving very slowly? I intone a quiet prayer at a dog-leg turn in the road and pick up my pace for the route ahead.

10.00 a.m.

From Clais na Muc the trail continues to a crossroads, where the local primary school, Scoil Mhuire, has fallen quiet for the Easter break. There is a group of a dozen or more cottages in the adjacent Rian Ard Park. The original trail at this point goes over a small stream and down to meet the main road above Grange Creamery. Jim Moloney advises me, however, to continue on the road that emerges nearer Grange Church. Although I have spotted two of the distinctive pilgrim-path waymarkers, one was discarded in a pungent bank of wild garlic. Now, as traffic hurtles by on the N25, the walking pilgrim must figure it out for himself. At least I have the long-out-of-print pilgrim map as I divert down to the disused creamery, sold off recently by Glanbia, and search for the route entrance. All I find is an old wooden gate entangled in briars and brambles. I turn on my tracks and head back east as far as Grange Chapel and the adjacent post office on the brow of the hill, then turn left and head north again on the small country road. The old pilgrim path on the high ground beyond the stream to my left is called Bóthar na Riológ at this point and Jim Moloney says I will 'really miss nothing' by avoiding it in its swamped condition. Soon I arrive at Áth na Ceardchan, where the road comes to a T-junction, the right heading off towards Grallagh Bridge, the left towards Drumgullane. A small derelict cottage at the junction features distinctive gates, which I know immediately were wrought by the Ó Rathaille family, and my pilgrim path leads me down the back of the cottage.

I will later learn from Mary Lincoln, owner of the Ardmore Pottery and Craft Gallery, that a casual enquiry on her part the year before identified this part of the route. She was talking to the elderly woman who lived in the cottage and asked where the lane at the back led.

'That's the road to Cashel,' the woman said casually. Mary Lincoln, whose family has been deeply involved in promoting and preserving the heritage of Ardmore, points beyond the village and says, 'For her, that was just as natural as saying that's the road to Youghal. As far as she was concerned it was the road to Cashel and it went down the back of her house.'

On down the mucky lane, a second gate features a staggered entrance through concrete pillars and is set off with a fresh bloom of primroses. Here the path turns into a marvellous medieval road, descending through brush and woodland banks to a final recess. A sign points the pilgrim to the right, over a rivulet and on to a pedestrian wooden bridge across the River Lickey, which flows slowly through a channel between thickets of woodland. At the far side of the bridge, a laminated notice on a wooden post has been utterly defaced by someone who went to the trouble of scoring out the Irish wording printed in the old Gaelic typeface. I try to read it: '*I ndíl chuimhne ar Bhaillin, teachta Phádraig Naofa, a bádh …*'[87] From there the defacement renders the rest of the notice virtually unreadable, except for those who know of the wondrous miracle it commemorates. For in the *Betha Decclain*, we are told of how Patrick sent his disciple Ballin to Declan 'with power and authority', but he drowned here in the River Lickey. When Declan heard of this he rushed to the scene in his chariot, cried and prayed over Ballin, whose face was 'dark and deformed', then invoked the Holy Trinity to raise him from the dead. Ballin was revived and eventually fully recovered and returned to Patrick, who 'gave glory and thanks to God and the name of Declan was magnified'.[88] It is beyond comprehension why anybody would wish to obliterate a simple public notice recording a miraculous legend that is so important to the neighbouring parishes of Grange and Clashmore, which assisted public officials in preserving the beauty spot.

11.00 a.m.

From the northern bank of the River Lickey, where sturdy stepping-stones provide an alternative crossing to the footbridge, the land rises into the parish of Clashmore through the townland of Ballycurrane and a series of three crossroads before reaching a point marked simply on the guide map as 'Cross'. The title of the trail has reverted from Bóthar na Riolog to St Declan's Road and this path through the Drum Hills reveals a marvellous vista to the west towards Youghal and the Blackwater Valley. While scouting the trail yesterday, I visited the picturesque village of Clashmore on the Creagagh River, where the bridge crossing is part of the Gaeltacht Drive in west Waterford. I was trying to locate Geosh, which seemed a good place to stop for lunch. At a local shop I asked the man standing at the door if he was familiar with the area. He said he wasn't local, but he was running the shop. When the next customer walked in, he asked him about Geosh and the customer gave precise details in a strong English accent. Today, Clashmore, with its impressive Protestant church on the site of a monastery founded by St Mochua, a disciple of St Carthage of Lismore, remains a distant presence down in the valley from my pilgrim trail.

11.40 a.m.

So far, the trek has been along small country roads, with the sole exception of the 'Cashel Road' across the River Lickey. It continues through Cross and progresses up and down the gentle Drum Hills, until it emerges on the busier R671 road, at a point where the Creagagh River crosses the townland of Ballindrumma. My old guide map tells me I should see the ruins of an old mill, but all I can see are newly built homes. Then the trail goes down a boreen and through a farm gate onto a small path bounded by an electric fence. Behind the fence is a fairly large herd of cattle in a meadow enclosed into actual grids. Further along, the trail goes straight ahead, while a branch of the path veers right through the townland of Monagally. A strand of the electric fence impedes my path but, determined to assert the public right of way for my B&B hosts in Ardmore, I use my staff to raise the wire and scramble underneath. From there, the trail goes down past some farm buildings into another quite difficult phase, where I have to climb over a couple of padlocked gates and negotiate the path through neglected thickets of unkempt brambles bursting out from the hedgerows. Finally, I emerge onto another small country road that leads back down to the R671. Here a home-made fingerpost sign at the junction points up towards the holy well. This is Toor Well, which draws large numbers of pilgrim visitors during the pattern day of St Declan, but it is not on the itinerary of the pilgrim path and is a considerable diversion of 6 kilometres or more off the walking route.

According to Daphne Pochin Mould, the popularity of 'St Declan's Well' at Toor took off in 1951. The 'insignificant spring in the moors' had already enjoyed a long reputation for having the cure of skin diseases.

> *But the action of a grateful pilgrim, whose failing sight was greatly improved by the water, in donating a concrete setting, bathing place, oratory for Mass, and statues of Declan and Our Lady, has brought this small spring back into the public eye. Cures are claimed by a number of people, and an impressively large and devout crowd, either striding through the gorse and heather in summer dresses on a fine day, or standing doggedly in pouring rain, gather for the annual Mass at the well on or near St Declan's Day. None of the alleged cures have been investigated, for they run on the lines, highly satisfactory for the sufferer of 'I was sick and now I am well'. Mostly, as in all Irish patterns and wells, it would be difficult to get full documentation of cures, but the overall impression is that they do, one way or another, take place.*[89]

Although the fame of Toor Well has spread far and wide, and today's pilgrims are more likely to arrive by car down the small lane to commodious parking facilities than to stride through the gorse in summer dresses, it is not marked on the Ordnance Survey map. The elaborate facilities put in place by the grateful client 60 years ago are still there, as is a sign asking pilgrims not to bathe their sores in the main well, but in another outlet below the raised altar, where a bush is draped with rags and other offerings.

12.15 p.m.
I arrive down at the scenic bridge over the River Geosh well ahead of schedule, passing a sign with a photo of a rather ferocious canine and a warning to 'Beware of the Guard Dog'. This is at the entrance of a private property, where a cottage is complemented by a mobile home with three rather formidable attack dogs gambolling around in the open without any sign of restraint. I cross the bridge quickly, to be greeted on the other side by the furious barking of another dog, smaller but unseen and possibly restrained. This sets off the trio in my wake. I abandon thoughts of this lunchtime venue and, with an advisory phonecall back to Ardmore, decide to press on to Knocknascagh, over the next series of hills to the north.

This phase starts out very impressively, with clear signage pointing me off the main road and onto St Declan's Road, a wide footpath ascending a fairly steep brae that has recently been paved to make a comfortable, even walking surface. As I continue, the surface becomes less elaborate, first with a grassy track down the centre – a more authentic pavement – and then a rutted surface. Then, over an intersecting road and past a house, the right of way is blocked by a carefully constructed gateway. I make my way through to a part of the ancient lane where the field boundaries on my left become sparse, with gates to the farmland removed. A large herd of cattle is enclosed in the space that now includes the public right of way and I reassure myself by raising my pilgrim's staff to my shoulder. Another gate is padlocked, so I scramble over it onto a lane that is so deeply rutted that a stream of water cascades along its channels from the adjacent fields, possibly diverted thus to deter walkers. My way is also made difficult by untended bushes on both sides, which encroach on the path in a profusion of unbridled growth. I negotiate another bolted and padlocked gate ahead by making my way around it on the bank, cursing the deliberate sabotage of this ancient, holy pathway and calling on St Declan to protect the pilgrims on his trail. Then, just off to the west comes the toll of the Angelus bell from the nearby village. It is appropriately named Aglish (an Eaglais, meaning the Church). I mutter my prayers and suppress feelings of rage. Then I hear musical chimes from the same source, recognise the tune and sing along to the glorious refrain of the Easter hymn:

> *Jesus Christ is risen today, Alleluia,*
> *Our triumphant holy day, Alleluia;*
> *Who did once upon the cross, Alleluia,*
> *Suffer to redeem our loss, Alleluia.*[90]

Almost immediately, the lane opens out into a comfortable expanse with a fairly sandy surface. At the next juncture, I spot a sign with the word 'gallop'. I take it to be for the benefit of the horseman passing by, not the pilgrim walker.

12.50 p.m.
The hike to Knocknascagh Crossroads continues across country through the Drum Hills and the townland of

Woodhouse. Some signage points to the site of a proposed wind farm to feature eight turbines on masts 70 metres tall with rotating blades of approximately 40 metres. According to the planning application, these will generate 22,000 kilowatts of power, enough to supply 15,000 homes while offsetting the use of an estimated 13,000 tonnes of fossil fuels. From previous walks, I wonder at the omission of the huge environmental cost of opening access across environmentally sensitive land. Virtual highways are needed even to put turbines of this size in place. During a brief lunch break, I mull over how much wind it takes to offset the energy spent in construction.

1.15 p.m.
I search out the next part of my pilgrim path, which takes me into the second map of the route from Ardmore. With no visible signage, I call to a house where the woman tells me that I am in the townland of Ballinameela. She points to the road for Clonmel. I explain that I need to follow the pilgrim trail, so we peruse the conjunction of my two maps briefly. She tells me that I have to go back through Knocknascagh Cross as far as the old 'tech' school – now a business premises with 'aluminium windows' – and turn to the right there. I locate the building with aluminium struts for a conservatory-type addition and move on to the second map for the back road to Cappoquin.

2.00 p.m.
About a kilometre up the road from Knocknascagh, the road for Cappoquin swings right at a junction for a bridge over the River Finisk, around the intriguing ruins of an ancient church with an old-style iron gate, which could have been forged near the banks of the River Lickey. The

gate is surmounted by a simple metal cross. The church, Cill Molaise, gives the townland of Kilmolash its name and its ruined walls now stand derelict in a graveyard that is overgrown and unkempt. At one gable end of the ruins, a mighty yew tree grows, the east side a tangle of branches without foliage. Yet the church and its surroundings certainly bear a few moments' respite for investigation. The erudite Revd Patrick Power, MRIA, of University College Cork, wrote an excellent account of this general area for the Waterford and South-East of Ireland Archaeological Society.[91] Contrary to the belief of some that the church is dedicated to St Molaise, founder of Devenish Monastery on an island of Lower Lough Erne, Power ascribes this church to another Molaise of the Déise, who is commemorated in *The Martyrology of Donegal* under the 17th of January. However, the interesting point about these ruins is that they illustrate various phases of Irish ecclesiastical architecture:

> *First the cyclopean doorway and the north wall of the Nave in which it is set belong to the early Celtic Oratory plundered, and no doubt burned, by the Danes at the beginning of the ninth century. Next in age comes the remainder of the nave, including the west gable with its features; this is of fifteenth century character. An eleventh century origin has been claimed for the Chancel, but to the writer it seems a comparatively modern addition – no older, in fact, then the inscription on the ashlar block of the arch: Fear God Honer the Kinge Ano Domn+ 1635.*[92]

I do not find this inscription, nor do I see the 'recumbent' monuments Power mentions, in particular the one of a 'much worn figure of an ecclesiastic or knight whose head rests upon a cushion' in the grass to the north of the ruin.

The presence of this 'knight' may attest to the even earlier reference to this church ruin by Samuel Lewis, in his 1837 work *A Topographical Dictionary of Ireland*, which mentions a ruin near the 'river Phinsk' said to have been a 'religious edifice' belonging to the Knights of St John of Jerusalem.[93] This medieval confraternity, also known as the Knights Hospitaller, was founded around 1023 to care for poor, sick and injured pilgrims to the Holy Land. After the First Crusade it became a religious/military order to defend the European conquest of Jerusalem, growing from there to wide temporal power based in Rhodes and Malta. As I take leave of Kilmolash, I cannot help wondering whether the pivotal presence of the Knights Hospitaller along this great medieval route related more to its initial role in caring for poor, sick and injured pilgrims or to its later temporal excesses.

2.30 p.m.

Up until lunchtime, I have followed St Declan's Road and Bóthar na Riolog. My guide map now tells me I am on Cosán na Naomh, or Saints' Road, as I cross the beautiful stone bridge over the Finisk just past the Kilmolash ruins and walk along a shaded country road with the entrance and boundaries of a large house on my right and the river on my left. I note the beautifully crafted stone wall that forms an elegant boundary here. However, my attention is also drawn to the litter that spoils this beautiful spot – plastic wrappers, cardboard and the ubiquitous plastic bottles. As several cars pass, the litter rankles even more. For while previous generations enhanced and maintained this place with craftsmanship and care, a single generation ruins it with debris thrown carelessly from cars that hurtle through without a second glance.

3.00 p.m.
Cosán na Naomh merges with Bóthar na Naomh on my guide map as I pass the impressive walled grounds of an old castle, which surprisingly is not annotated on my map. I take it to be a great house linked to Affane, home to the FitzGeralds of Desmond, who held sway locally. This may well have been the place where, according to Power's archaeological tour notes, the first cherry tree was grown in Ireland – a horticultural distinction to offset the claim of nearby Youghal as the first place in Europe where potatoes were grown (on the estate of Sir Walter Raleigh). Yet there is no sign of this wonderful history in either the marvellous old graveyard or the ruined parish church at Affane on my right. The only public information is the bright yellow notice, which says, 'DANGER', and then, 'Keep Out – Falling Masonry'. Yet the old belfry defies the warning and rises proudly above the ivy-covered walls, with their great arch windows. Below are the lawns and rhododendron bushes, with row upon row of impressive headstones in all directions.

I would love to enter the church, for it is here in the aisle that one of the greatest charlatans of all time is said to have been buried in November 1682 alongside his father. The faith healer Valentine Greatrakes may well have given rise to the Hiberno-English term 'pulling a stroke', for he was known as 'the Stroker'. Born here in Affane in 1628, Greatrakes is the subject of a play by Jim Nolan, *Blackwater Angel*, staged at Dublin's Abbey Theatre in 2001. Waterford County Museum curator Willie Fraher wrote a fascinating account of Greatrakes in the programme foreword.[94] It tells how, after serving as a lieutenant in the Cromwellian army regiment of the earl of Orrery, Greatrakes returned home to farm in Affane, but soon took up office as clerk of the peace for County Cork and registrar of transplantation, in which role he would have been responsible for deporting many Irish slaves to the West Indies after the Cromwellian conquest. He was also involved in the witchcraft trial of Florence Newton of Youghal, in which, gruesomely, he lanced her skin and pierced her body with awls to prove she was guilty. Such aversion to the occult notwithstanding, Greatrakes was soon in the mystical realm himself as a healer, even ignoring an order of the Bishop's Court in Lismore to cease his laying on of hands. His effrontery and defiance paid off in a reputation that spread to England, where he was invited – via the archbishop of Dublin – to cure Lady Anne Conway at Ragley Hall in Warwickshire. He failed to ease her migraine but pulled enough strokes while there to go on a healing tour of England; his clients even included King Charles II. His reputation was much enhanced in 1666 by a published account of his great healing powers – which he wrote himself. That led to other lucrative visits across the water until his death and burial, which, according to the Herald's Office in Dublin, was at Lismore Church. However, Revd Samuel Hayman, writing in the 1860s, was adamant that Valentine Greatrakes lies here in Affane. So west Waterford's trickster may even have cheated the gravediggers through bilocation.

3.30 p.m.

From Affane, the road turns at a right angle at the junction of the scenic Dromana Drive along the east bank of the Blackwater, which still cannot be seen. In a dog-leg route, St Declan's Road enters Cappoquin through a suburban industrial zone, where several motorists seem amused at the sight of a walking pilgrim. One carload of young men even blesses my progress with a beeping horn and raucous cheers from the open window as it speeds by.

It is here, in a precise spot now hidden, that the old route led down to the ford of the great river to which Cappoquin owes its origin. The crossing, known as the Áth Mheadhon (Middle Ford), was used by St Carthage and his cortège to reach Lismore and has always been a strategic point in the region, the scene of many battles. One notable battle in 1564 is mentioned by Revd Power in his notes. This was a mighty clash between the Anglo-Irish forces of Ossory (Butlers) and Desmond (FitzGeralds) that resulted in the death of 300 of the latter on the bloody field. The earl of Desmond was taken prisoner:

> *As he was borne wounded from the field of disaster the proud chieftain was tauntingly asked by the men of Ormond who borne him: 'Where now is the great Earl of Desmond?' The answer was incisive as the taunt was bitter – 'In his proper place, on the necks of the Butlers.'*[95]

I continue my trek through the junction with the main road, the N72, and enter the town of Cappoquin over a humped bridge across the Glenshelane River, past the local GAA grounds. As I trudge along, I reflect that the men of Desmond and Ossory are still clashing on such hurling pitches in great derby matches between the men of the Déise (Waterford) and the 'cats' of Kilkenny. And, in every notable encounter of recent years, the Leinster men are still doling out punishment to their Munster neighbours.

4.00 p.m.
The Blackwater appears at last on the far side of Cappoquin, where the main road spills along the north bank of the river towards the west. Above it, a formidable hill begins the ascent to the Knockmealdown Mountains. The riverscape

is idyllic but for the busy road, made even busier by the removal of the Great Southern Railway services. The railway once crossed the river on a strong metal bridge, which now comes to an abrupt stop on reaching dry land again. I am jealous of the times when, in his Archaeological Society notes, Revd Power paid homage to the inspiration of the river for poets and painters, even noting that 'fatuous guidebooks have called it the Irish Rhine'. He tells us that ancient Irish pagans named the river Nemh, 'a word cognate with the Irish name for heaven' (*neamh*). The learned reverend professor also quotes an unidentified verse in its praise:

*From all the rivers which son or daughter*
*Of Adam prizes, the world within.*
*The 'Branch of Beauty' you bear, Blackwater*
*From Youghal Harbour to Cappoquin.*[96]

It is here at Cappoquin that the river decides almost arbitrarily to abandon its eastward flow through Waterford and turn sharply south for Youghal Harbour. The great bend in the majestic river is confusing also for this modern pilgrim, who again finds no waymarker to indicate the ancient pilgrim road to Lismore. My trusty borrowed route map helps by indicating a course along the south bank and I turn gratefully from the hectic N72 onto a beautiful old stone bridge that arches its way across the torrent. As the traffic deliberately ignores this route, there is ample time to stand and survey the river and the town at its turn. An information board tells me this is the Avonmore Bridge. It stands upriver of the old wooden bridge that was built near the ancient ford in the seventeenth century. It was started during the Great Hunger in September 1847 with a £4,000 loan from the Office of Public Works; when it was completed four years later it was officially named Victoria Bridge in honour of the monarch who had donated £5 to famine relief in Ireland. That name was chiselled out and it became the Avonmore Bridge. It was of particular strategic importance during the Troubles and especially during the Civil War in 1922, when it was blown up by General Liam Lynch's southern command of Irregular forces. It was rebuilt as the main route to the west through Lismore and then made redundant by the new road.

Today, its seven elegant arches provide a majestic crossing for the pilgrim on foot, with a marvellous view of the old railway bridge, before another right turn to follow the south bank above the river's edge. The high, wooded bank oppositeis dotted with stately homes and the sound of the traffic becomes an almost inaudible buzz on this wonderful afternoon, the roadside banks bursting with new spring growth. It is worth recording Power's observation from a hundred years ago on this 'ancient highway': 'This is perhaps the oldest roadway at present in use in Ireland; its centuries of existence number at least a dozen, and it has been in constant use all those ages!'[97] A century later, I walk it alone and undisturbed.

5.00 p.m.

Despite forewarning from the map guide, I miss the ancient cemetery known as Reilig Déagláin (Declan's Graveyard) – which, ironically, is said to be the place of Declan's birth. Power suggests that a fort on this site was the home of Dobhran, a kinsman of Declan, whom his parents were visiting when he was born. Perhaps the site is no longer visible for some reason, but I miss it completely as I amble along the ancient highway to St Carthage's holy city. However, there is no missing the next notable feature a few kilometres further along the way. At a turn in the road, the Round Hill soars to the heavens with trees that have now become home to the 'caw-cophonous' assembly of a parliament of rooks. There is no mistaking the importance of this ancient place, a prehistoric mound that commanded the intersection of two ancient Celtic Christian highways – Bóthar na Naomh, which I now walk, and Rian Bó Phádraig (the Path of Patrick's Cow), which crosses the Knockmealdown Mountains from Cashel to Lismore and continues southwards. My guide map and other sources suggest that this mound is the site of the great fort for which Lismore is named and that it determined passage through an area that was once known as Magh Sciath (Plain of the Shields). Certainly it was fortified as a motte during the Anglo-Norman conquest of the twelfth century and thereafter.

As I sidle down a path at the back of a cottage that now sits below the ancient hill, I imagine it within a wicker enclosure for livestock, the ancient chieftain's mud-and-wattle dwelling presiding over it from the summit, where the rooks now circle. The thought of mud is hardly fortuitous, for soon I am on the final stretch of St Declan's Road to Lismore, called the Riverside Walk. The guide map has an advisory: 'Caution! Care needed on Riverside Walk when wet underfoot.' On this dry and bright Easter weekday, I wrongly presume that the passage will be fair for the final stretch of little over a kilometre. I am wrong. Climbing up a small bank onto the path, I quickly discover yet another vital use for my pilgrim's staff, which acts as a lever when plunged into the sticky yellow mud of the riverbank. From here on, it provides a safety fulcrum on several occasions, as the treacherous muddy path threatens to jettison the pilgrim into the river. It occurs to me that this may well be a time-honoured penitential trial that must be undertaken before entering the holy city. While negotiating the treacherous path, however, I pause several times to wonder and admire the fast-flowing torrent that threatens to consume the bank along which I edge my way.

5.30 p.m.

Finally, over a small metal pedestrian bridge that provides little help with the huge mud puddles on each end, the path enters a riverside plain and cuts through swampland. To my left, a man out walking his dog talks to a youth who is reclining along the almost-horizontal bough of a tree, while his own dog ferrets around the brush. As the man moves off, the youth gives me a friendly wave and I pick my way through the mud and swamp over to a metal turnstile in the formidable cut-stone walls. This corner entrance features fingerposts pointing inside and also along the outside wall to the left, both identifying it as Lady Louisa's Walk. I walk through and find immediately that I have exchanged the yellow muddy clay of the riverbank for rich brown loamy mud. I traverse the walkway that rises gently on an incline, allowing wonderful views of the river below, before entering a small courtyard beside a car park and another gate to the road ascending from the river to the cathedral city of St Carthage. On weary legs that have been given a good workout in the mud below, I walk slowly up the hill, passing a sign for a walkway to the cathedral, and enter the town centre. It is quiet as the business day draws to a close.

I walk back down to the main intersection, where, eschewing the Lismore Heritage Centre, which is now closing for the day at the former courthouse, I look for a friendly tavern to slake the thirst of a weary pilgrim. An atmospheric-looking hotel stands at the cross, a blue plaque on the wall recalling the great nineteenth-century novelist William Makepeace Thackeray, author of *Vanity Fair*. Thackeray recorded glowing impressions of Lismore in his *Irish Sketch Book*, published in 1843. Despite his sojourn – and the sojourns of many other travel writers – at the hotel, where the terrace tables looked most appealing, I drag my muddy hiking boots to a more humble hostelry across the street. The woman behind the bar seems highly suspicious of a bedraggled pilgrim. Yet, after an enjoyable pint of stout, I rally my resources and make my way back up the main street and down an attractive avenue to the Cathedral of St Carthage.

In the pleasant evening sunlight, I pass through the gateway to the cathedral grounds, where scaffolding has been erected for maintenance work on the chancel arch, drawing attention to the slender steeple soaring to the heavens from the rectangular belfry. A woman and a man, whom I take to be the dean of the cathedral, chat at the gate, their northern accents carried in the hushed atmosphere with references to places such as Ballyclare in Antrim and Dungiven in Derry, far off on the other side of the island. Past gnarled old tree-stumps sprouting spring life, the doorway leads under the scaffolding into the ancient place of worship founded by and named for St Carthage, also called Mochuda.

In the seventh century, Carthage founded a monastery here, which grew into one of the great ecclesiastical centres of Christendom. Lismore attracted pilgrims even in its early years and sent missionaries to distant lands. Lismore Castle, across a ravine from the cathedral, was the home of the bishop until, in a less-than-chivalrous exchange, Sir Walter Raleigh took it from Bishop Myler McGrath. He sold it on to the earl of Cork. Since the mid eighteenth century, the dukes of Devonshire have owned it. Even with Myler's ouster from the castle, the McGrath presence in Lismore is most secure in the family tomb, an altar-style structure of carved marble that commands attention inside the cathedral – even for a weary pilgrim who has walked St Declan's Road in mucky boots.

*Thursday, 8 April 2010*

There is a warm greeting on entering the Pottery and Craft Gallery on the Cliff in Ardmore for the 'man who walked St Declan's Road'. Last night after dinner in Youghal, I called into Keever's pub in Ardmore, a few doors down from the bed and breakfast, to find almost the entire village community gathered for a whist drive in aid of the local primary school. In conversation, I mentioned that I had walked the pilgrim path and soon I was a centre of attention, even receiving an invitation from the chairman of the local GAA club to join a walk of the entire route to Cashel by club members.

Potter Mary Lincoln was at the fund-raiser, and soon she has a morning mug of excellent coffee in my fists and is recounting her own role and that of her husband in resurrecting the pilgrim route. Her husband's aunt was Siobhán Lincoln, the visionary promoter of Ardmore's Christian archaeological heritage, whose 1979 guide to walking the ancient monastic sites of Ardmore prompts a morning stroll around the earliest Christian settlement in the land.

Starting at the car park on the seafront, the route takes a little over an hour of leisurely walking – from St Declan's Stone, which miraculously carried his bell across the waves, to the holy well and tiny church perched on the clifftop, which is said to have been founded as a seminary around AD 416, 16 years before Patrick's arrival. From there the path wends its way around the cliff, past the castle tower and

Fr O'Donnell's Well (an impressive structure known as a source of cures for eye ailments, although its associations are mysterious), then back towards the village. We reach the route's crowning glory in the perfectly preserved and elegant round tower and the adjacent cathedral with its fabulous west gable, both built almost a thousand years ago. Finally, the village walk ends at St Declan's Oratory, said to be the final resting place of the saint, where generations of humble patients scooped up the earth as a protection against illness. Down to the Pottery and Craft Gallery, then, for a final demonstration of Déise hospitality in another reviving cup of coffee, and the Ardmore residents' delighted anticipation that pilgrims will come again to walk the first steps taken in Ireland in the name of Jesus Christ.

# Chapter 10

# Wells along the Way to Barra's Bower

## To Gougane Barra

*Friday, 30 April 2010*

At 11.10 p.m., the shadows of pedestrians loom in the moonlight on the raised bog road outside Kilmacrennan. Once caught in the headlights, most are wearing high-visibility jackets; several carry torches and all are heading back towards the north Donegal village. I enquire of a couple of women what is happening, and they explain that the procession is coming from the local church and is expected to arrive at Doon Well at midnight for the Rosary and blessing of the waters.

'Father has it timed exactly,' one of the women points out, and they head off.

I decide to park at the well and then join the procession for the final part of the route. On each side, the road drops precipitously down steep banks, a raised causeway covering a prehistoric *tóchar* to Doon, which brought pilgrims to the centre of a 'termon' comprising some 20 townlands of north-west Donegal. At the well, the car park is already full, with a couple of small buses tucked in behind the cars, close to the public toilets. One of the buses, like me, has come from Castlederg in County Tyrone and its passengers remain seated inside. I turn to drive back to a parking spot, but a car begins a very laboured three- (or five-) point turn in the narrow corridor. A man in a car alongside signals to offer me his spot at the foot of the steep path up Doon Rock, where the chieftains of the mighty O'Donnell clan were inaugurated in the days of the old Gaelic order.

11.30 p.m.
It must be 35 years since I last visited Doon Well, prompted by curiousity, on a diversion from an Easter student break in Gaoth Dobhair. It was a well-hidden location with a rough path leading down to a bushy enclosure. Back then, it was little more than a rough hole in the ground surrounded by branches festooned with rags and trinkets, yet it evoked all the mystic power of a forgotten pagan place, where people at the ends of despair made furtive visits to invoke ancient powers. Tonight, it is barely recognisable, with an ample car park – although full to overflowing on this special night – and other 'improvements' surrounding the well. The well itself is encased behind tiny wooden doors and has a plaque outlining the pilgrimage prayers that 'must be recited with bared feet'. A low wall surrounds an expanse of lawn with the well at its centre now. The path is paved and the undergrowth has been cut back save for a lonely pair of raggy bushes.

A group is circling the bushes, reciting the Rosary, while other pilgrims pray at the well. The atmosphere is hushed, with mere glances for newcomers. Others sit in their cars as

I climb the steep path with railings to the rock where colourful pagan rituals of the past marked the secular inauguration of the O'Donnell. These rituals followed a church inauguration at Kilmacrennan Abbey and were presided over by 'lectors' drawn in a hereditary line from the O'Frighil sept.

The ritual was described in the twelfth century by Giraldus Cambrensis:

> *When the whole people of that land has been gathered together in one place, a white mare is brought forward into the middle of the assembly. He who is to be inaugurated, not as a chief, but as a beast, not as a king, but as an outlaw, embraces the animal before all, professing himself to be a beast also. The mare is then killed immediately, cut up in pieces, and boiled in water. A bath is prepared for the man afterwards in the same water. He sits in the bath surrounded by all his people, and all, he and they, eat of the meat of the mare which is brought to them. He quaffs and drinks of the broth in which he is bathed, not in any cup, or using his hand, but just dipping his mouth into it round about him. When this unrighteous rite has been carried out, his kingship and dominion has been conferred.*[98]

While Professor Charles Doherty of UCD judges the accuracy of this description as 'unlikely' for the twelfth century, he concedes that it parallels the horse-sacrifice rituals of ancient India like the Aśvamedha, and provides thereby a vital link with the whole Indo-European concept of kingship and 'world dominion' echoed in poetic accounts of ceremonies at the Navan Fort outside Armagh City.[99] Today, a recess has been created at the base of the huge rock for a Marian shrine in the Lourdes/Fátima model, and a couple of people are praying there. As I arrive, they move off silently, descending to the car park where vehicles are still arriving and squeezing into every available space. I try to get to the top of Doon Rock but it is too dark to see anything, even though I can feel the latent power of the mammoth boulder.

*Saturday, 1 May 2010*
12.30 a.m.
The amplified strains of a hymn invoking Our Lady of Fátima carry on the night air as midnight passes and, upon the arrival of the ancient festival of Bealtaine, spring turns to summer. The procession from the church arrives, a huge crowd filling the road. It breaks up when confronted by the throng of cars parked higgledy-piggledy in every nook and cranny. The lead party with a few torches presses through and we follow, spilling through the narrow gaps to reach the walled enclosure. Many simply move further along the road and stand in a throng at the wall, facing in, as the priest calls out for the 'colour party' to gather in at the centre.

Explaining that a company from Ardara is filming the proceedings for a DVD about holy wells, he says that he told them to expect between 3,000 and 4,000 people tonight and that his forecast is borne out in the pilgrim crowd present. I scan the crowd with a rough count and calculate that it is just over a thousand people. Perhaps the others lurk in the shadows beyond. The priest then explains 'for the benefit of visitors' that the well at Doon has been known and accepted as a holy well since the fifteenth century, when a local man called Lector O'Friel, 'who may have been a professor of theology', invested his powers of healing in the spring water before his death. As pilgrims flocked to the well for healing, it was subsequently blessed by a Fr Gallagher, who 'invested his power of priesthood' in the well, as many other priests have done since then.

Our chief celebrant of the night then invites the two other priests present to join him in blessing the well waters with their combined 'power of priesthood' before we begin the Rosary. Since it is after midnight, he announces that we will say the Joyful Mysteries. During the course of the recitation he invites those from parishes he names individually to lead the prayers. However, he also invites his fellow priests and those selected as members of the colour party to lead. Their amplified voices virtually drown the soft murmur of the lay pilgrims present. Beginning with the parish of Kilmacrennan and others in close proximity, the net widens to include all the parishes of Raphoe Diocese. For the third mystery, celebrating the Nativity, it is the turn of the Gaeltacht parishes of west and north Donegal and we recite that in Irish. The Rosary concludes with the contribution of those who have come from the dioceses of Derry, Clogher and Elphin. I also note that we invoke the intercession of the Virgin Mary at the conclusion of each mystery. Finally, the formal ceremonies are concluded with the singing of a hymn to St Brigid, the 'Mary of the Gael'.

12.45 a.m.

The priests and members of the colour party have departed, leaving only a close press of pilgrims at the well. At the centre of the throng some women are busy filling bottles from jugs of the blessed waters. Pilgrims on the periphery proffer their empty bottles as those kneeling and crouching at the well perform their task without comment, much less complaint. On the outside of the crowd at the head of the well I meet John McAteer, the colourful founding editor of the *Tirconaill Tribune*. He raises his flash camera above the heads in a bid to capture the moment, but successive attempts are frustrated because faces are bowed. As I wait for the waters and he for the lifting of eyes, I chat to him about this pilgrimage and about his former reporter, Lawrence Donegan, who wrote a best-selling book detailing the year he spent with the tiny paper after forsaking London's Fleet Street.[100] His former editor tells me Lawrence 'never settled since' and is now in America, writing about golf. I am reminded of a former pastor in Canada, who used to announce each year that he was off to 'visit the 18 holy shrines' when leaving for his winter golf holiday in Florida.

So, as the crowd at Doon thins out and the car park and access road become sufficiently clear to allow me out, I leave with my plastic bottle of Doon's miraculous water. On my way home, the raised road of the *Tóchar* is lit by a bright and almost full moon. Bathed in its light, I greet the start of summer by heading south to the north and my thoughts turn to that glorious poem of Seamus Heaney's about the pre-Christian rituals of Bealtaine and the words '*fionn uisce*' or 'fair water':

*So on a day when newcomers appear*
*Let it be a homecoming and let us speak*
*The unstrange word, as it behoves us here,*
*Move lips, move minds and make new meanings flare*
*Like ancient beacons signalling, peak to peak,*
*From middle sea to north sea, shining clear*
*As phoenix flame upon fionn uisce here.*[101]

*Thursday, 14 May 2010*

9.15 a.m. My long pilgrim trek south to Finbarr's sanctuary begins with a brief visit to St Patrick's Well at Magherakeel, near Killeter in west Tyrone. Just a short distance from the Derg River, which flows from the patron saint's purgatory, and adjacent to the ruins of St Caireall's Church, founded about 1,500 years ago, Patrick is said to have quenched his thirst here when returning from pilgrimage. The well water is reputed to cure toothache. It has been beautifully restored as a wayside shrine and tastefully enhanced as a sacred place by a proud local community. I linger and recite the prayer to St Patrick displayed on a plaque. For this first part of my pilgrimage through the Black Gap and on through Pettigo, Belleek and south Donegal, the news is of volcano-cloud disruptions and possible pension cuts. I reflect on the lines from my prayer:

> *Give security to those shaken by doubt; strengthen the weak; help the elderly; comfort those who are ill; bless those who travel the roads and airways of the world.*

11.15 a.m.
By inadvertently taking the wrong road at the first sign-post for Lough Gill, I reach Tobernalt on a circuitous – but fabulous – route through Dromahair, County Leitrim. Just on the edge of the sprawling town of Sligo, Tobernalt and its natural setting come with rave reviews. Not least is the evocative poem, 'The Lake Isle of Innisfree' by W.B. Yeats, which extols the beauty of Lough Gill. Almost equally poetic is the ecclesiastical description by Archbishop John Healy, who wrote in his 1911 essay on holy wells:

> *One of the most picturesque holy wells in Ireland is that which is known as Tubbernaltha, on the shore of Lough Gill, near Sligo. The well gushes out from the face of the cliff to which it owes its name. The pellucid stream at first lingers under the shade of embowering shrubs, the centre of a scene of enchanting loveliness, and then steals away with gentle murmur to mingle with the waters of the lake.*[102]

It is just as beautiful today, despite the encroachment of suburbanity on its environs and the politely prohibitive notices posted everywhere: 'Please do not drink the water'; 'Please do not put coins in the well'; 'Please do not place candles on the altar rails'; 'Please do not leave items at the Holy Well'; and 'Please maintain a sacred silence.' I cannot testify to how the final rule is observed, but I did observe a mug for water at the well, coins at its bottom, candle wax on the rails and a few trees adorned with traditional pilgrimage tokens of beads, socks, ribbons, medals, soft toys and more.

Archbishop Healy noted:

> *…the well has a double sanctity, for it was not only blessed by St Patrick, who, it seems, baptised his converts there on his way southward through Tirerrill, but in the penal days its waters were used in the celebration of Mass, which was solemnised there beneath an aged tree when no priest dare venture into the town of Sligo.*[103]

In acknowledgement of this, the well is surmounted by a full altar of stone with the aforementioned rails and a Mass lectern, all used during the pilgrimage period at the end of July. Below the well, on both sides of the rivulet burbling to the nearby lough, are quiet havens with appropriate plaques for the Sorrowful, Joyful, Glorious and the recently inaugurated Luminous mysteries of the Rosary and benches for pilgrims to rest on and ponder. There is also a large stone indented by Patrick's touch, where pilgrims rest for the cure of back problems. As wings to the altar, there is a crucifixion scene beside the rag-tied trees to the left. Even more elevated on the right is a Lourdes grotto, which again I found an unnecessary intrusion on the traditional shrine. However, the entire scene is enfolded in lush trees, with banks of pungent wild garlic and other early summer growth. Most touching is the carved wooden notice recalling the generations who worshipped at this spot, with the carved figure of a bearded pilgrim with staff and the admonition, 'Pilgrim walk softly – this is holy ground.' The lines echo Yeats in his 1899 poem, 'He Wishes for the Cloths of Heaven':

*But I, being poor, have only my dreams,*
*I have spread my dreams under your feet;*
*Tread softly because you tread on my dreams.*[104]

On the next stage of my pilgrimage south, I carry the dreams of the multitude that still gathers at Tobernalt on Garland Sunday and the thought that the deep and abiding love of poetry among Irish people is a secular form of prayer, which continues to elevate our spirits and our souls even in times of despair.

12.30 p.m.
The young man on duty at Cruachan Aí, the interpretative centre in Tulsk, County Roscommon, is enthusiastic about Ogulla Well. Perhaps it's a welcome change from discussing the comings and going of the kings of Connacht who resided at Rathcroghan and also of Queen Medb, who brooded over the land and coveted the livestock of rivals to the north.

'It was always a holy well,' he explains, 'even before Christianity, because there are three springs at Ogulla. That had spiritual significance for the Celts, but it was taken on by Christianity to represent the Trinity. Ogulla is close to the ancient druidic school of Cashel Manannáin, where they studied for 20 years before they could practise as druids. It would have been a very important site for their rituals and probably for that reason, it was where Patrick chose to carry out the baptism of the druids and of Eithne and Fidelma and their foster parents. Ogulla is a sacred place. There is no doubt about that.'

With clear directions, I have no trouble finding the well, about a kilometre from the centre of the village. It is in a glade with a small open space incorporated right beside the three springs and the rivulet running off from them as the young River Tulsk, which flows down through the village and on to Lough na Fulla. This is the essence of life for the surrounding area and it is for this reason that the well at Ogulla is identified as the Tobar Cliabhach where St Patrick baptised Eithne and Fidelma, daughters of King Laoghaire of Tara. They were attending the school of Cashel Manannáin at Rathcroghan and were fostered by leading druids Mael and Coplait, who were also christened by Patrick. It was a crucial breakthrough, which established Patrick as the Apostle of Ireland and ensured that our ancient forms of Celtic spirituality would be incorporated rather than routed in the new dispensation.

The site is dominated by three features of pilgrimage – a glass-walled oratory, a statue of St Patrick and a small statue of the Blessed Virgin, situated strangely right beside a pile of metal pipes. I find surprising comfort in the general run-down appearance of the shrine. It signifies that it is part of the traditional landscape, a place of folk ritual with no need to dress itself up as anything other than what it is. And it is clear that it is a popular place of pilgrimage. Pilgrim tokens are everywhere – draped around Patrick and the Virgin, tied to trees at the first well, strewn around the oratory interior, piled on the small altar and scattered on the ground beside Our Lady's statue and the pipes. The votive offerings are holy pictures, beads, statues and other religious objects, but also personal effects, including a few toothbrushes and a barely used tube of toothpaste. I find the open door to the oratory and kneel to pray at one of the five long pews inside. Outside again, nesting birds tweet and twitter as the day warms up and I imagine what it was like on that day when Fidelma and Eithne accepted the scripture and were baptised in Christ's name. It was a ritual of transformation, of transcendence; a magnificent rebirth of spirit in revealed truth. It showed a remarkable willingness to embrace enlightened change on the one hand and to accept deep and abiding traditions of spirituality on the other.

2.45 p.m.
The older man working in his small garden plot on the narrow ground between the road and the shore is delighted by my interest.

'It's back there along the road about two hundred yards,' he informs me. 'You'll see it clearly if you walk that way.' He points off down the Lough Atalia Road towards Galway's city centre and the docks, both within a remarkably short stroll. We talk of the well and its association with St Augustine through the nearby abbey church, just off Eyre Square. 'This would have been no more than a boreen going back because it was only used by the fishermen,' the gardener explains. 'Then they started bringing in horses and carts and the road was built about 1960. They took about 20 feet or so from the people's gardens along here. You see, the gardens of the houses on College Road would have gone all the way back to the sea. But we still paid rates on these gardens back when there was rates.'

Clearly he is fonder of the spiritual legacy than the temporal and, with his blessing and a request for a prayer for himself, I walk back, keeping an eye on the shoreline. The well is immediately recognisable, despite changes carried out through the efforts of the garden owners hereabouts, along with Galway Civic Trust. I've seen it before, in a print that caught my eye at a used-book sale. Entitled 'Pilgrims at the Holy Well, West Highlands, Connemara', it depicts two barefoot women in shawls kneeling on the pebbled shore, Rosary beads draped through their fingers. One of the women supplicates herself before the well beneath a big boulder with 'IHS' etched beneath a cross. A young girl peeps from beneath her raised shawl and a smaller, prone child looks in fascination at the supplicant. In the background, two men seem unconcerned as they work amid moored boats. A train with a tall, smoking funnel trundles across the bridge and causeway towards Renmore.

The picture, now framed on my living-room wall, was published in *The Graphic*, a London publication, on 16 September 1871. I note the despair in the posture of the women, their entreaty for divine intercession and the poverty of their garb in an Ireland still recovering from the tragedy of the Great Hunger. I know that hidden now on the reverse of my framed picture are unrelated words written by a correspondent from Dresden as he indulged in the finer aspects of life at the time. He describes how he listens with 'breathless attention' to 'Haydn's Symphony in G' at a café where the audience 'paid five silver groschen (6d)' and ate and drank as they listened. He goes on:

> *Surely coffee, lemonade and lager beer must be intimately associated in the German mind with all the choicest morceaus of the great composers. They sip and listen daily, and never tire of the occupation. Their visitors follow their example willingly. Very good fare was to be enjoyed on that particular*

> *evening at the Belvedere. We selected pfannkuchen from the menu, especially some choice kind of cake – good cakes and confectionery abound in Germany – and found familiar pancakes placed before us, cooked to perfection. On my right, some Americans were indulging in bread and cheese; to my left some delicious-looking baked puddings with cream were rapidly disappearing.*[105]

The contrast of that idyllic scene with this well of hope for the desperate on the shoreline of Galway city could hardly be starker.

Archbishop Healy noted in 1908 that cures at St Augustine's Well had been 'formally attested by more than a dozen of the first citizens of Galway, both clerical and lay'. Prime among these was the case of Patrick Lynch, who had 'a most grievous, desperate dangerous disease, and given over by all doctors to be incurable, and could not eat one bite since Easter last'. He was brought to the well on 11 June 1673 and 'totally dipped therein, and having also drunk a cup of water out of the well three times in the name of the Father, Son, and Holy Ghost, he at once got up of himself and walked about the well, and recovered his strength and his appetite, and "doth sleep well as before, for which the eternal God be glorified and praised for the same for ever",' Archbishop Healy related.[106]

Despite fears when the well ran dry in July 2008, it is in robust health now.[107] There are hand-railed steps from the roadside, a retaining wall/bench and a stone cross. I wonder momentarily at the name of the building opposite, Salt Lake House, but it is just a blunt translation of Lough Atalia (Loch an tSáile). This is the sole remaining spring well of three along this shoreline, the others dedicated to the Blessed Virgin and John the Baptist. All were possibly associated with a pagan site dedicated to the Celtic god Crom Dubh, according to an informative article by Ronnie O'Gorman in the *Galway Advertiser*.[108] Citing a number of experts, he tells us that all three wells are identified as 'St Augustine's wells' in James Hardiman's history of Galway and that an Augustinian friary was founded on Fort Hill in 1508. With the Elizabethan conquest, the friary was taken over as a garrison post. O'Gorman writes: 'Whatever its origins, the present St Augustine's well was long a place of pilgrimage and veneration.' He goes on:

> [Antiquarian scholar Máire] *Mac Neill tells us that during the Cromwellian régime, a crowd of pilgrims at the well were, by the governor's orders, fired upon. Some of them were severely injured while others were stripped of their clothes and goods, and taken into prison.*[109]

I complete my pilgrimage to the sacred site in the centre of Galway and make good my escape.

5.30 p.m.

There is an overwhelming primeval atmosphere at the sacred well dedicated to St Brigid in Liscannor. The narrow, gently curved passage to the underground well is a dank cave that is literally packed with the votive offerings of pilgrims. They are crowded onto the stone shelf, set in crevices, pinned to the whitewashed (but greening) walls and even suspended on roots of plants that have grown down from the ancient cemetery above. There are pictures, ribbons, beads, statues, crucifixes, soft toys, *in memoriam* cards, flowers, pendants, caps, socks, ultrasound images of internal body organs and everything else imaginable that could possibly evoke something of the spirit of those for whom prayers have been offered up.

Yet it is the photos of real people – on Mass cards, tucked into frames, attached to typewritten sheets, carefully arranged into collages or simply set into nooks and crannies – that choke back the breath and tears of this pilgrim wayfarer. For example, there is the collage of Eileen, pinned above the door at the well itself. It has images of a very beautiful, vivacious young blonde woman and the pretty girl she had been, with a typed prayer offered for her repose. Right beside it is an image of Mother Teresa of Calcutta in prayer, then a framed picture of St Francis with lots of Mass cards tucked into the rim; among them are more images of the smiling Eileen. All around is the heartfelt detritus of desperation, final recourse in the melted wax of a burnt-out candle.

And there are the scrawled names of those who have come – not the mindless graffiti of visitors, but the supplicant prayers of pilgrims. It is so much more than one expects on entering the flagstone-floored cave through the arched entrance guarded by pots of flowering geraniums, the statue of St Brigid presiding over the entrance gate from a flower-shrouded pedestal featuring her iconic crosses. Travellers passing the entrance and the fingerpost opposite for the holy well probably assume that it is simply another wayside shrine and attention is drawn to the big stone column on the opposite side of the small byroad at the graveyard. Those who venture inside may see no more than the statue of Brigid before venturing up the nearby steps to the graveyard. There can be found an impressive paved path to the sunken tomb of the Uí Bhriain chieftains of the Dál gCais – kinsmen of Brian Boru, high king of Ireland in the early eleventh century, who defeated the Vikings at the battle of Clontarf in 1014 and was then slain himself.

While Brian Boru rests in Armagh City, his family tomb is surmounted by a cross-topped steeple rising proudly to the heavens. Yet underground a sacred nook survives the ages in the spring that trickles from the rock face into a stone basin. Tradition has it that a white trout lives in the well and that those who see it are sure to have their prayers answered. The trout links the tradition of the well to the Salmon of Knowledge in the Fenian Cycle, the legend of Finn McCool. With the main focus of pilgrimage around the Lughnasa festival (from the last Sunday of July to 15 August, the Christian feast of the Assumption), stations are located on the circuitous path of the Ula Uachtarach (Upper Sanctuary) and the Ula Íochtarach (Lower Sanctuary). Having completed the pilgrimage ritual, moreover, there is the added option of a sojourn in Murphy's pub, which almost seems to be incorporated into the shrine and cemetery. However, it is closed today, as is Considine's Bar about a hundred metres along the road. Most traffic heads that way to the tourist stop at the Cliffs of Moher. Even this evening, visitors are filing to and fro from the expansive car park across the road.

With kerbed slip-roads, one-way systems and traffic-calming features in abundance, this much-promoted tourism venue is almost a Disneyworld replica of the wonder of the world I visited as a child. I drive by, promising myself another visit soon to the more secluded and loftier cliffs at Bun Glas on the seaward side of Sliabh Liag. Further along, I am even more concerned by the changes in Doolin, which, since my last visit about a dozen years ago, seems to have fallen victim to the Celtic Tiger. It is now a half village of higgledy-piggledy development, with features that look like suburban shopping malls strung out along a narrow coast road. Overlooking the village is a field of 'tax-exemption' holiday homes, near the junction with the main road. If that is the best Irish experience we have to offer, we have lost our soul and our hope.

I drive back through Liscannor to Lahinch and note that it is a town that seems to be wrestling with its identity. Signage offers the town's name in English as both 'Lahinch' and 'Lehinch'. I settle for the Irish name, Leacht Uí Chonchubhair, and stay the night. Even dressed up and expanded, at least it is still a real place from my fond childhood memories of west-Clare holidays.

*Friday, 14 May 2010*
11.30 a.m.
Across the mighty Shannon and on to where my mother had that seemingly rare experience of a very happy Limerick childhood in the 1930s and 1940s. The small town of Kilfinane is tucked into the south-east corner of the county, perched proudly at an elevation of 150 metres (the highest in Limerick) in the foothills of the Ballyhoura Mountains, presiding over the Golden Vale meadows below. Set under Seefin, it is midway between the north-Cork towns of Charleville and Mitchelstown. Off the beaten track and with a population of fewer than a thousand souls, it has probably changed little since my mother moved here from Bandon when her dad (my grandfather Jack Bowen) was posted as a first-time manager to the local Munster and Leinster Bank. The bank branch is gone now and there is little activity in the commercial heart of Kilfinane as I search for directions to Thomastown and the sacred well of my mother's childhood. My interest has been piqued by a poem by Gabriel Rosenstock, who also grew up here. Writing about the locality's ancient Moat or Motte, he begins with the lines:

*I think I understood*
*Even back then that it would outlive us,*
*That it was more ancient, more permanent*
*Than the sweet clash of hurleys.*
*There were things around us when we were growing up*
*That blessed us with sweetness and terror:*
*A Holy Well … do they still visit it?*[110]

An older lady suggests I talk to the priest, Fr Michael Hanley, a 'lovely man', and she walks me to the parochial house, slowly and with difficult conversational exchanges as she points to her earphone which, I suspect, is turned off. Fr Michael himself answers the door at the priest's house beside the impressive church named for St Andrew, even though Kilfinane means Church of St Finian. He is happy to give me directions to the well, then enquires about my interest. Happy to hear of my mother's memories of his parish, he tells me that Ladyswell is still a central part of the traditional worship.

'We say Mass there every August and some people actually gather at the church here and walk there to make it a real pilgrimage,' he informs me. 'Every year also we have a pilgrimage to Lourdes and we bring back Lourdes water and we add it to Ladyswell to make a real connection between the two places, which are of course in two different countries but carry the same message.'

With Fr Hanley's blessing and directions, I set off to retrieve my car and search for the wayside grotto that will mark my passage to the ancient site of pilgrimage. I miss the grotto twice while driving by because the statue of the Virgin is in a high alcove, yet somehow I find my way to the farm home of the O'Briens, on whose land, Fr Hanley has told me, the well is situated. John Joe O'Brien greets me hospitably and points to where the well is located, just a couple of fields below the traditional-style farmhouse. He advises me, however, to drive around onto the low road, where there is stile access to the field – he has horses grazing in the field beside the house.

I drive around and along a beautiful wooded road, past parkland fields, and soon spot a neat sign for the holy well. The stile takes me into a field of rich spring grass leading down to a rushy bottom, before rising again majestically past the O'Briens' house to a whin-covered hill. Behind me the land also rises into the Ballyhoura Mountains, as if cupping this sacred place. About a hundred metres along, I come across the first of the two wells in the field. Called Sundayswell, it is apparently a souterrain that is no longer a focus of pilgrimage, although it is covered neatly in a flagstone structure. Just 50 metres ahead, Ladyswell nestles undisturbed in a clump of bushes with access through a neat green gate. The well itself is surmounted by an ornate metal cross with a ladle suspended from a hook on its base. Two pairs of Rosary beads have been draped over the cross. Opposite it, a statue of the Blessed Virgin is protected by a neat wooden case with a glass door and votive trinkets have been placed on the stones in front – tiny statues, medallions and coins – and a few ribbons have been tied to the bushes. I take a good drink of the sweet spring water, fill a small bottle for my mother and pray for her health at the sacred spot which she visited herself as a sprightly, happy Limerick girl with her entire life – and all it would bring – ahead of her.

3.15 p.m.

Through Mallow and Macroom and into the deep southwest, my pilgrim path enters the land of Múscraí and the west-Cork Gaeltacht. At a fork in the road, I halt briefly to ask directions. The woman who assists me has a 'Back Home in Tyrone' sticker from the *Ulster Herald* on her rear window, celebrating the double all-Ireland football victories of 2008. Her husband is originally from Cookstown, she informs me, and we discuss football briefly. Then back on the road through Inse Geimhleach and Béal Átha an Ghaorthaidh, with a Celtic-Tiger Taj-Mahal home on the village edge, and at last I find the sanctuary of Finbarr and the spring sources of the lovely River Lee:

> *There is a green island in lone Gougane Barra,*
> *Where Allua of songs rushes forth as an arrow;*
> *In deep-valley'd Desmond – a thousand wild fountains*
> *Come down to that lake from their homes in the mountains.*
> *There grows the wild ash, and a time stricken willow*
> *Looks chidingly down on the mirth of the billow;*
> *As, like some gay child, that sad monitor scorning,*
> *It lightly laughs back to the laugh of the morning.*[111]

Just inside Cronin's Café, I read J.J. Callanan's exultant poem celebrating Gougane Barra and wonder over tea and a sandwich why it does not mention Finbarr. Perhaps it's a given that any pilgrim needs no reminder that the patron of Cork founded a hermitage here in the sixth century and the breathtaking valley itself is testimony enough to that. Certainly the tiny green island with its picturesque church oratory, linked to the mainland by a brief causeway, is a striking focal point. I sit at a window table and gaze out on a bridal party marching proudly and happily back to the adjacent hotel. Pictures taken, the celebrations begin. The woman at the café till, from Carndonagh in Donegal's far north, tells me I'll find information on walking routes at the gift shop next door. There, for €1.70, I buy a small booklet on Gougane Barra Forest Park, first planted in 1938 and open to the public since 1966. It informs me that it 'is unusual among Forest Parks in that it provides drive-around facilities for the motorist'. Given its relatively modest size of 350 acres, I decide to forsake the car and undertake my pilgrim path on foot.

First stop, of course, is the island sanctuary, where a plaque embedded on the gatepost announces: 'This is a Holy Place; Here may you, pilgrim and visitor, find peace and the love of the Lord,' with a warning against camping and picnics in the hallowed ground. On the other gatepost, the plaque tells us that here in the sixth century Finbarr 'communed with God. The surrounding mountains were his cloister and the lake was for him the mirror of God's grandeur.' From here, it adds, he journeyed along the Lee to found the church and city of Cork before he died in AD 623.

Immediately inside the gates, I encounter Finbarr's holy well, the final one of my southward odyssey. While the beautiful sanctuary has been lovingly restored, it rests on solid traditions of pilgrimage lasting more than a thousand years. Through the ages, cattle were driven though the water here to ensure that they would thrive for the coming year. The small causeway to the island had a wooden pole on which 'votive rags and spaneels of cattle were hung. Part of the lake was enclosed and treated as a holy well for bathing. This was often the only bathing and was considered to ensure good health for the whole year. Unlike at other times, there was no danger of drowning during the midsummer bathing.'[112] Instructions for the modern pilgrim are clearly outlined on a notice with a colourful sketch comprising 13 steps. They begin at the cross in the centre of the walled enclosure (Creed, Confiteor, Pater, Ave and Gloria) that marks the site of Finbarr's cell, and carry on to each of the eight cells built into the beautiful stone wall – at the old altar in the shady bower between the enclosure and the oratory, at the holy well and at the Slannán (Health Stream) that trickles down from the mountain outside. The final prayers are said at the tomb of Fr Denis O'Mahony, who retraced Finbarr's steps to the sanctuary 300 years ago and lived as a hermit here during those penal times. The old altar and other aspects of the pilgrim site date from his time.

Finally, the instruction of rounds suggests 'optional prayers' in the oratory for a particular person. 'Then,' it goes on, 'get a half bottle of water from the Holy Well, and a half bottle of water from the Slannán to sprinkle on the person(s) for whom the intention is for [*sic*].' I enter the oratory, bathed in shades of warm pink, to complete my pilgrimage thus and pause to gaze on Harry Clarke's stained-glass-window representation of Finbarr, a Patrician figure in the top left (north-east) window of the nave, just where the chancel begins. In the south-west corner, a plaque commemorates Cardinal Timothy Manning, the local boy who became primate of Los Angeles until he 'fell asleep in the Lord' on 23 June 1989.

4.30 p.m.

With formal pilgrimage rounds completed and blessed water on board, I climb into the small graveyard that overlooks the island. Amid beautifully tended graves, the sounds, smells and sights induce a pervasive sense of tranquillity at the end of my quest. Across the way, a woman bends to fill a white bucket from the lake and carries it into the oratory, perhaps to replenish the holy water there, since all the water of Gougane Barra is blessed. Invigorated, I set off on foot into the forest park, past the thatched mushroom-shaped toilets and further along. The new gate barrier is under construction behind steep enclosures; two fingerposts saying 'Pedestrian gate' point at each other and nothing else. A few cars pass, coming and going, before I reach the lower car park with its toilets and bright, clearly posted information about walking routes. In the spirit of pilgrimage, I eschew Slí Dhoire na Coise as too gentle, along with the other routes marked 'moderate'. Instead, I choose Slí an Easa, with its promise of 'tumbling waters and magnificent views' and an hour's 'strenuous' walking to a viewing point just under the peak of Tooreen Beg in the Shehy Mountains.

The short trail keeps its promise, even if the climb of steps, path and stepping-stones takes just 40 minutes to complete, with several lingering pauses to take in the view and a considerable rest at the top. There I drink in the vista down to the shores of the saintly lough below Derreennacusha and the slopes opposite of Faill Duibh, Bealick and Coomroe with the lush forest in between.

A green baseball cap lying on the bench says '101st Airborne' and I wonder if its owner lost it on the way down from the blue skies peeping though wispy clouds. I don't wonder long, because at the stepping stones over the stream that provides one of the sources of the River Lee, I meet the owner on his way up to retrieve it.

'If it was any other hat,' he tells me, 'I'd just leave it.' At the base, his partner waits with their dog, sitting on a bench to the side of the car park, and she laughs when I tell her I met him almost at the top.

'That didn't take him long,' she says, acknowledging his concern for the prized possession. Still energised and anxious to walk off the effects of my long journey south to this sacred bower of Barra, I wander off along the motor trail. It is a short route to the head of the canyon, where I find another trail notice for Slí Sléibhe – the Mountain Trail – also described as 'strenuous', with a climb of 130 metres and an estimated time of an hour and three-quarters. I weigh my options and reluctantly decide against it, continuing on past a couple of streams signposted 'Laoi' to identify them as the infant River Lee, where visitors can step out of their cars for a snapshot photo. But the trail is tranquil now and I march briskly back to the island sanctuary and leave Gougane Barra. As I pass the crucifixion scene opposite the signposted entrance on the road to Bantry, I offer a final prayer of thanks.

# Chapter 11

# Between a Cnoc and a Hard Place

## Cosán na Naomh

*Saturday, 15 May 2010*
3.45 p.m.

He is standing at the side of the road in an Clochán looking for a lift, just beyond a small bridge at the very end of the tiny village nestling beneath the feet of mighty Brandon. His grey-flecked beard is long enough to cover part of his chest, and it is only when I stop and he climbs in beside me that I notice he wears a crucifix around his neck. He is going to Daingean Uí Chúis, the peninsular Gaeltacht town also known as Dingle. Since I am going on to Ceann Trá, I can take him the whole way. And so begins a journey that is incredible not only because we are driving through an Chonair (the Conor Pass), the highest mountain route in Ireland and a place of stunning natural beauty. As we climb the narrow road, pulling into sporadic recesses to allow oncoming vehicles to edge by, he points down to the valley floor and tells me of the families who once lived there before moving into an Clochán, of how they return each year to re-establish their links. The Conor Pass, he remarks with a laugh, really means the Pass Pass. I steal wary glances down the cliffs and shift down another gear to make the climb.

He talks on with the calm demeanour of one who has seen it all before and yet cannot quell his enthusiasm for the place where he lives, although he tells me that he is actually a native of Killorglin, in the very heart of Kerry. When he learns that I have come from Tyrone, he tells me he travelled to Bosnia with a friend from Tyrone, who has now moved into Omagh from Castlederg because he found the latter too quiet. I tell him I moved the opposite way, but why did they go to Bosnia?

'Why not?' he replies, and then tells me of other places he has visited – Jerusalem and the Holy Land, Rome. When he learns that I plan to walk the Cosán na Naomh pilgrim path on the feast of St Brendan tomorrow, he tells me that he did it only last week and that he has also walked the Camino de Santiago de Compostela from the Portuguese side. We talk some more of pilgrim paths as we crest the mighty mountain pass between Cnoc Bhaile Uí Shé and an Cnoc Maol Mór and begin our descent to the coast. By now we are discussing our own ancient pilgrim paths in Ireland and their huge importance as spiritual heritage. He tells me he has walked them all, or as many as he could find, and he has actually walked around Ireland twice – or was it three times? A dog in Gleann Cholm Cille bit him, he says; I tell him of my encounter with Rex on the *Tóchar* Phádraig.

'He told you his name, did he?' he asks with a laugh. 'The dog that sneaked up and bit me didn't reveal his.'

By the time we reach an Daingean, I am almost exhausted at the thought of all the walking he has done, yet he is full of energy, stimulated by memories, inspired by the spiritual essence and at ease with himself and where he is now. I wonder if there is something special happening along Cosán na Naomh tomorrow and he tells me of plans for a televised Mass from Cuas an Bhodaigh. He suggests I pull in at the Catholic church so he can get me a parish bulletin, which should have all the details of anything taking place. I do and he emerges a few moments later with a local free newspaper – the bulletin hasn't arrived yet. He is going into the library just down the street and we part with farewells through the car window. I ask his name and he tells me he is called Columbanus. When I enquire whether he plans any more pilgrim journeys, he smiles: 'I've been everywhere I want to go to, the places I felt I needed to see,' he says. 'To do any more now would just be titillation!'

With a laugh at that and the blessings of Columbanus on my own pilgrimage, he saunters off happily down the street, leaving a mighty wave of goodwill in his wake.

5.00 p.m.

My second encounter of the afternoon is equally fortuitous. I call to the tourist office on the harbour-front, where a friendly assistant gives me the official guide book to Cosán na Naomh. Published in 2002, it was the first in a planned series on the Heritage Council pilgrim trails. After a brief read over coffee, I call in to the church, where the parish bulletin has brief details of the Mass at Cuas an Bhodaigh. Then I call in to the large building next door, once a Presentation convent, now the Irish campus for the Sacred Heart University, Connecticut (among other cultural and educational functions). A wedding has just ended in the chapel and the bridal party is posing for photos. A visiting priest directs me inside and there the receptionist responds to my enquiry about Cosán na Naomh and St Brendan's Day by summoning T.P. Ó Conchúir from an adjoining room.

His advice is focused: the noon Mass at Cuas an Bhodaigh is the place to be and there will still be time for the trek to the 'hill' afterwards. It is here that I notice the ultimate Kerry art of understatement. In all references to Mount Brandon, he refers to it as the 'hill', even though it is the fourth highest peak in all Ireland and the loftiest outside the Macgillycuddy Reeks at 951 metres.[113] His term is a direct translation of the Irish, of course, where the bulk dominating the skyline and northern horizon of the Gaeltacht area known as Corca Dhuibhne is named Cnoc Bhréanainn (Brendan's Hill). When he learns that I have come from Tyrone and our conversation turns to Gaelic football, I notice that this wily Kerry understatement is also employed to assess prospects of a challenge to the Kingdom's reign as all-Ireland champions. Cork is talked up, as are Dublin, Tyrone and several others, while the possible fortunes of his own beloved county are underplayed and set against the loss of key players. One suspects his faith in Kerry football is as unshakable as his faith in the rich Christian heritage of his home under the 'hill'.

10.00 p.m.

The third encounter of the day is with fellow pilgrim Róisín, who takes me to see Tobar Gobnait, a striking holy well in Dún Chaoin out beyond Ceann Sléibhe, with its crucifixion scene overlooking na Blascaodaí. The well is right beside the schoolhouse built for the filming of *Ryan's Daughter* 40 years ago, a lingering reminder of a Hollywood interlude that changed the district forever and alerted the world to its breathtaking beauty. The well itself has an ornamental head to represent Gobnait, a cross suspended over her forehead:

*By Gobnait's sculpted lump*
*a slab of a woman on a frieze of stone buds*
*and the locked bodies of bees …*[114]

The patron saint of the parish – and also of Baile Bhuirne, hub of the west-Cork Gaeltacht – is said to have been the daughter of a sea captain from Clare who founded a church in Inis Óir on the Aran Islands, another at Baile an Fheirtéaraigh, another in Baile Bhuirne and yet another in Kilgobnet in the Déise of Waterford near Dungarvan. Her feast day is on the 11 February and, although for some her name will evoke memories of comedian Frank Kelly's monologue recordings, she has commanded huge devotion in the Gaeltachts of Munster:

> *In 1601, the Gobnait devotion was sufficiently famous for Pope Clement VIII to grant an indulgence of ten years and quarantines to those who visited the parish church of Gobnait on the feast, went to Confession and Communion, and prayed for peace amongst Christian princes, expulsion of heresy and the exaltation of the Church.*[115]

A prayer for St Gobnait's intercession merits the indulgence of a few tasty pints of stout in Kruger Kavanagh's pub, another famous shrine in Dún Chaoin well worth a visit and only a short stroll to my bed and breakfast, Lóistín de Mórdha.

*Sunday, 16 May 2010*
11.30 a.m.
Another glorious day begins with the mellifluous Irish of the *bean an tí* at Lóistín de Mórdha in Dún Chaoin, high above the cliffs, with commanding views of the most

northerly of na Blascaodaí, Inis Tuaisceart. From this angle one can see why it is called an Fear Marbh (the Dead Man). Then an awe-inspiring drive around the western reaches of Corca Dhuibhne, past Ceann an Chloichir, Cuan Aird na Caithne and an Triúr Deirféar and through Baile an Fheirtéaraigh, an Mhuiríoch, Baile na nGall and on to Cuas an Bhodaigh. Here stewards direct the faithful into a large field car park. The television crews are in place, with cameras covering every angle, and big trucks are drawn up in the recess beside the statue of Brendan, a bronze figure almost hidden by the bronze sail of his tiny craft in a small enclosure at the top of the cove. According to T.P Ó Conchúir, 'There is only one statue of St Brendan in this district and it is at the top of Brandon Creek. Brendan is shown inside his little boat and it is written, "We will not allow our oars to be taken by the current". But there is no need for a statue here, for Brendan is in the mountains, the hills and the sea and in the consciousness of the people of this place. He is alive in this place.'

11.45 a.m.
Kairos Communications director Finbarr has a vantage beside one of his cameras on the road leading down to the quay, where a huge boom camera and two others have been arranged between the tiny table altar and the general congregation seated on tubular steel chairs. Another camera has been placed on a rocky overhang of the tiny cove. We greet Finbarr and wish him well, but he is clearly concerned that everything will turn out all right and the weather will stay dry.

'It will be OK on the night,' I reassure him, as we head off to take our pews across from the canvas sail with a red cross – the same one used by explorer Tim Severin when he set out from here on a tiny leather craft exactly 30 years ago to re-enact the Brendan Voyage, the most dangerous expedition he ever undertook. Yet Brendan faced an even more uncertain and dangerous outcome when he set out all those centuries before. T.P. Ó Conchúir acknowledges 'the bravery, the courage, the ability that he and his mariners had. And of course he depended on God and placed himself in God's hands.'

Yet the pivotal importance of that voyage and its recording and dissemination throughout Christendom is often overlooked in modern times. Fixation on the subsequent voyages of Columbus and others in the golden age of exploration have relegated Brendan's accomplishment to the shadows of the Dark Ages, the stuff of myth and legend. Yet there is a sound historical basis to the account of Brendan's epic voyage into the vast unknown and strong reason to believe that it sent others in his wake, including Columbus. Tim Severin points out that the lands described by Brendan appeared on medieval maps as 'Brendan's Islands'. Columbus actually went off in search of 'Brendan's islands when he was on his way to Cathay,' says the intrepid modern explorer.[116]

Donnchadh Ó Corráin, professor of medieval history at University College Cork, says:

> *Brendan is one of the best known of the Irish saints, a saint of the sixth century associated with the north of county Kerry and the Dingle Peninsula. His cult travelled widely along the Atlantic coast and devotion to him stretches southward as far as the Azores. His influence is enshrined in the* Navagatio Sancti Brendani *– the voyage of Brendan – written around the year 775 and carried in a single copy to continental Europe. It became the great wonder tale of*

> *Europe in the Middle Ages. The* Navagatio *tells us the story of man against the sea, man experiencing dramatic events. Both as an academic and as a human being, I find it fascinating. They encounter killer whales; they encounter icebergs; the text contains the first description of a North Atlantic volcanic eruption in the mountains of south-eastern Iceland. It may even be Eyjafjallajökull. It is also profoundly religious and volcanoes and killer whales and the ocean and the icebergs are all the products of a Creator. To discover them and to admire them is an act of religious devotion to their Creator.*[117]

12.15 p.m.
The prelude of commentators and experts has ended and the Mass has begun with a spirited processional – the local hymn to Brendan by Caoimhín Ó Cinnéide, OS. It is sung by the local choir of adults and children led by a button accordion and the concelebrants take their place on chairs beside the small table altar – Fr Eoghan Ó Cadhla, SP, Fr Pádraig Ó Fiannachta and Fr Tomás Ó hIcheadha. Then, with a welcome from Bosco Ó Conchúir to those present and those viewing, especially those who are old, infirm and in hospital, the Mass is under way. Still the weather is uncertain – until children dressed in bright yellow robes step out from the choir and take their places for a Peruvian-style dance to the Gloria. As they rise and kneel in synchronised movement, the sun breaks the clouds. From then on the scene on the quay at Cuas an Bhodaigh is bathed in a gentle sunshine. By another happy coincidence, meanwhile, a last-minute rearrangement of seats to fill up the front has me sitting right beside John Ahern, a contemplative monk in the tradition of Celtic Christianity, who lectures and leads field trips from the Sacred Heart

University. I was urged to contact him prior to my visit, but decided to treat this pilgrimage as the others and leave my encounters to chance, or God's will. When I tell him of my plans to walk Cosán na Naomh after Mass, he offers to accompany me for part of it.

12.45 p.m.
The readings for Ascension Sunday progress, followed by the Prayers of the Faithful by a succession of local people, especially youngsters – and the spirited response from the congregation: 'A Thiarna, bí ceansa agus éist linn' ('Lord, graciously hear us'). Then come the Offertory gifts – including an iconic picture of a swarthy Brendan and a model of his boat – followed by the Consecration and the Communion rite. By the time we are asked to exchange a sign of peace, there is an overwhelming sense of bonhomie in our small quayside congregation. And it continues through to the final hymn, which provides a rousing chorus for the Blessing of the Boats. Those of us at the front can follow this ceremony below on the slipway by looking at the boom-camera monitor. Fr Ó Cadhla climbs aboard a small motor craft and moves out into the water to bless the currachs and other vessels as the closing credits play on screen and the sun shines down on Cuas an Bhodaigh. Then it's over and we move *en masse* to the end of the pier and watch the boats bobbing about on the gentle swell as they head for open seas.

2.00 p.m.
The pilgrim path of Cosán na Naomh starts at the beachside car park in Ceann Trá, where it is intersected by another walking route, Slí Chorca Dhuibhne. While walkers on the latter follow the waymarker hidden behind the recycling bins, pilgrims simply head off uphill and inland along the

small road. With a waymarked right turn into a narrow lane and left along another uphill road, the route swings left along the base of Leataoibh, passing the round enclosure called Cill na gColmán and its boulder with the ancient ogham inscription of the name 'Colman the Pilgrim'. The tradition of pilgrimage to Cnoc Bhréanáinn has followed this route down the ages, with pilgrims arriving by sea to walk through the concentration of archaeological sites associated with the holy men who lived here. There are other pilgrim routes, including one from an Clochán. Yet the contrast of perspective on Cosán na Naomh is surely hard to match – the initial view across Bá an Daingin as far as Skellig Michael on a clear day and then the spectacular views to the west. Ceann Trá was the scene of a mythical battle between Finn McCool and Dáire Domhain, the 'Emperor of all the World'.[118] That epic battle lasted a year and a day and the pagan god of the sea, Manannán Mac Lir, eventually assisted Finn to victory.

Rounding Leataoibh Beag in a big loop past the tower-castle of Ráth Sheanáin, the view is of Cuan Aird na Caithne and an Triúr Deirféar, headlands that dip their toes into the most westerly waters of the Irish coast. On the right, the loftier slopes of Leataoibh Mór (318 metres) are hummocks formed by the melting glaciers of the last Ice Age. Across the main road, then, past the monastic enclosure of Teampall na Cluanach with its church, oratory, huts and cross-inscribed pillars. This marks the first in a rapid series of fascinating archaeological sites along this central part of Cosán na Naomh.

3.00 p.m.

Our Celtic spiritual mentor and guide, John Ahern, keeps apologising for delaying our pilgrimage schedule. He needn't bother, for the extra time spent in perusing this trove of wonders is entirely welcome. And what a guide he proves as we move from Gallarus Oratory through several other wonders, parting company with a blessing at Cill Maolcheadair. Nor are his observations on these sites the standard stuff of guide books. The Celtic Christian monk and lecturer constantly challenges popular interpretations and, while at it, draws in other visitors who simply have the luck to be at these sites at the same time as our small pilgrim party. With his trusty walking cane, which he proudly introduces as a stick cut from a hedge and fashioned by his father into a great drover's tool, he points constantly at features that might escape the casual tourist. And so we come to Gallarus, described with remarkable repetition as like an 'overturned boat' in all the guide books. I much prefer the description of poet Seamus Heaney, who observes that it is 'like going into a turfstack, / A core of old dark walled up with stone / A yard thick'.[119] John Ahern invites us to notice something that contradicts the received wisdom about this ancient place.

'There are 140,000 visitors to this place every year,' he notes, 'and hardly any of them spot this – and it goes against what is in the guide books and what you will hear in the interpretative centre down there.' He points in the direction of the main private car park, where visitors pay at the entrance for a video introduction to the site, unaware that there is a free public entrance just a hundred metres further up the road. John then points his stick upwards and I realise that the curvature of the two side-walls, which forms the stone roof, stops just short of meeting. The gap is bridged by a series of capstones that give the illusion of an intricate junction.

Our mentor is delighted at my observation and says, 'Yes, the wonderful thing about this building is that you could knock down this wall ...' he points with his stick, 'and the rest would still be standing. I don't think engineers today could do as good as that.' He also points out that, rather than being a hermetically sealed enclosure, there is a spot where the narrowest gap between the stones penetrates all the way through. It is tiny and can be seen from an angle, perhaps only by those who know of its existence. I think of Patrick Kavanagh's line in his poem 'Advent': 'We have tested and tasted too much, lover – Through a chink too wide there comes in no wonder,' and decide that this chink is narrow enough to encapsulate all the wonder of this ancient place of worship. As Revd Patrick Power of UCC wrote so colourfully in his description of the 'oldest church in Ireland', it 'has seen the snows of fourteen hundred winters upon Brandon mountain, and was contemporary with St Columba. It saw the Danes come and go, and it was hoary when Strongbow landed.'[120]

Yet attempts by eminent archaeologists such as Peter Harbison to date the structure have come up with nothing more definite than that it was constructed some time between AD 700 and AD 1200. In other words, between St Brendan's voyage to the Americas and the Anglo-Norman invasion of 1169. For centuries, however, it has continued to fascinate pilgrims and tourists. Already we have been introduced to the doorway flaw that signifies the builders' humble desire to demonstrate imperfection in the face of the Almighty and now John leads the way to the bed of stones to the left of Gallarus, with its small standing stone just over a metre in height. This is described as a 'burial place' in my Cosán na Naomh guide book, but John prefers to think that the jury is still out. He would welcome a modern archaeological study of this and other important sites in the district. He points out the inscription, 'Colum Mac Dinet', written vertically from the right facing the stone. The man of that name is not remembered or known beyond the inscription, yet the 'Colum Mac' can be clearly seen in the uncial script of medieval scholars – all capital letters developed from old Roman cursive writing. The 'Dinet' is less clear but the old Gaelic 'D' can be made out. John says several times that this is the clearest he has ever seen the inscription in all his years of visiting and studying the site. Clearly this bright sunny St Brendan's feast is a day of wondrous revelation.

3.45 p.m.
From Gallarus, the pilgrim path takes a dogleg turn towards the ocean, past the nearby castle which was built in the fifteenth century by the FitzGeralds, the Norman interlopers who remained in residence there until the Williamite Wars and who still reside scattered among the indigenous seed of Corca Dhuibhne. Then it's back inland to Cathair Deargáin, a substantial stone *cashel* with ruins of circular buildings that may have constituted as many as five large rooms within the defensive wall. John points out the formidable walls facing an incursion from the sea with its panoramic view of an Triúr Deirféar. Inside the one of the circular rooms, a souterrain built under the wall may have been used for cooler food storage or hiding. We proceed just up the road to Fothrach an tSainsiléara (the Chancellor's House), a long run of rectangular rooms, with a large pizza-type oven built into the fireplace at the side of one of them. This would have been the home of successive representatives of the diocese of Ardfert during the later medieval period. It was a substantial dwelling whose occupants were supported by Cill Maolcheadair Church and the offerings of pilgrims passing along Cosán na Naomh towards the sacred hill of Brendan beyond.

4.15 p.m.
Even though our mentor John apologises again for delaying the pilgrims on Cosán na Naomh, our visit to Cill Maolcheadair provides just a cursory examination of this trove of archaeological and ecclesiastical treasures. The church, attributed to Brendan but more likely founded by St Maolcethar, who died in AD 636, enshrines many of the finest examples of medieval church architecture in Ireland. Unlike Gallarus, which clearly follows a Celtic tradition, this Romanesque structure up the way marks a period when strenuous efforts were being made to draw Irish Christians into the fold of Christendom throughout the rest of Europe. It retains Celtic aspects, which John points out, but they are incorporated into structural norms that are evident in other ecclesiastical remains from the period.

Starting outside in the old graveyard, our brief lecture incorporates various standing stones and crosses – some with Celtic ornamentation, one used as a sundial and another that has been used in a custom to signify betrothal, much like the meeting stone in Gleann Cholm Cille. Then it's on to the beautiful archway leading into the church itself. John and I agree that it is strikingly similar to the doorway of Teampall na gCailleach at Clonmacnoise. Inside we study the various strata of stones, showing where the building materials originated; one ogham-inscribed stone brings us the name of Mael Inbir Mac Brocán, if not his story. At the far gable wall of the chancel, built as an extension to the church a century later, John points out the 'Eye of the Needle' window. Tradition has it that anyone who can squeeze himself or herself through is sure of eternal salvation. I decline to try, feeling rather more like a camel at that point. Then outside and through the new cemetery, where the headstones provide a modern who's who of Corca Dhuibhne. Among these is the headstone of poet Caoimhín Ó Cinnéide, who died in 1985 and whose hymn to Brendan was sung at the procession for today's Mass. His succinct epitaph reads: 'Níl sa tsaol seo ach naíscoil na síoraíochta' ('This life is only the kindergarten for eternity').

Next, we move out into the lane and up towards the next waymark for Cosán na Naomh, beside a padlocked galvanised-steel gate. Over it, John points out the substantial remains of a sturdy two-storey building known as Fothrach Bréanann (Brendan's Ruins). The robust walls seem blanched and have a chancel-type window along with narrow slits and an attic window high in the northern gable. This building may have housed the parish priest of a later period (thought to be the sixteenth or seventeenth century) than Fothrach an tSainsiléara below. It was once part of the tourist trail, but now the landowner has closed off access. Scattered around the neighbouring fields, our mentor tells us, are many other archaeological sites – for another time, perhaps. So, with bowed heads, we receive a solemn yet uplifting blessing from this Celtic Christian monk for the remainder of our pilgrimage along Cosán na Naomh on the feast of St Brendan. We part ways – he heads off for a late Sunday lunch and two pilgrims trudge off up the gentle slope of Cnoc Rinn Chonaill.

5.15 p.m.

The first part of the route after Cill Maolcheadair is along a lane that has an old cobbled base, thought to be the remains of the old pilgrimage road trudged for generations, especially on this blessed day of Brendan. Today, it is deserted but for a pair of pilgrims who move towards the summit in expectation of another spectacular view of the holy hill of Cnoc Bhréanainn. The pilgrims pass through fields of rough mountain pasture via stiles over the dry-stone walls. Sporadic waymarkers show the route, but are hardly needed as the unseen mountain presides over the rest of Corca Dhuibhne. Finally to the summit, where a rocky outcrop is decorated with the Celtic circular symbol of eternity and the vista opens up to mighty Brandon.

The spectacular valley below the mountain spills into a coastal plain around an Mhuiríoch and then into the ocean. The middle valley, tucked into the mountain, follows Abha na Feothanaí and the march of small, walled green fields that spill from its banks are pock-marked here and there by the remains of circular ringforts. As the pilgrims descend, the valley to the right, or north-east, opens up into the vale of Com an Lochaigh. Just beyond the ruins of Corráilí at the base of Rinn Chonaill, a stone-wall enclosure containing the remains of a beehive hut and standing stone with a cross and Celtic symbols, is a small country road. The pilgrim path continues across land but, in the absence of a way-marker, we take the road that follows a circuitous path back towards the base of Brandon. Just beyond the pub called an Bóthar in Baile na nGall, the road turns sharply right and starts to rise. Past fields of grazing sheep with lambs, it turns sharply right again at an unoccupied house whose front lawns are a blanket of daisies. The tiny white flowers with yellow centres even grow from the old concrete path to the front door. A little way ahead, a solid concrete silo-type structure commands a magnificent view of the coast and an Triúr Deirféar.

Finally, in the car park at an Baile Breac, a plaque on a stone monument recognises Dáithí Ó Gríofa, Liam Ó hUigín, Berní Ní Concubhair and Jane Power, who each have walked the path of Cosán na Naomh 'for the cure of cancer' in each successive year from 2006 to 2009. There is ample space for more names to be added to the list of those to follow 'ar Chosán na Naomh faoi choimirce Bhréanainn' ('on the Saints' Trail protected by St Brendan'). At a standing stone marked by a simple cross, across a crystal-clear stream from a small grotto, the Heritage Council route for Cosán na Naomh ends. From here, pilgrims can follow the traditional path to the summit 'at their own risk'.

7.00 p.m.
The television news ends after coverage of the day's Gaelic sports. In the bar/restaurant of an Bóthar, many of the local people linger in clusters, reluctant to leave and bring the weekend to a close. As we chat about the health of vernacular Irish in the Gaeltacht locality, where a generation gulf has opened up, with young people choosing the English they speak at school, Leo Ó Murchú tells us they have been there since Sunday lunch. The crowds came in after the Mass at nearby Cuas an Bhodaigh and many of them stayed on to celebrate St Brendan's Day by watching the Munster football championship match against Tipperary at Thurles. Kerry won easily in the end – but, in the heart of the Kingdom, they are still talking deferentially about the odds being stacked for a big Cork year.

8.00 p.m.
I make the spectacular journey back across an Chonair, heading north through an Clochán to the village of Cé Bhréanainn, which nestles under the mighty mountain that protects its picturesque bay. I have been offered hospitality and enjoy an evening's chat at one of the local pubs before retiring early. Outside, the village is deserted, the last outpost on this long finger that juts out into the mighty ocean, the refuge of a holy man who climbed to the summit of the 'hill', looked out

and saw beyond the waves. This man climbed into a leather-skinned vessel (known hereabouts as a *naomhóg*) one day and set a course for the Island of Promise he had heard about from a hermit who lived off the coast of Donegal. In times to come, many more would follow in his wake in search of the Island of Promise, leaving their fate to the intercession of St Brendan and the God he trusted implicitly as he and his fellow mariners pushed out and beyond:

*I think especially of Brendan setting sail*
*One day the sea was blueblack*
*As his body that overnight he had beaten.*
*Drifting along wherever God liked*
*And the people living by bread alone*
*Shouting after Good Luck, Good Luck.*[121]

*Monday, 16 May 2010*
10.30 a.m.
Ken Roddy says his boat is fully booked for today's sailing and asks if I can wait until tomorrow. I tell him that I plan to head back north this evening, and he says to come on ahead and he will make sure I get passage. I finish my roadside coffee and press on for Cahirciveen and Portmagee beyond, where pilgrims embark for Skellig Michael, the last refuge of Christendom in the known world – a tiny monastic settlement clinging to the edge of a cliff on top of a volcano-shaped rock that juts 700 feet into the heavens.

After I arrived late from west Cork through Kenmare on Saturday, I enquired at the tourist-information office in Cahirciveen and my name and phone number were passed on to Ken Roddy. Ken's family has been associated with the Skelligs for generations – first as lighthouse keepers on the remote rock, then as ferry operators. He tried to call me but was unable to get through to my Northern Ireland mobile number. Yet all is well when I arrive in Portmagee after a two-hour drive from the foot of Brandon, including another spectacular mountain pass on Rock Road between Lock Mountain and Caherconree and between Camp and Aughils to take me off the peninsula. Now at the dockside in Portmagee, I find Ken and he tells me to climb into a boat moored at the quayside, inside another small vessel with a group of American women on board. I take a photo of them on their camera before their boat pulls off with many waves and *bon voyages* and heads out the bay. Heedless for a moment of Ken's caution to stay on board, I climb up onto the pier, walk out to the end and watch the small flotilla of four boats bobbing on the swell as they head for open seas. By the time I get back, boatman Michael Pat Murphy is already on board with a couple of others. As I get on I am followed immediately by a group of seven, making ten passengers in all, the full complement for the passage. Our boatman dispenses oilskin jackets and trousers to all and casts off. Soon we are bobbing along after the other boats through relatively calm waters on another beautiful day.

10.45 a.m.
By the time we pass the outer headland with its Martello fortification, the swell is more pronounced and occasional splashes punctuate our voyage. What must it have been like in a small leather-skin boat such as the one on which Brendan sailed off into the vast unknown? Passage to Skellig Michael takes an hour and I chat occasionally with the others on board. They are German and one with fairly good English tells me that this is his thirteenth trip out to the Skelligs and his forty-fifth visit to Ireland. I ask why he doesn't just move here permanently, but my irony is lost in translation.

Then, after a few moments, he smiles at me and points off the port side of our boat. The inner Skellig is now visible, a stark rock plastered with white bird droppings. I stand and lean out the starboard side, beyond the cabin where Michael Pat is steering our voyage, and there it is – a vision to impress even the most jaded pilgrim. Skellig Michael juts abruptly upwards from the waves, a huge grey mass with pointed summit shrouded in the mist of the heavy clouds as waves lash its nether regions. We get closer; the other boats are bobbing about in a small cave-like cove, taking turns to approach and nestle up to the small jetty and empty themselves of their pilgrim passengers. Closer in, the grey austerity of the rock has mellowed somewhat to reveal a light sheet of green vegetation clinging to its rocky surface. The boats seem hopelessly fragile and insignificant as they nestle into the jetty to disgorge, like tiny insects depositing eggs on a larger being. Then each empty boat motors out onto the waves and assumes an idling position, waiting patiently until it is time to collect the passengers. It would take all of the allotted two-hour stopover on the rock to travel back to shore and then return for the rendezvous.

Soon it is our turn. Michael Pat expertly nudges up to the jetty. The boat rises and falls on the swell as we hop ashore onto the steps on Michael Pat's arm. He informs each in turn that he will be back in for us at two o'clock.

11.30 a.m.

Ascending from the jetty along the railed and then walled path that skirts the lower cliffs induces a feeling of huge excitement. Pilgrim passengers from the earlier boats have congregated along the wall, taking photos and delighting in the huge flocks of puffins resting on the rocks just beneath them. A veranda covers a large section of the path here, presumably to protect users from the bird droppings that fall from the huge nesting area above. Round a corner and through a gate, the helicopter pad perches precariously on a tiny ledge on the leeward side of the rock, barely big enough for the aircraft, while a refuge-type building on the inward side of the path is locked against intrusion. I pass by, imagining the scenes of terror, panic and concern that must have unfolded here only last year when, in separate incidents, two American visitors had to be airlifted from the rock after falling from the path above us – two tragedies that proved fatal.[122] In such a confined area, where access to and from the rock is channelled along such a narrow passage and contact with the mainland is remote and fragile, the impact must have been truly frightening for other pilgrims and almost impossibly difficult for the rescue personnel.

I press on along the wall and come to the bottom of the steps that begin to climb in a course that zigzags along a narrow path hewn from the rock. Pilgrims from earlier boats have already begun the ascent and I climb after them, easing my way up the slope and momentarily thankful that I feel fit, fresh and exhilarated from my pilgrimage along Cosán na Naomh yesterday. Under a big overhanging rock, where others pause to have photos taken as they pretend to hold up the boulder to stop its collapse, the path comes to its first major recess on a natural ledge. Here, a big standing rock, weather beaten through the ages and pierced with several small eye-openings, has drawn the attention of others, who pause. Beyond the rock across the wide ocean channel, the inner Skellig is clearly visible with its flocks of seabirds. Beyond, the shore of the mainland, 12 kilometres away, is shrouded in mist. We are alone and at peace, except for the circling birds in the sky and the few tiny boats bobbing on the waves below us.

From here, the gentle zigzag of the climb gives way to stone steps that lead heavenwards in lines that vary little from a straight course up the rock. Pilgrims from the earlier boats climb and pause, turning to drink in the ever-widening view from the loftier perspective. Up and up the stone steps lead. I pass others who have paused for breath and a view, just as they pass me in turn. Then on to a level area, where the rock splits in two – like two giant rocky horns – with the steps leading up one side. There is a small area of vegetation and a makeshift security fence about 5 metres ahead to prevent anyone straying too close to the cliff edge there. The majority of those who have pressed ahead are gathered here, preparing for the final assault. They include a group of excited American students and the first trio of these takes the lead in the push for the summit. I follow immediately in their wake with a young woman in their group. We chat briefly through laboured breath as we near the top, then arrive through a narrow gap in the crown of rocky thorns into the sacred place where the cloud mist swirls. I look back and down. The other horn of rock, where a tiny hermitage once provided an even more arduous sanctuary for the holy people who came here to live and pray, is almost lost in the mist. Below, the pilgrims in the recess area seem like tiny entities in this overwhelming place and far, far below, the cliffs fall down and down to the sea, which appears calm and vast. It is a huge watery barrier between the world and this sanctified place in the last fragile outpost of Christendom, far out from land's end. Here, communion with the Creator seems much more accessible than communication with the mortal world over the waves and beyond the mists.

12.15 p.m.

The monastic settlement perched on the cliffs near the very summit of this island rock dedicated to Michael, the archangel with a sword who led the souls of the saints into heaven, is bigger than I expected from photos I have seen. Yet in the expanse of its setting, it is small and precipitous. Surrounded by a formidable dry-stone wall, access is through a narrow portal surmounted by a large lintel. Attached to the wall is a 'Fógra' ('Notice'), pockmarked with rust, declaring in the first and second official languages of the state that this 'Séadchomhartha Náisiúnta' ('National Monument') is in the care of the Commissioners of Public Works under the 1930 act. The old Gaelic typeface with archaic lettering appears to have been there since then. Certainly it would be incomprehensible in Irish to anyone who is unfamiliar with the alphabet taught before the introduction of standardised Roman script in the mid-1960s, which dispensed with the *sí buailte* dot marking *séimhiú* and removed the confusion of the letters replaced by the Roman r and s. Yet if that notice seems ancient at less than a century old, then the passage along the path and up past a garden enclosure, through a second narrow portal in a massive dry-stone wall, is a time-traveller's dream sequence.

In a tiny group we walk in silence, as three of the American students lead the way into the sacred past of Skellig Michael. Entry is up more rough stone steps, through the narrow passage in the vast stone wall that has protected what survives within from the wintry blasts of the north for more than 1,500 years. The monastic buildings within remain intact in all their humility, yet larger again than I had envisaged from photos. Indeed, the cluster of buildings, dry-stone beehive huts built close together for protection and practicality in the minimal space available, evokes images of a busy little cloister inhabited by holy people who made every provision possible for their survival in such a harsh environment. Between the huts, a flagstone-paved path with steps to each of the buildings is dominated by a relatively large, striking but simple, cross hewn from stone. It reminds me once more of the ancient cross in Carndonagh, far off near the most northerly point in Ireland. It has none of the elaborate carving of the Celtic high crosses that were used for instruction of the faithful. This is an elegant testimonial wrought in a single piece of stone to the Christian faith of those who lived and prayed here for more than half a millennium.

About midway through the monastic 'street', a raised bed covered in peat and grass has rows of small crosses and slabs along the sides – about two dozen in all. It is believed to be the final resting place for the mortal remains of those who lived here, more than halfway to the heavens to which they aspired. I pause by the bed, counting the headstones, and pray for the repose of those within and all who have visited their monastic eyrie. Back though the narrow street we move in silence, crouching through the low doorways into the beehive dwellings, where the ancient darkness opens up into a shadowy interior that is more spacious than anticipated, relatively commodious accommodation for the dozen or so monks who would have lived here.

One building in particular, near the entrance, seems huge inside. It is rectangular, with four walls coming together at an apex surmounted by a headstone, reminiscent of Gallarus Oratory on Cosán na Naomh. Unlike the smaller beehive buildings, it has small window openings that allow the light of God to pierce the gloom within. Back outside, the mist still enfolds the clifftop settlement as I scramble up the back, past another enclosed area containing a smaller rectangular building thought to be another oratory. The small, flat area may also have been a meagre garden, where the monks cultivated what they could in the lee of the summit to supplement their diet of fish, seal meat and birds' eggs scavenged from the rocks and cliffs below them.

As fellow pilgrims move in silent reverence from one building to another, pausing for photos with friends, I seek out the solitude of the heights. I gather my thoughts and eat my lunch with the birds, who settle momentarily and then rise into the misty heavens. Though a relatively frugal repast of an apple, a banana and an orange, with a bottle of water, it seems positively sumptuous and exotic in such a spartan place.

1.00 p.m.
I am joined by some of the students who arrived with me in the vanguard of today's pilgrims, and I discover that they have been studying in Ireland for the past year. The two male students seek out the most precipitous places for souvenir photos of each other. I learn they are from Montana, but they admit that even that land of mountain peaks has nothing compared to this. The young woman I chatted to on the final ascent sits down beside me. Her name is Chelsea and she tells me that she has been studying at Trinity College Dublin, where one of her lecturers told them about this place. Chelsea says, 'I really needed to come here after that and it is more than I even dared to hope it would be. It is so hard for us who have grown up with everything we wanted or needed to imagine that anybody could have lived out here. It must have taken all their ingenuity, all the resources they could gather and a heck of a lot of faith in God to survive, but it is so beautiful. It is more than worth it.' Chelsea tells me she hopes to become a writer some day, but she is returning to complete her final year of study at Notre Dame University in Indiana.

As we 'bond' (the term she uses to her friends), she asks me frankly about my faith. For the first time in many years, I have absolutely no hesitation in asserting my belief in Christ. I tell her briefly of my spiritual reawakening in the Catholic Church in which I was baptised and confirmed, yet which has seemed peripheral, inconvenient and irrational for much of my life. She confirms her own Catholic faith with a candid freshness and I ask her about her impressions of faith in Ireland as she has experienced it over the past year. Chelsea pauses to find the words and then looks me straight in the eye.

'People my age here don't seem to know that there is a difference between organised religion and spiritual faith,' she says. 'They have lost faith in religion because of what has been happening and they have rejected it outright but they don't have anything else to fall back on. They don't seem to have any sense of spirituality – not those I have met, anyway.'

Seated beside me on a slab of rock at the summit of a huge pointed crag where saintly men once prayed for the salvation of their people, this young American woman drops her eyes and plucks at a stony knob momentarily. 'I feel so sorry for them, and for all those who have no faith,' she tells me quietly, 'and I pray for them, because we all need spiritual hope. We all need faith in our lives.'

1.45 p.m.

Back down in the monastic site, Chelsea takes a photo of me on my camera as pilgrims move from one building to another. Of the 40 to 50 people who have come out today, I estimate that only a dozen or so have come all the way up here to the crowning glory of this sacred rock. We move from enclosure to enclosure, lost in our thoughts and prayers, and pause to read the inscription on a slab to the memory of Patrick Callaghan and his brother William, aged two and four in the successive years of 1868 and 1869. I learn later that they were the children of one of the families that kept the signal alight in the two lighthouses that once sat on this offshore rock, which in turn kept a spiritual flame alight through the Dark Ages. Slowly, then, we all descend the rocky path for the rendezvous with the boat.

I linger as long as I can, drinking in the spiritual essence left here by the holy inhabitants of six successive centuries. They finally moved their monastery to the mainland as the asceticism of the Celtic Christian Church was weathered away and absorbed into the Augustinian pomp and majesty of the Roman Church, solidified in Ireland after the Anglo-Norman conquest. Down through the inner portal, I realise that spiral steps in what I had taken as a walled garden enclosure lead into a hole that leads to a ledge, where a hoist once allowed cargoes to be hauled up from the shoreline cave hundreds of metres below. I go through the second portal and back down the narrow path, with the cliffs plunging to the side below, then along a shelf pathway. The helicopter pad is far below, and other pilgrims down near it scramble around the island's nether regions. Down and down and down, following the path of the American students directly below me, past the small recesses where climbers paused earlier and into what seems like a verdant region of mossy grass with blankets of delicate white flowers. Puffins roost and pose nonchalantly for photos as cameras inch closer and closer to them.

I pause to absorb the tranquillity of a place where wildlife seems so dismissive of human incursion, oblivious to any predatory fears. A seagull lands beside me, its vivid orange beak and yellow eyes and feet a beautiful contrast to the grey plumage, jet-black tail and striking white breast and belly. I notice that it has a metal ring on its right leg.

Together we stand on the cliff path of Skellig Michael, at one with our surroundings and each other.

I move further down, where the steps reach the wall path, and spot clusters of tiny pink blossoms growing from the crevices of the cut stone – the same gentle pink flowers I see here and there on rocky ledges and shelves – clinging to life and survival in a starkly inhospitable place and bringing to it a glimpse of beauty and hope beyond the utilitarian world we inhabit. High above, the cliffs rise to the monastic summit and I notice the crevices of growth and life going all the way up, natural successors to the sacred dwelling of the past. I am asked to delay on the pass by a woman, one of several keeping guard while a female companion has a 'rest stop' along the path, as the Americans might say. There are no public toilet facilities on Skellig Michael.

The students come along, and I point out a series of steps and parts of an alternative path I have spotted hewn from the cliffs above. We wonder again at the faith that drove the need to scale this rock and inhabit it for the greater glory and honour of the divine Creator. We move on, and I pause beside the Germans who came out in the same boat. They are ranged along the veranda, their intricate and expensive cameras trained on the puffins below. The man I spoke to on the passage out tells me they have been here since landing.

'We only come to photograph the puffins,' he tells me. 'It is best to come in July because then you can photograph them with little fishes in their beaks. It is good.'

I move along down to the pier as they begin to dismantle and pack their gear, confident that not even the delight of nature down here can begin to compare with the path to the peak and what lies high above the cameras trained on the birds below.

3.00 p.m.
Down at the jetty, the boats heave to and the pilgrims board. Turning about, they come alongside, facing into a cavernous opening where the rock is a striking shade of pink. A boat called the *Flying Horse*, which arrived later with its passengers from Ballinskelligs, unhitches and nudges into the cave to allow Michael Pat to heave to. We clamber aboard once more. I secure a seat at the stern as we cast off and the engine guns our way into a billowing wake from the rock. Above in the heavenly height, the ancient monastic village is lapsing into its sanctified solitude. We move further and further offshore and soon move in a set course around the shores of Little Skellig, where cameras click and snap pictures of the huge flocks of shearwaters that nest there, a population barely dented by the kestrels and other predators that hover in its environs. Then, passing a small fishing boat, where two men wave in a greeting I alone return, we make for the shore. Skellig Michael recedes further and further from view across the waves.

I retrace my pilgrim path back to the harbour of Portmagee, where Michael Pat Murphy lends me a helping hand as I climb from his boat and pay him the €40 ferry passage he has not asked for directly. He asks me where I have come from and I tell him Tyrone.

'I thought so,' says he with a smile, and we part as friends. Michael Pat is another who has assisted my pilgrim path to its remote conclusion on Skellig Michael and brought me back to shore for the long drive home to the north – back to the real world, where:

*There is a wind of politics*
*A wind that blows about our walls*
*Not just our European history*

*Hitler and St Francis of Assisi –*
*For all that we may walk today*
*In Harold's Cross among laburnums*
*From Sceilg Mhichíl to the Albaicín*
*Do penance in Jerusalem*
*Or make the journey from St Jacques*
*The pilgrim road to Santiago*
*With silver wings upon our heels*
*Tomorrow in Bohemian Grove*
*Or Berchtesaden*
*Or some other version of the Bunker*
*Serious heads of state will sit*
*Drinking from a human cup*
*Without reflecting surfaces*
*Greek Fire or Pepper's Ghost*
*Or the magician's smoky glass –*
*It will be real no artifice*
*No mime of tinsel there or heartbreak*
*But toasts to commerce and to murder*
*Drinking to the dispossessed*
*Whose unforgiving skulls they use*
*Ai Ai Hieronymo*
*Ai Ai Alhambra*

*And still we carry on*
*While there is sunlight in the corridor*
*The news ticks in piles up*
*From all points of the compass –*
*The winter will be hungry*
*And the hard winds blow …*[123]

# Conclusion

# Salvation in Sight

*Tuesday, 8 June 2010*

My pilgrim path began a year ago on the shores of a lonely Donegal lake in the sanctified surrounds of St Patrick's Purgatory. Since then, it has brought me through some of the most beautiful places I could ever hope to visit. That alone is more than worth the effort. Yet I have gained so much more. Along the way, I have enjoyed the privilege of meeting some of the most humble and reflective people I could possibly encounter. I have seen the resilience of faith, the healing power of humour and fellowship and the strength of fundamental hope based on real and lasting values, which were honed through the generations before hope died in so many hearts, minds and souls. I have sensed the spiritual essence of my heritage in all its evocative glory. I have been to places that have harboured holiness down the ages, through times that were a lot more austere and bereft of hope than anything we can imagine, even in our jolting and rapid descent from the clutches of the Celtic Tiger.

Along my penitential path, I have learned that pilgrimage is at the core of a spiritual search fundamental to the human condition. In our spiritual quests through organised religion and even alone, in our personal search for inner peace, it is a driving force of our lives. It involves both a real journey and an inner odyssey to special places that have already drawn countless people just like us. I have learned beyond doubt that this journey is at least as important as actually getting there.

Yet I firmly believe that the path to the special solace to be found in these places is not open to those who travel in air-conditioned coaches, jetliners or comfortable cars. I doubt that it is open to those who take a tourist jaunt by bicycle or on foot along the *route* à *la mode*, with a race to the next hostel or hotel and the empty boast that that is another experience chalked up and what is next?

The pilgrim path is at best a rough-hewn, barely detectable *tóchar*, a lane that follows ley lines of our earth with a magnetic pull. It traverses mountain passes, bogs and mires, follows rivers and crosses streams, scales rocky inclines and plunges into secluded valleys, climbs to cliff crevices and crests the ridge of an ancient geological fault line on an ancient high road. It follows medieval highways now consigned to cattle and sheep paths with precious, precarious rights of way for pilgrims; it skirts and nips across the modern borders of man; it crosses stiles on lesser land boundaries; and it is often shrouded in freezing fog, pounded by driving rain or bathed in glorious sunshine. Along the way, it visits ancient wells that have provided the essence of spiritual belief as well as life-giving water, encompassing the ancient monasteries, hermitages and places of worship of those who have long gone to their eternal reward. It is enshrouded in silent reverence, yet it is alive with the sounds and wonders of nature. It defies the passage of time and the emptiness of earthly fixations. Its steady decline by age enhances an inner beauty that contrasts with the corruption of the world surrounding it and the empty values of those who have strayed from the path to wonder and worship.

It is a slow, often painful trek, invariably tiring to the point of exhaustion. Yet it leads to a place of rest and trust. It begins with a first step on the same path taken by all those who have gone before. That initial, tentative footstep takes the pilgrim on a voyage of discovery – not just in the actual world that reveals itself along the way, but also in the thoughts and values of those who walk it in wonder. Along the way, the true pilgrim path empties our minds and spirits of all the dross that comforts but blinds our lives to the focus on what we need. Then it fills the void with a peace that passes understanding.

I began my journey in the jaded cynicism of a world where I shared the panic and pain of material concerns. I feel slightly more comfortable now in acknowledging that I continue it in a spirit of growing grace and gratitude for all that I have and the inner peace I am finding. My journey continues because the path goes on and there are still many places to visit in prayer and wonder. I have missed so much because I did not know how to look. Not least among the places I have neglected is the ancient monastic town of Clones, where I grew up, founded by Tigernach in the pivotal year of Our Lord AD 500 – a holy place still rich with the spiritual essence of its past. Within the environs of my childhood home, there is the attendant monastic site of Tigernach across the adjacent border at Galloon Island and Aghalurcher, where the chieftains of the Maguires lie in repose. A short distance from there is the monastic island of Devenish in all its earthly splendour on Lough Erne.

Further afield, there are countless places I have learned of along my pilgrim journey – fascinating places such as Inis na mBeo at Monaincha, just outside Roscrea. Giraldus

Cambrensis described an island monastic retreat there as the island of eternal life. Once upon a time it ranked alongside Lough Derg in Ulster, Croagh Patrick in Connacht and Glendalough in Leinster as one of the four great pilgrimage sites of medieval Ireland. Today it is virtually forgotten, in a world that has let go of the wealth of its spiritual past. Then there is the Saints Island on the Shannon; the remainder of the pilgrim path from Ardmore through Lismore to Cashel; the alternative course of St Kevin's Way from Valleymount, with the walk this time through the Wicklow Gap; and so much more.

The path of the pilgrim is as long as life itself. It has many starting points, yet it has only one destination. As I have endeavoured to follow it, I have learned that it is a path truly worth taking, for it leads the true pilgrim through wondrous places to the most wondrous place of all … thanks be to God.

# Notes

1 Paulo Coelho, *The Pilgrimage* (Alan R. Clarke, trans.) (London, 1992), p. 32.

2 Louis MacNeice, 'The Truisms', *Louis MacNeice: Poems* (Michael Longley, ed.) (London, 2001), p. 96.

3 Returning to Lough Derg in September 2009, I find it transformed, with a walkway down to the water's edge here and a stainless-steel cross marking the spot where pilgrims once crossed the causeway bridge to Saints Island.

4 Patrick Kavanagh, 'Lough Derg', *Collected Poems* (Antoinette Quinn, ed.) (London and New York, 2004), p. 109.

5 Lady Augusta Gregory, *Gods and Fighting Men: the Story of the Tuatha Dé Danann and of the Fianna of Ireland* (Oxford and New York, 1970), p. 111.

6 Michael Dames, *Mythic Ireland* (London, 1992), pp. 22–4.

7 Joseph Duffy, *Patrick in his Own Words* (Dublin, 1972), p. 66.

8 William Grattan-Flood, 'St Patrick's Purgatory', *The Catholic Encyclopedia*, vol. 12 (New York, 1911), <http://www.newadvent.org/cathen/12580a.htm> (accessed 25 September 2011).

9 Michael Haren and Yolande de Pontfarcy, *The Medieval Pilgrimage to St Patrick's Purgatory: Lough Derg and the European Tradition* (Enniskillen, 1988). The story was popularised in a medieval long poem, *L'Espurgatoire Seint Patriz* by Marie de France.

10 Filip Coppens, 'Ramon's Voyage to Purgatory', *Société Périllos*, <http://www.perillos.com/purgatory.html> (accessed 25 September 2011).

11 Carol G. Zaleski, 'St Patrick's Purgatory: Pilgrimage Motifs in a Medieval Otherworld Vision', *Journal of the History of Ideas*, vol. 46, no. 4 (October–December 1985), pp. 467–85.

12 See 'Historical Chronology', *Lough Derg*, <http://www.loughderg.org/heritage/historical-chronology> (accessed 25 September 2011).

13 Peggy O'Brien, *Writing Lough Derg: From William Carleton to Seamus Heaney* (New York, 2006), p. 77.

14 James Reston, *Dogs of God: Columbus, the Inquisition and the Defeat of the Moors* (New York, 2005), p. 287.

15 Kavanagh, 'Lough Derg'.

16 Seamus Heaney, 'Triptych III At the Water's Edge', *Field Work* (London, 1979), p. 14.

17 Ian Bradley, 'When All Roads Lead to a Sense of the Sacred,' *The Times*, 7 April 2009.

18 Gregory, *Gods and Fighting Men*, p. 132.

19 Kavanagh, 'Lough Derg'.

20 Katie Donovan, 'On a Spiritual Journey', *The Irish Times*, 5 July 1994.

21 Oideas Gael, *Gleann Cholm Cille: Treoirleabhar Ildaite le Léarscáil* (Glencolmcille, 2005).

22 Caroline Madden, 'CSO Figures Show Financial Assets of Irish Households Down by 42%', *The Irish Times*, 17 June 2009.

23 Frank McNally, 'An Irishman's Diary', *The Irish Times*, 27 August 2009.

24 Michael Herity, *Glencolumbkille: A Guide to 5,000 Years of History in Stone* (Dublin, 1971).

25 Oideas Gael, *Gleann Cholm Cille*, pp. 18–19.

26 Lawrence J. Taylor, *Occasions of Faith: An Anthropology of Irish Catholics* (Dublin, 1997), pp. 35–76.

27 Cary Meehan, *The Traveller's Guide to Sacred Ireland: A Guide to the Sacred Places of Ireland, her Legends, Folklore and People* (Glastonbury, 2004), p. 114.

28 Gabriel Rosenstock, '20', *Uttering her Name* (County Clare, 2009), p. 20.

29 Oideas Gael, *Gleann Cholm Cille*, p. 41.

30 Ballintubber Teamwork, *Tóchar Phádraig: Patrick's Causeway from Ballintubber to Croagh Patrick – A Pilgrim's Progress* (Ballintubber, 2006), p. iv.

31 John Healy, 'St Patrick in the Far West', *Irish Essays: Literary and Historical* (Dublin, 1908), *Library Ireland*, <http://www.libraryireland.com/HealyEssays/Patrick1.php> (accessed 25 September 2011).

32 Ballintubber Teamwork, *Tóchar Phádraig*, p. 57.

33 Ibid., p. 78.

34 Duffy, *Patrick in his Own Words*, p. 35.

35 Michael Longley, 'The Cairn at Dooaghtry', *Collected Poems* (London, 2006), p. 191.

36 Patsy McGarry and Tom Shiel, 'Harsh Conditions for Croagh Patrick Climbers', *The Irish Times*, 27 July 2009.

37 Hermann Geissel, *A Road on the Long Ridge: In Search of the Ancient Highway on the Esker Riada* (Newbridge, 2006), pp. 57–69.

38 'Cill Chais', *An Duanaire 1600–1900: Poems of the Dispossessed* (Thomas Kinsella and Seán Ó Tuama, trans.) (Portlaoise, 1981), pp. 328–31.

39 Elizabeth Shee Twohig, 'Context and Chronology of the Carved Stone at Clonfinlough, County Offaly', *Journal of the Royal Society of Antiquaries of Ireland*, vol. 132 (2002), pp. 99–113.

40 Offaly Historical and Archaeological Society, 'Offaly Historical and Archaeological Society Newsletter – April 2005', *Offaly Historical and Archaeological Society*, <http://www.offalyhistory.com/articles/35/1/Offaly-Historical-amp-Archaeological-Society-Newsletter---April-2005/Page1.html> (accessed 25 September 2011).

41 Patrick Kavanagh, 'The One', *Collected Poems* (Antoinette Quinn, ed.) (London and New York, 2004), p. 229.

42 Ian Bradley, *Celtic Christianity: Making Myths and Chasing Dreams* (Edinburgh, 1999), pp. 9–11.

43 J.J. Ó Ríordáin, CSSR, *St Brigid of Ireland: Faughart Pilgrim's Manual* (Dundalk, 2000), pp. 31–2.

44 Ibid., p. 30.

45 Daphne Pochin Mould, *The Irish Saints: Short Biographies of the Principal Irish Saints from the Time of St Patrick to That of St Laurence O'Toole* (Dublin, 1964), pp. 41–7.

46 Carole M. Cusack, 'Brigit: Goddess, Saint, "Holy Woman" and Bone of Contention', *On a Panegyrical Note: Studies in Honour of Garry W. Trompf* (Victoria Barker and Frances di Lauro, eds) (Sydney, 2007), pp. 82–3.

47 Ibid., pp. 75–97.

48 Ibid, p. 89.

49 Dorothy Bray, 'The Image of St Brigit in the Early Irish Church', Études Celtiques, vol. 24 (1987), cited in Bradley, *Celtic Christianity*, p. 11.

50 Cusack, 'Brigit', pp. 91–2.

51 Séamas Ó Catháin, The Festival of Brigit the Holy Woman', *Celtica*, vol. 23 (1999).

52 T.G.F. Paterson, 'Brigid's Crosses in County Armagh', *Journal of the County Louth Archaeological Society*, vol. 11, no. 1 (1945), pp. 15–20.

53 Seán Duffy, *Robert the Bruce's Irish Wars: The Invasions of Ireland 1306–1329* (Stroud, 2002).

54 Domhnall Ó Néill, 'Remonstrance of the Irish Chiefs to Pope John XXII', *University College Cork*, <http://www.ucc.ie/celt/published/T310000-001/index.html> (accessed 25 September 2011).

55 'Annals of Ulster', *University College Cork*, <http://www.ucc.ie/celt/published/T100001A/> (accessed 25 September 2011).

56 Kitty Holland, 'Visitor Figures Could Be Down 13%,' *The Irish Times*, 11 February 2010.

57 Darach MacDonald, *The Chosen Fews: Exploding Myths in South Armagh* (Cork, 2000), pp. 187–90.

58 Translated by Thomas Kinsella as follows: 'Through the deep night a magic mist led me / like a simpleton roaming the land, / no friend of my bosom beside me, / an outcast in places unknown'. Eoghan Rua Ó Súilleabháin, 'Ceo Draíochta', *An Duanaire 1600–1900: Poems of the Dispossessed* (Thomas Kinsella and Seán Ó Tuama, trans.) (Portlaoise, 1981), p. 186.

59 The Chieftains, 'Changing Your Demeanour', *The Long Black Veil* (1995).

60 Martin Critchley (ed.), *Exploring the Mining Heritage of County Wicklow* (Wicklow, 2008), pp. 23–32.

61 Glendalough Mining Heritage Project Committee, 'History', *Glendalough Mining Heritage Project*, <http://www.glendaloughmines.com/history.html> (accessed 25 September 2011).

62 The Dubliners, 'The Glendalough Saint', *Finnegan Wakes* (1966).

63 Pochin Mould, *Irish Saints*, p. 80.

64 'St Kevin's Way, Co. Wicklow', *The Heritage Council*, <http://www.heritagecouncil.ie/recreation/heritage-council-initiatives/the-pilgrim-paths/st-kevins-way/?L=0> (accessed 25 September 2011).

65 W.B. Yeats, 'Stream and Sun in Glendalough', *W.B. Yeats: The Poems* (Daniel Albright, ed.) (London, 1992), p. 305.

66 Duffy, *Patrick in his Own Words*, p. 68.

67 Ibid., p. 20.

68 Ibid., p. 23.

69 Ibid., p. 55.

70 Patrick Kennedy, *Legendary Fictions of the Irish Celts* (London, 1866), p. 321.

71 J.P. Donnelly and M.M. Donnelly, *Downpatrick and Lecale: A Short Historical Guide* (Newtownards, 1980), pp. 42–3.

72 John Montague, 'History Walk', *Selected Poems* (London, 2001), p. 182.

73 'Betha Decclain/Life of St Declan of Ardmore' (P. Power, trans.) (London, 1914), *Christian Classics Ethereal Library*, <http://www.ccel.org/d/declan/life/declan.html> (accessed 25 September 2011), section 2.

74 Ibid., section 13.

75 Ibid.

76 Ibid., section 16.

77 Ibid., section 26.

78 Siobhán Lincoln, *A Walking Tour of Ardmore, Co. Waterford* (Cork, 1979).

79 Ibid., p. 24.

80 Ibid., p. 25.

81 Ibid., p. 24.

82 Ibid., p. 25.

83 James T. Quain, 'St Declan's Church, Ardmore: 1. The Early Years' (2003), *Waterford County Museum*, <http://www.waterfordcountymuseum.org/exhibit/web/WAIVersion/article/178> (accessed 25 September 2011).

84 'Betha Decclain', introduction.

85 Pochin Mould, *Irish Saints*, p. 138.

86 Ibid., p. 141.

87 'In memory of Ballin, delegate of St Patrick, who was drowned …'

88 'Betha Decclain', section 43.

89 Pochin Mould, *Irish Saints*, pp. 141–2.

90 'Jesus Christ is Risen Today', *Compleat Psalmodist* (London, 1749).

91 P. Power, *Dromana to Lismore: Notes on the Antiquities to be Visited on Society's Annual Excursion* (Waterford, 1907).

92 Ibid., pp. 5–6.

93 Samuel Lewis, *A Topographical Dictionary of Ireland* (London, 1837), vol. 2, p. 181.

94 Willie Fraher, 'Valentine Greatrakes – The Stroker' (2001), *Waterford County Museum*, <http://www.waterfordcountymuseum.org/exhibit/web/Display/article/45/1/> (accessed 25 September 2011).

95 Power, *Dromana to Lismore*, p. 5.

96 Ibid., p. 4.

97 Ibid., p. 10.

98 Giraldus Cambrensis, *The First Version of The Topography of Ireland* (John J. O'Meara, ed.) (Dundalk, 1951), pp. 93–4, cited in Charles Doherty, 'Royal Society of Antiquaries of Ireland Spring Outing Friday April 20–Sunday April 22, 2007: Flight of the Earls/Teitheadh na nIarla, Field Guide', *Royal Society of Antiquaries of Ireland*, <http://www.rsai.ie/photos/RathmullanGuideSc.pdf> (accessed 25 September 2011), p. 9.

99 Doherty, 'Field Guide', pp. 6–7.

100 Lawrence Donegan, *No News at Throat Lake* (London, 2000).

101 Seamus Heaney, 'Beacons at Bealtaine' (2004), *Ireland's Presidency of the European Union in 2004 Web Archive*, <http://web.archive.org/web/20041221223016/www.eu2004.ie/templates/news.asp?sNavlocator=66&list_id=641> (accessed 25 September 2011).

102 John Healy, 'The Holy Wells of Ireland', *Irish Essays: Literary and Historical* (Dublin, 1908), *Library Ireland*, <http://www.libraryireland.com/HealyEssays/Wells1.php> (accessed 25 September 2011).

103 Ibid.

104 W.B. Yeats, 'He Wishes for the Cloths of Heaven', *W.B. Yeats: The Poems* (Daniel Albright, ed.) (London, 1992), p. 90.

105 *The Graphic*, 16 September 1871.

106 Healy, 'Holy Wells of Ireland'.

107 'City's Holy Well Runs Dry Mysteriously', *Connacht Tribune*, 29 July 2008.

108 Ronnie O'Gorman, 'St Patrick Passed Us By, but Some Magic Remains …' *Galway Advertiser*, 19 March 2009.

109 Ibid.

110 Gabriel Rosenstock, 'The Moat at Kilfinane', *Portrait of the Artist as an Abominable Snowman: Selected Poems*, (London, 1989), p. 13.

111 J.J. Callanan, 'Gougane Barra', *Gougane Barra*, <http://www.gouganebarra.com/poem.htm> (accessed 25 September 2011).

112 Meehan, *Traveller's Guide*, p. 537.

113 'What Are the Highest Mountains in Ireland?', *Ordnance Survey Ireland: National Mapping Agency*, <http://www.osi.ie/en/faq/faq3.aspx#faq1> (accessed 25 September 2011).

114 Thomas Kinsella, 'Harmonies', *Collected Poems 1956–1994* (Oxford, 1996), p. 263.

115 Pochin Mould, *Irish Saints*, p. 193.

116 *Mass on Sunday*, RTÉ One (broadcast 16 May 2010).

117 Ibid.

118 Peter Harbison and Joss Lynam, *Cosán na Naomh: Corca Dhuibhne, Co. Ciarraí* (Dublin, 2002), p. 25.

119 Seamus Heaney, 'In Gallarus Oratory', *Door into the Dark* (London, 1969), p. 10.

120 P. Power, *Early Christian Ireland: A Manual of Irish Christian Archaeology* (Dublin, 1925), cited in Peter Harbison, 'How Old Is Gallarus Oratory? A Reappraisal of the Role of Gallarus Oratory in Early Irish Architecture', *Medieval Archaeology*, vol. 14 (1970), p. 40.

121 Paul Muldoon, 'The Lives of the Saints', *Poems 1968–1998* (New York, 2001), p. 23.

122 Anne Lucey, 'Review of Safety on Skellig Michael', *The Irish Times*, 22 September 2009.

123 Macdara Woods, 'Blues Note for John Jordan', *Knowledge in the Blood: New and Selected Poems* (Dublin, 2000), pp. 131–2.